Tort Law in Slovenia

Tort Law in Slovenia

Nataša Samec Berghaus
Andrej Bitrakov
Klemen Drnovšek

This book was originally published as a monograph in the International Encyclopaedia of Laws/Tort Law.

Founding Editor: Roger Blanpain
General Editor: Frank Hendrickx
Volume Editor: Britt Weyts

Wolters Kluwer

Published by:
Kluwer Law International B.V.
PO Box 316
2400 AH Alphen aan den Rijn
The Netherlands
E-mail: lrs-sales@wolterskluwer.com
Website: www.wolterskluwer.com/en/solutions/kluwerlawinternational

Sold and distributed by:
Wolters Kluwer Legal & Regulatory U.S.
920 Links Avenue
Landisville, PA 17538
United States of America
E-mail: customer.service@wolterskluwer.com

ISBN 978-94-035-4038-2

e-Book: ISBN 978-94-035-4048-1
web-PDF: ISBN 978-94-035-4058-0

This title is available on www.kluwerlawonline.com

The Authors

Dr Nataša Samec Berghaus was born in 1974 in Maribor. She currently serves as an Associate Professor at the Faculty of Law, University of Maribor. There, she imparts knowledge on several subjects: Law of Obligations, Substantive Civil Law, Capital Market and Securities Law, as well as European Union (EU) Capital Markets Law and Rules on Liability. In addition to her academic role, she is a permanent arbiter at the Central Securities Clearing Corporation of Slovenia. During her academic journey, she received the Chancellor's Award for Best Law Student of the Generation from the University of Maribor. Her outstanding Master's thesis also earned her the Young Lawyer Award for Remarkable Achievements from the Association of Slovenian Lawyers' Societies. She successfully passed the bar exam in 2003 and later achieved her PhD under the guidance of a distinguished professor from the Faculty of Law at the University of Ljubljana, Slovenia. Her expertise encompasses not only the law of obligations, where she delves deeply into compensation claims across various sectors but also capital market and securities law, as well as commercial law. With over two decades in research, she initially delved into areas like corporate law, with a special interest in good corporate governance. Since 2013, her research pivoted towards medical law, environmental, and energy law. As a testament to her dedication, she spearheaded two research projccts and contributed to six other research initiatives and four research programs in her chosen fields. In 2019, Dr Samec Berghaus had the privilege of serving as a Visiting Professor at the University of Zagreb's Faculty of Law in Croatia, specifically in the civil law department. Her literary contributions include two scientific monographs titled 'Corporate Takeover Defence: Preventive and Curative Defence Mechanisms' and 'Stock Options: Aspects of Law of Obligations, Corporate Law, Labour Law, Insider's Perspective, and Tax Aspects'. Additionally, she co-authored 'Energy Law in Slovenia' and has to her credit twenty-four original scientific articles published both in Slovenia and internationally.

The Authors

Andrej Bitrakov graduated from the University of Maribor's Faculty of Law and currently works there as a Teaching Assistant for the Law of Obligations. For his outstanding academic success, namely the highest average grade in his generation at both the First Cycle University and the Second Cycle master's study program, he received several awards from the Dean of the Faculty of Law of the University of Maribor and was also rewarded the Rector's Award for the Best Academic Achievements of Students at the University of Maribor. In addition to his position as a teaching assistant, he is currently employed at the Centre for Legal and General Affairs of the University of Maribor, where he deals with contract law, real estate law, labour law, personal data protection law, and many others. He is actively engaged in academic research in various legal areas, including the law of obligations, intellectual property law, real estate law, and labour law. He fluently speaks four languages: English, Slovenian, Macedonian, and Serbo-Croatian, and is well-versed in German.

Klemen Drnovšek is a Research and Teaching Assistant of Civil Law and Commercial Law at the Faculty of Law, University of Maribor. He graduated with honours and, in recognition of his outstanding achievements, was awarded the Grawe Excellence Award and the Rector's Award for the highest academic accomplishments among students at the University of Maribor. In 2019, he held the position of a Visiting Research Fellow at the University of Washington. He is employed as the head of the Department for Legal, Personnel, and General Affairs at the University of Maribor and holds the role of President at the Lawyer's Association in Maribor. In addition to his commitment to teaching and practice, he actively engages in scholarly research. His research contributions span across various legal domains, including contracts, torts, public procurement, environmental law, and labour law.

Table of Contents

List of Abbreviations

ABGB/ODZ	*Allgemeines Bürgerliches Gesetzbuch/Občni državljanski zakonik* (Austrian General Civil Code)
BGB	*Bürgerliches Gesetzbuch* (Civil Code)
CAA	Collective Actions Act
CC-1	Criminal Code
CJEU	Court of Justice of the European Union
CP	Civil Division
ECHR	European Court of Human Rights
ECLI	European Case Law Identifier
EPA-2	Environmental Protection Act
EU	European Union
GZ-1	Building Act
HSA	Health Services Act
LPC	Law of Property Code
MSA	Medical Services Act
NATO	North Atlantic Treaty Organization
OZ	Obligations Code
RS	Republic of Slovenia
SMA	Spatial Management Act
UL RS	Official Gazette of the Republic of Slovenia
UPRS	Administrative Court of the Republic of Slovenia
URS	Constitution of the Republic of Slovenia
VDSS	Higher Labour and Social Court of the Republic of Slovenia
VSCE	Higher Court in Celje
VSKP	Higher Court in Koper
VSLJ	Higher Court in Ljubljana
VSMB	Higher Court in Maribor
VSRS	Supreme Court of the Republic of Slovenia
ZAID	Architecture and Civil Engineering Act

List of Abbreviations

ZDLov-1	Game and Hunting Act
ZDR-1	Employment Relationships Act
ZGD-1	Companies Act
ZKP	Criminal Procedure Act
ZN	Notariat Act
ZNB	Communicable Diseases Act
ZOJed-1	Nuclear Damage Liability Act
ZON	Nature Conservation Act
ZOR	Act on Obligation Relations
ZOSRL	Obligations and Real Rights in Aviation Act
ZPP	Civil Procedure Act
ZPPCP-1	Road Transport Contracts Act
ZS	Courts Act
ZVPot-1	Consumer Protection Act

General Introduction

§1. General Background of the Country

I. Geography

1. Slovenia became an independent country on 26 June 1991, after having been one of the constituent republics of the Socialist Federal Republic of Yugoslavia since 1945.[1] Its geography includes the Alpine, Pannonian, Karst / Dinaric Alps and Mediterranean areas. Slovenia is located at the crossroads of Southeastern and Central Europe, where the Eastern Alps border the Adriatic Sea. It lies in the heart of Europe and borders other European Union (EU) Member States, namely Austria, Italy, Hungary and Croatia. Ljubljana, the capital and largest city of Slovenia, is geographically close to the centre of the country.

2. The country covers an area of 20,271 km^2, has the third-highest forest cover in Europe and has some of the richest water resources on the continent. Slovenia is predominantly mountainous and has a population of 2.1 million (2,106,215 people).[2] Slovenians constitute over 80% of the country's population. Slovenian, a South Slavic language, is the official language. Slovenia has a predominantly continental climate, with the exception of the Slovenian Littoral and the Julian Alps.

3. Due to its position on the small Adriatic Plate, which is sandwiched between the Eurasian Plate to the north and the African Plate to the south and rotates counterclockwise, Slovenia is in a rather active seismic zone. Compared to Western Europe, Slovenia is not very windy, as it lies in the lee of the Alps. Average wind speeds are lower than in the plains of neighbouring countries. The highest peak in Slovenia is Triglav with 2,864 m (9,396 ft); the average height of the country above sea level is 557 m (1,827 ft).

---

1. Between the First and Second World Wars it was part of the State of Slovenes, Croats and Serbs, then joining the Kingdom of Serbs, Croats and Slovenes, which became the Kingdom of Yugoslavia. Before that it was part of the Habsburg Monarchy and Austria-Hungary.
2. For more on the population in Slovenia in 2022, *see V 1. četrtletju število prebivalcev upadlo*, Statistical Office of the Republic of Slovenia, (1 Apr. 2022), https://www.stat.si/StatWeb/News/Index/10463.

II. History

4. The name Slovenia means ‘the land of the Slovenes’. The name for the Slovenes (nowadays more commonly referred to as Slovenians) comes from the word ‘Slovani’ (Old Church Slavonic: ‘slověnьsky’), although the origin of this word is unclear. It is derived from the root *slov-, which is also preserved in some water-related names throughout Eastern Europe. Therefore, in its original meaning, it could refer to ‘inhabitants by the river *Slova or *Slovy’ (the name of the river is nowhere preserved). According to another interpretation, it derives from the Proto-Slavic *slövo, meaning ‘word’, so it could be understood as *‘people with whom it is possible to exchange words, to speak’*.[3]

5. Although the territory of present-day Slovenia has been inhabited since prehistoric times[4] and one of the most important finds from the Stone Age, dating back approximately 55,000 years,[5] was discovered within its borders, the name Slovenia, in a sense that roughly corresponds to its present-day meaning, did not appear until 1834 in the book *Ancient and Modern Slovenes* (*Starodavni in današnji Slovenci)* by the Russian historian Yuri Venelin. Ten years later it also appeared in the poem by Koseski (real name Janez Vesel).

6. Based on numerous studies, it can no longer be claimed that Slovenes are exclusively the descendants of a single ethnic group, namely the Slavs who settled in the Eastern Alps and the river basins in the sixth century. Although this historical migration gave our area its linguistic identity, which it retains to this day, it is essential to note that Slovenes are a blend of various ancestral roots. Like all modern nations, they have a diverse range of ancestors ranging from ancient indigenous peoples to the Slavs, Avars, Carantanians, Carniolans, Croats, Germans, Uskoks, Friulians, and others. In this sense, Slovenes are considered indigenous though not as the first inhabitants of Slovenian territory, but as the result of a historical development that led to their emergence in this region. Throughout different historical periods, various identities were documented in this area, with the Slovene identity being one of the last to emerge.

7. At the end of the Bronze Age and in antiquity, the territory of present-day Slovenia was inhabited by Illyrian tribes that relied on agriculture for their livelihood. In the Late Iron Age (eighth–fourth century BC), a princely society emerged, and some hill forts began to have features of urban settlements (such as Stična). The

3. Marko Snoj, *Slovenski etimološki slovar* [electronic format: https://www.fran.si/193/marko-snoj-slovenski-etimoloski-slovar], (Ljubljana: Založba ZRC, Znanstvenoraziskovalni center SAZU, 2015); Janez Cvirn et al., *Ilustrirana zgodovina Slovencev* (1st reprint, Mladinska knjiga 2000), p. 15.
4. The oldest evidence of human habitation in today’s Slovenian territory consists of two stone tools from the Loza Cave near Orehek, dating back approximately 250,000 years. For more information on the history of Slovenia, you can refer to the following sources: Cvirn et al., *supra* n. 3, 526 pp; *Veliki splošni leksikon part of the series Der Knauer – Universallexikon im 15 Bänden*, seventh book (S-Te), (Marija Javornik ed., 2. dopol. izd., DZS 1998), pp. 3949–3957.
5. This is probably the oldest musical instrument in the world – a flute from the Divje Babe cave near Cerkno.

flourishing of domestic iron production facilitated the development of Situla culture. Later, in the fourth and third centuries BC, the area of present-day Slovenia was also occupied by Celtic tribes, who founded the first state entity, known as the Noric Kingdom.

8. During the early years of the first millennium, the Roman Empire expanded into what is now Slovenia, dividing the area into three provinces: Venetia and Istria, Noricum, and Pannonia. In various towns, the residents engaged in trade, crafts, and commerce. The ones in the coastal areas were involved in maritime activities, olive cultivation, and salt production. Notable Roman towns in present-day Slovenia include Emona (Ljubljana), Petovio (Ptuj), and Celeia (Celje). A road system was also established at the time.

9. At the beginning of the fourth century, the migrations and invasions of various peoples into the territory of the declining Roman Empire began. To escape the eastern invaders, the inhabitants of present-day Slovenia sought refuge in mountainous shelters, where they sustained themselves mainly by raising cattle. An understanding of mining and metallurgy was also preserved. In the early fifth century, the Western Goths (Visigoths) invaded Italy through the territory of present-day Slovenia, followed by the Huns, Eastern Goths (Ostrogoths), and Lombards. From the second half of the sixth century onwards, the Slavs began to settle in our territory. Between about 623 and 658, Samo united various Slavic tribes and resisted the incursions of the Lombards, Avars, and others. Samo's tribal alliance represented an important consolidation of the Slavic tribes in their struggle against external influences and violence. Under Samo's leadership, they managed to maintain the independence of the Slavic tribes during this period.

10. In the seventh century, Carantania emerged in the region between the rivers Drava, Danube, and Mura. The Carantanians found themselves entangled in conflicts with the neighbouring Avars, Bavarians, and Lombards. The heart of Carantania was Krn Castle, located on the outskirts of the Zollfeld Field (*Gosposvetsko polje*) in what is now Austrian Carinthia. The Carantanian leader, solemnly installed on the Prince's Stone in the Gosposvetsko polje, was elected by the military nobility and the free peasantry (*kosezi*). The pledge, in which the leader swore to uphold the rights and wishes of the populace, was still held in the Slovenian language long after Carantania lost its political autonomy in the eighth century. This coronation ritual was a remarkable instance of democratic practice within the broader European context of that era. It was later documented by the French jurist Jean Bodin, and according to some accounts, Thomas Jefferson drew inspiration from it when formulating the American Constitution. When the Carantanians sought help from the Bavarians against the neighbouring Avars, they consequently lost their political independence. Carantania was missioned by Christian missionaries and the land that today forms modern-day Slovenia became part of the Holy Roman Empire of the German Nation, which was divided into distinct regions: Styria, Carniola, Carinthia, and Istria. The Counts of Celje were the most powerful feudal family, ruling over almost the entire Slovenian territory in the fourteenth century.

11. The Middle Ages were characterised by the colonisation of extensive parts of Slovenian territory by immigrants from the Germanic world. The ethnic boundary between the previously dominant Slovenian population and the Germanic immigrants underwent significant changes. The convergence of Southern German influences from the north and Venetian influences from the west can be seen in many buildings, which feature Romanesque and Gothic architectural styles.

12. The late fifteenth to the late sixteenth century was a period marked by a series of events, including Turkish invasions, urban expansion, peasant uprisings, the influence of the Renaissance and Humanism, and the emergence of the Protestant Reformation. It was in this era that Slovenian literature found its roots with the publication of the first books in the Slovenian language by Primož Trubar in 1550 and the translation of the Bible by Jurij Dalmatin in 1584, which was the fourteenth such translation worldwide. Slovenian literature played a pivotal role in shaping Slovenia's national identity. Although supported by many townspeople and the nobility, the Slovenian Protestant movement was largely suppressed during the Counter-Reformation. The development of Slovenian national consciousness gained greater momentum during the Enlightenment period.

13. In the eighteenth century, under the rule of the Austrian Empress Maria Theresa, the territory that comprises present-day Slovenia saw advancements in various sectors, such as agriculture, horticulture, and livestock breeding. From 1774, the foundations were laid for elementary education in the Slovenian language. Her successor, Joseph II, granted freedom to the peasants, thus establishing the basis for economic growth in the Slovenian regions. Towards the close of the eighteenth century, enlightened intellectuals endeavoured to bring the Slovenian language up to the same level as German and Italian. This period witnessed the publication of numerous works, including a new translation of the Bible, the inaugural scientific history of the Slovenian people, the first theatrical productions, and the maiden newspaper in the Slovenian language.

14. The Slovenian territory in the first half of the nineteenth century was marked by a series of noteworthy events that had a lasting impact on the region. Among these events was the period of French occupation (from 1809 to 1813), which brought significant changes to the area. Additionally, the construction of the Vienna-Trieste railway line, a major infrastructure project, was completed in 1857, connecting Slovenia to a wider European trade network. During this time, there was a notable resurgence in the development of national identity, marked by key moments such as the Spring of Nations and the formation of the first Slovenian political programme known as United Slovenia (*Zedinjena Slovenija*) in 1848. This programme called for national autonomy within the Habsburg state, reflecting the desire for self-governance and recognition of Slovenian culture and language within the broader political landscape. In the realm of culture, the poet Dr France Prešeren played a pivotal role. His literary contributions and advocacy efforts helped elevate the Slovenian language and culture to a level comparable to that of the more culturally advanced European nations of the time.

15. The period preceding the outbreak of the First World War witnessed a significant surge in economic growth and increased political engagement in Slovenia. This period was characterised by large-scale outdoor political gatherings, the so-called *tabori*, and the proliferation of newspapers and other publications. It was during this time that the first political parties were founded, reflecting the growing interest in shaping the political landscape. However, the advent of the First World War left an indelible mark on the region and its populace. The western part of Slovenian territory, particularly the Isonzo Front (1915–1917), became one of the deadliest battlegrounds of the entire war. Numerous Slovenians participated in the conflict, mainly as part of the Austro-Hungarian army, and tragically many of them lost their lives in the course of the war. In 1917, Slovenian delegates submitted the May Declaration (*Majniška deklaracija*) to the Austrian Emperor, campaigning for greater autonomy for Slovenian territory within the framework of Austria-Hungary. The declaration received broad support and garnered a substantial number of signatures.

16. After World War I, the Slovenians initially became part of the State of Slovenes, Croats and Serbs, and by the end of 1918, they were integrated into the Kingdom of Serbs, Croats and Slovenes, which later became known as Yugoslavia. The economic and social progress of the Slovenian nation was significantly shaped by a complex political landscape. This included political tensions between the unitarist Serbian authorities and the Slovenian People's Party, which was the predominant political entity in Slovenia, advocating vigorously for greater autonomy for Slovenians. In this transformative period, General Rudolf Maister emerged as a key figure in the establishment of the northern border of present-day Slovenia. His leadership and military efforts were instrumental in securing the northernmost regions, known as the Maribor territory, for the nascent Yugoslav state. General Maister's actions helped delineate the border of contemporary Slovenia and ensure that it included areas with a significant Slovenian population. This achievement bolstered the territorial integrity of the Slovenian nation within the newly formed Kingdom of Serbs, Croats and Slovenes. During this period, Slovenian national identity received a boost from notable sporting achievements, including those of Leon Štukelj in gymnastics and Milan Vidmar in chess. The construction of the Planica ski jumping hill also helped strengthen Slovenian national consciousness.

17. World War II brought a tumultuous period for Slovenia, as it found itself partitioned into occupation zones controlled by German, Italian, and Hungarian forces. The Slovenian nation endured immense challenges and grave threats during this time, including forced deportations, conscription into foreign armies, restrictions on the use of the Slovenian language, and widespread violence. Within this context, different political factions pursued varying courses of action. Some politicians chose collaboration with the occupying forces, while the communist forces initiated a resistance movement, which eventually led to a full-scale revolution. The turning point came with the German invasion of the Soviet Union in June 1941. In response, the communist-led resistance called for an armed uprising, marking the beginning of the partisan struggles against the occupying forces. As the conflict progressed, the non-communist factions found themselves increasingly marginalised and excluded from the resistance efforts. Amid the turmoil of war, the communists managed to seize political power and establish their dominance in Slovenia through undemocratic means in 1945. The post-war period also saw the tragic events of May 1945, when many Slovenians attempted to flee to Austrian Carinthia but were forcibly repatriated to Yugoslavia by British soldiers. This resulted in a grim chapter in Slovenian history with over 14,000 extrajudicial killings and the scattering of human remains in various locations throughout the country. To date, over 700 sites of such atrocities have been documented, serving as grim reminders of the challenges and sacrifices endured by the Slovenian people during World War II.

18. After the end of World War II, Slovenia became one of the six constituent republics of the newly formed Socialist Federal Republic of Yugoslavia. Despite it being part of the Yugoslav Federation, the country maintained its unique identity, characterised by a mosaic of national, economic, social, religious, and cultural differences. In the post-war period, Yugoslavia consolidated as a one-party state, with power concentrated in the hands of the ruling Communist Party and a charismatic leader, Marshal Josip Broz Tito. Tito's leadership, marked by a lifelong dictatorship, garnered support from both the Communist Party and the military, which helped maintain stability in the diverse Yugoslav republics. However, after Tito's death, Yugoslavia entered a challenging and multi-faceted crisis. The country grappled with mounting economic woes, ethnic tensions, and political fragmentation among its republics. Within the context of Slovenian history, the significant contributions of Slovenian companies such as TAM (*Tovarna avtomobilov Maribor*), known for its car manufacturing, and Zlatorog, a prominent brewery, to the Yugoslav economy are worth mentioning. Slovenia also became renowned for hosting the annual alpine skiing competition *Zlata lisica* (Golden Fox) in Maribor. This international event, which is part of the Women's World Cup, has become a cherished tradition and a highlight in the global sports calendar.

19. In the 1980s, two divergent visions for the future of Yugoslavia emerged: The economically better-developed republics, most notably Slovenia and Croatia, advocated a decentralised and democratised state structure. In contrast, the central authorities, supported by the military and Serbia, pushed for a centralised and unitary Yugoslav federation. The increasing influence of the Serbian authorities, under the leadership of Slobodan Milošević, exacerbated tensions, particularly in the restive Kosovo region, and deepened divisions among the diverse nations within the country. Slovenia experienced a political awakening in the late 1980s, marking the onset of a 'political spring'. This transformative period was characterised by a series of significant events, including the legal proceedings against the Janša, Borštnar, Tasić and Zavrl quartet, the emergence of a vibrant and independent civil society, widespread protests against the existing regime, the formation of the first political alliances and movements, constitutional revisions, and the publication of the May Declaration, which called for a democratic and sovereign Slovenia. Towards the end of 1989, the democratic opposition movement known as Demos coalesced under the leadership of former dissident and political prisoner Dr Jože Pučnik. The turning point came with Demos securing their victory in the first multi-party elections in the spring of 1990, ushering in a new era. A defining moment was the successful plebiscite for an independent Slovenia in December 1990, which set the stage for Slovenia's triumphant War of Independence in 1991. By the end of October 1991, the Yugoslav army had withdrawn from Slovenian territory. A denationalisation act was passed in November, legislation on denationalisation was enacted and a new constitution was adopted in December 1991.

20. Slovenia was internationally recognised as an independent nation, although various European and global powers initially expressed reservations. The Republic of Slovenia (RS) was recognised by the EU in mid-January 1992 and formally admitted to the United Nations in May 1992. In February 1999, an Association Agreement with the EU came into force, marking a significant step towards deeper European integration. Slovenia further reinforced its international presence by becoming a member of North Atlantic Treaty Organization (NATO) on 29 March 2004 and officially joining the EU on 1 May 2004. On 1 January 2007, Slovenia introduced the common European currency, the euro, which facilitated trade and economic integration within the EU. In the summer of 2008, Slovenia held the presidency of the European Council, a pivotal role in shaping European policy within the EU. This was an important opportunity for Slovenia to contribute to the European agenda. Slovenia assumed the presidency of the European Council once again in 2021, reaffirming its commitment to active participation in European affairs and decision-making processes.

III. Political System

21. As regards the form of government in Slovenia, it should be noted by way of introduction that according to the Constitution of the Republic of Slovenia (URS),[6] Slovenia is organised as a democratic republic in which executive power is vested in the people, who in this sense have primacy and exercise their power directly and through elections, which is consistent with the principle of separation of the legislative, executive, and judicial branches.

22. According to the Slovenian constitution, all organs of state power, acting as representatives of the people, must (directly) uphold human rights and fundamental freedoms, including the principles of the social state and the state based on the rule of law, the consequences thereof, and other obligations set out by regulations. The principle applies that organs of state power and other persons under public law may act only in the cases and in the manner set out by law, while persons under private law may do anything that is not prohibited by law.

23. The National Assembly and the National Council exercise the governmental function of a bicameral parliament,[7] although it should be noted that the legislative

6. The English version of the *Constitution* is available on the website of the Constitutional Court of the Republic of Slovenia: http://www.us-rs.si/en/about-the-court/legal-basis/constitution/.
7. In the formal sense, it is not a bicameral parliament, as the National Council is (merely) defined as a separate body and is not formally part of the parliament in organisational terms, although it does

function lies with the National Assembly. The latter alone is a purely representative body[8] with the exclusive right to pass laws, while the National Council, which represents certain precisely defined interest groups, has limited powers, as it can merely propose laws to the National Assembly for adoption, submit (non-binding) opinions to it, or request a parliamentary investigation or a revote on a particular law.

24. The government exercises the executive function[9] and consists of the prime minister and ministers. The government and ministers are independent and accountable to the National Assembly within the framework of their powers. Ministries are each established to perform administrative functions in one or more administrative areas. Expert or professional support is provided to the ministries by the civil service or the administration, which performs the administrative tasks set out by law.

25. Bodies within a ministry are established to perform specific expert tasks, executive and developmental administrative tasks, tasks related to inspections and other types of supervision, and public service tasks, where this ensures greater efficiency and quality in the performance of the tasks or where the nature of the tasks or the field of work requires a higher degree of professional independence in the performance of tasks, while administrative units are established to perform state administration tasks that need to be organised and provided on a territorial basis.[10] It is common to all these bodies that in the formal-organisational sense they fall within the remit of the state administration, although it should be noted that administrative tasks can be delegated to bodies outside the state administration in the legal-organisational sense, i.e., to holders of public authorisations. A public authorisation to perform specific administrative tasks may be obtained by a legal person under public or private law or by a natural person, by or pursuant to law. In exercising these public authorisations, the holders have the rights and obligations of administration as set out in the law or other regulations.

26. Slovenia is divided into 212 municipalities (twelve of which have the status of urban municipalities).[11] The municipalities are the only bodies of local autonomy in Slovenia. Each municipality is headed by a mayor (*župan*), elected by popular vote every four years, and a municipal council (*občinski svet*). In most municipalities, the municipal council is elected according to proportional representation; only in a few smaller municipalities, the plurality voting system is used. In urban municipalities, the municipal councils are called town (city) councils. Each municipality

have certain powers that are customary for an upper house, which is why the National Council can be labelled the second chamber of the Slovenian parliament in terms of content.

8. It consists of members who are directly elected by eligible voters.
9. The executive branch also includes the administration and the president, who has very limited operational powers.
10. The Constitution also envisages local self-government, with the powers of the municipalities being defined by law. In principle, it can be said that the powers of the municipalities are relatively modest.
11. For more information on municipalities in Slovenia, *see Občine v. številkah*, Republika Slovenija, Sektor za lokalno samoupravo (15 Jan. 2023), https://www.gov.si/teme/obcine-v-stevilkah/.

also has a head of the municipal administration (*načelnik občinske uprave*), who is appointed by the mayor and responsible for the functioning of the local administration.

27. Among the holders of public authorisations, certain public agencies are worth mentioning – they are persons under public law established to perform regulatory, developmental, or expert tasks in the public interest, insofar as any other status is not envisaged by law. In general, they can be said to be established when the performance of administrative tasks thereby becomes more effective and more efficient than would be the case with an administrative body, in particular when the performance of administrative tasks can be financed entirely or mainly by administrative fees or user payments or when, given the nature or type of the (administrative) tasks, continual direct political control of the performance of the assigned (administrative) tasks is neither necessary nor appropriate. Put simply, one could say that the essence of a public agency is its specialisation, expertise, and autonomy and independence from politicians, political pressures and lobbying in general, which should be a key attribute of the sector regulator.

IV. Economic and Social Values

28. Slovenia, a small but vibrant country in Central Europe, is known for its rich economic and social values that have evolved over the years. These values form the bedrock of the nation's identity and play a crucial role in shaping its modern society.

29. Slovenia's economy is organised along the lines of a social market model. The protection of private property, freedom of economic enterprise and market competition are enshrined in its constitution. Economically, Slovenia boasts a well-developed and diverse economy that combines elements of both capitalism and social welfare. The country has a strong industrial base, with manufacturing, the technology sector, and the automotive sector contributing significantly to the country's GDP. In terms of wealth, it ranks in the middle of EU Member States (GDP per capita was at EUR 24,678 in 2022). Nominal GDP in 2023 is USD 68,108 billion, and nominal GDP per capita (GDP/pc) in 2023 is USD 32,214.[12] By far the largest part of Slovenia's economy is the services sector, which has for some time accounted for well over a half, while manufacturing accounts for about a quarter, construction for about a tenth, and agriculture for 2% of economic output. The economy is strongly export-oriented, but also heavily dependent on imports – imports and exports account for almost three-quarters of GDP. Additionally, Slovenia's strategic location at the crossroads of European trade routes has made it a

12. *Report for Selected Countries and Subjects: April 2023: Republic of Slovenia: 2022 Article IV Consultation-Press Release; and Staff Report* (18 Jan. 2023), https://www.imf.org/en/Publications/CR/Issues/2023/01/17/Republic-of-Slovenia-2022-Article-IV-Consultation-Press-Release-and-Staff-Report-528232.

gateway for commerce, fostering a culture of entrepreneurship and innovation. Slovenia remains committed to the objectives of increasing productivity, ensuring fiscal sustainability, and green and digital transition.

30. The country joined the EU in 2004 and adopted the euro three years later. It is a member of numerous other international organisations, both economic and non-economic, such as the UN (IAEA), the Council of Europe, NATO, the WTO, the OECD (NEA) and the ICSID.

31. Slovenia's commitment to social values is reflected in its comprehensive welfare system. The country gives high priority to healthcare, education, and social security, ensuring that its citizens have access to quality services and a high standard of living. The healthcare system is renowned for its efficiency and accessibility, while the education system is characterised by its emphasis on quality and inclusiveness.

32. One of Slovenia's most cherished social values is its commitment to environmental sustainability. The country takes pride in its stunning natural landscapes, including the Julian Alps and picturesque lakes, and has implemented policies to protect its environment. Slovenia is a leader in eco-tourism and sustainable agriculture, demonstrating its dedication to preserving its natural heritage.

33. Culturally, Slovenia is a melting pot of influences from neighbouring European nations, resulting in a rich tapestry of traditions and values. The Slovenian people take pride in their heritage, which is reflected in their strong sense of community and respect for diversity.

34. Slovenia, which like the rest of Europe struggled with the consequences of the crisis caused by the COVID-19 epidemic in 2020, saw a rebound in economic growth in 2021.[13] During the inter-pandemic period, Slovenia took unprecedented emergency measures that significantly mitigated the impact on the economy and population and contributed to high growth in 2021. The measures, which were adopted in ten legislative packages, mainly addressed challenges related to the health system, maintaining employment, supporting businesses, and improving the socio-economic situation of the population. In Slovenia, measures have already been taken to mitigate the rise in energy prices and changes are planned to strengthen independence from Russian energy imports.

35. In recent years, Slovenia has also embraced digitalisation and innovation, further enhancing its economic and social values. The country has made strides in promoting digital literacy and fostering a thriving startup ecosystem.

---

13. *See Commission Proposal for a Council Implementing Decision amending the Council Implementing Decision of 28 July 2021 on the approval of the assessment of the recovery and resilience plan for Slovenia* (29 Sep. 2023), https://commission.europa.eu/system/files/2023-09/COM_2023_575_2_EN_.pdf.

§2. Legal Systems

I. Primacy of Legislation and Codification

36. The Slovenian legal system consists of formal legal acts of domestic origin and transposed formal legal acts. Abstract legal norms are adopted in Slovenia at both the state and local levels. The legal instruments at the state level are the Constitution (*ustava*), laws/acts (*zakoni*) and implementing regulations, which fall into two main categories: Decrees (*uredbe*, sometimes translated as regulations) and rules (*pravilniki*).

37. Under the principle of primacy, EU law generally takes precedence over all other legal acts that are part of the Slovenian legal system. The Slovenian Constitution stipulates that legal acts and decisions adopted within the framework of the EU are applied in Slovenia in accordance with the EU legal system. In simple terms, this means that EU law, and not the Slovenian Constitution, determines the manner and conditions for the penetration of EU law into the Slovenian legal system, its position within the Slovenian legal system, and the conditions that must be met for an individual to be able to exercise the rights set out in EU law in proceedings before a national authority. In the event of a conflict between EU rules and (other) Slovenian rules, the EU rules generally take precedence and are applied in the specific case, while a national rule that contravenes a supranational rule is simply ignored. By contrast, the situation is different from classical international law, which consists of (traditional) international treaties, general legal principles, and international customary law, since all the aforementioned aspects are determined by the Constitution. Namely, the latter stipulates that international treaties penetrate the Slovenian legal system upon their ratification and publication, whereas this condition is not stipulated for the general legal principles recognised by civilised nations and international customary law. In the hierarchical sense, the Constitution stipulates that international treaties ratified by Parliament through a law, general legal principles, and international customary law are directly under the Constitution and above laws and secondary legislation, while international treaties ratified by the government through a decree are under laws but above secondary legislation.

38. So, in terms of hierarchy, one could say, somewhat simplified, that the apex of the Slovenian legal system consists of EU law and the Slovenian constitution; the second rank consists of international treaties by which Slovenia is bound and which have been ratified by the National Assembly through a law (the legislator), and the general principles recognised by civilised nations and international customary law; the third rank consists of laws or acts; the fourth rank consists of international treaties by which Slovenia is bound and which have been ratified by the government through a decree; and the fifth rank consists of secondary legislation and other general acts.

39. The Slovenian civil law approach is based on the idea of legislative supremacy, which means that the country's primary source of law is the statutory law created by the legislative body, the National Assembly. This principle emphasises that the legislature has the ultimate authority to enact, amend or repeal laws and that these laws are binding on everyone, including the courts.

40. The emphasis on the primacy of legislation and codification contributes to legal certainty and stability in Slovenia. Citizens and businesses can rely on clearly-defined legal rules and a predictable legal environment. This fosters trust in the legal system and encourages both domestic and foreign investment, which further promotes economic development.

41. The Slovenian legal system does not recognise judicial precedence as a mandatory source of law. However, lower-instance courts tend to respect and follow the case law of higher-instance courts and the Supreme Court (*Vrhovno sodišče*). The Supreme Court, sitting in a plenary session, may adopt principled legal opinions (*načelna pravna mnenja*) on issues important for the uniform application of laws/acts. Under the Courts Act (ZS),[14] such principled legal opinions are only binding on the Supreme Court panels and may only be changed in a new plenary session. However, the lower-instance courts tend to follow the principled legal opinions.

42. Slovenian law adheres to the conventional classification into public law and private law (*see* General Introduction, §2, III). Within the realm of private law, tort law deals with civil wrongs and damages inflicted by one person on another. Its foundations lie predominantly in statutory law. Specifically, the Slovenian Obligations Code (*Obligacijski zakonik* or the OZ)[15] serves as the primary legislative source for governing tort liability. This codification provides clarity and predictability to individuals and businesses when it comes to their rights and obligations in tort cases. Victims of tort in Slovenia rely on the legislative framework to seek remedies and compensation for the harm they have suffered. The OZ establishes the legal basis for determining liability, calculating damages, and enforcing judgments in tort cases. Victims can bring lawsuits in civil courts to assert their rights and seek compensation for various types of harm (e.g., physical harm, emotional harm, damage to property, damage to reputation or defamation, financial harm). Legislative supremacy ensures that victims of tort are clearly protected by the law. They can rely on the established legal framework to hold wrongdoers accountable and seek compensation for their losses. Additionally, this approach promotes legal predictability and consistency in the adjudication of tort cases.

43. While legislative supremacy is a key principle, the Slovenian legal system also allows for judicial interpretation and development of tort law based on court decisions. Courts play a significant role in applying and interpreting statutory law to specific cases. If a civil case cannot be resolved based on existing regulations,

14. Official Gazette RS, Nos 94/07 – official consolidated text, 45/08, 96/09, 86/10 – ZJNepS, 33/11, 75/12 – ZSPDSLS-A, 63/13, 17/ 15, 23/17 – ZSSve, 22/18 – ZSICT, 16/19 – ZNP-1, 104/20, 203/20 – ZIUPOPDVE and 18/23 – ZDU-1O.
15. Official Gazette RS, Nos 97/07 – official consolidated text, 64/16 – Constitutional Court decision and 20/18 – OROZ631.

the judge will consider the regulations that govern similar cases. If the solution to the case is still legally questionable, the judge decides in accordance with the general principles of the country's legal system. In doing so, the judge follows the legal tradition and the established principles of legal science (Article 3(2) of the ZS).

II. Position of the Judiciary

44. The courts exercise the judicial function and judges are independent in their work, bound solely by the Constitution and the law. In accordance with the Constitution, they are also bound by the general principles of international law and ratified and published international treaties. The arrangements and powers of the courts in Slovenia are set out by law. A distinction is made between general courts, specialised courts and the Constitutional Court of the Republic of Slovenia.

45. The general courts decide on all matters other than those reserved for the specialised courts. The courts of first instance are the local courts (*okrajna sodišča*) and the district courts (*okrožna sodišča*); in simplified terms, one could say that the district courts have jurisdiction over civil cases where the amount in dispute exceeds EUR 20,000, or, in other words, over more complex cases.[16] There are (four) higher courts of second instance, which are primarily responsible for deciding on appeals, which are ordinary legal remedies. The court of third instance is the Supreme Court of the Republic of Slovenia (VSRS), which is primarily responsible for deciding on extraordinary legal remedies.

46. The specialised courts rule on matters of labour and social law (Labour and Social Court of the Republic of Slovenia) and administrative law (Administrative Court of the Republic of Slovenia (UPRS)).

47. Also worth mentioning is the Constitutional Court, which is entirely independent of the other bodies. It is the most senior judicial body for the protection of constitutionality, legality, human rights and fundamental freedoms, and is responsible, *inter alia*, for ruling on the constitutionality of laws; the compliance of laws and other regulations with ratified international treaties and the general principles of international law; the compliance of secondary legislation with the Constitution and with laws; the compliance of general (legal) acts adopted for the exercise of public authorisations with the Constitution, laws and secondary legislation; and constitutional appeals against violations of human rights and fundamental freedoms by individual acts.

---

16. *See* Art. 32 of the Civil Procedure Act (ZPP – Official Gazette RS, Nos 73/07 – official consolidated text, 45/08 – ZArbit, 45/08, 111/08 – Constitutional Court Act, 57/09 – Constitutional Court Act, 12/10 – Constitutional Court Act, 50/10 – Constitutional Court decision, 107/10 – Constitutional Court decision, 75/12 – Constitutional Court decision, 40/13 – Constitutional Court decision, 92/13 – Constitutional Court decision, 10/14 – Constitutional Court decision, 48/15 – Constitutional Court decision, 6/17 – Constitutional Court decision, 10/17, 16/19 – ZNP-1, 70/19 – Constitutional Court decision, 1/22 – Constitutional Court decision and 3/22 – ZDeb).

III. Distinction Between Public and Private Law

48. In Slovenian law, there is no strict demarcation between public and private law. Slovenian legal theory draws on German differentiation theories to define the distinction between these two areas.[17] Specifically, the widely accepted concept in the Slovenian context is the 'Special Law Theory' (*Sonderrechtstheorie*), which posits that a legal relationship falls under public law when it involves a party with authority that is acting in an official capacity.[18]

49. Public law encompasses various branches, including constitutional, administrative, criminal, international, and procedural law. It is inherently coercive (*ius cogens*) and individuals cannot deviate from these norms. In contrast, private law is characterised by the discretionary nature of legal norms and individual autonomy. However, public law exerts its influence on private law, as the state intervenes in several areas of private law with mandatory regulations, such as consumer protection, liability insurance in traffic, restrictions on the inheritance of agricultural land, and environmental protection. It is worth noting that entities governed by private law are also subject to public law regulations if they engage in public functions or provide public services, as seen in the field of healthcare.

50. Private law is divided into two main categories. On the one hand, civil law, often referred to as the general part of private law or private law in the narrow sense, comprises classic civil law areas, including the general part of civil law, law of obligations, property law, family law, and inheritance law. The special part of private law, on the other hand, consists of branches that have evolved in the course of recent developments and have a mixed character. These include commercial law, labour law, private international law, intellectual property law, consumer law, insurance law, and capital markets and securities law.

51. Tort law, a crucial component of the law of obligations, falls under private law. Consequently, the law of obligations is characterised by its dispositive provisions (Article 2 of the OZ), which allow parties to contractually tailor their relations as long as these agreements do not violate the Constitution, laws, or moral principles (Article 3 of the OZ).

52. In contrast, the primary characteristic of tort law is the protection of injured parties through mandatory norms stipulating the obligation to compensate for legally recognised damages. In cases involving contractual tort liability, there is a possibility of contractually excluding liability for slight negligence. However, such agreements are prohibited by the mandatory rule set forth in Article 243(2) of the OZ if they result from an unequal bargaining position of the parties.[19]

---

17. Cf. Viktorija Žnidaršič Skubic, in Juhart et al., *Uvod v civilno pravo* (2011), p. 27; Verica Trstenjak, *Pravne osebe* (2003), p. 96; Marijan Pavčnik, *Teorija prava* (1997), p. 438.
18. Trstenjak, *supra* n. 17, at 97.
19. *See* General Introduction, §5 for the differences between contractual and tortious liability.

53. Similarly, mandatory tort provisions are found in sectoral laws, such as those pertaining to consumer protection or liability for nuclear damage.[20] It is important to note that the injured party's decision to seek compensation is always voluntary and discretionary.

IV. Sources of Private Law in General and of Tort Law in Particular

54. In the hierarchy of legal acts in civil and tort law, it is necessary to first mention the URS,[21] which was adopted on 23 December 1991. Of particular importance for civil and tort law are the provisions regarding human rights and fundamental freedoms. These provisions primarily govern vertical legal relationships between individuals and holders of authority, i.e., they determine whether and under what conditions holders of authoritative functions can encroach upon human rights and freedoms. In horizontal legal relationships between individuals, constitutional rights are realised indirectly based on laws. Nevertheless, the Constitution serves as a guide for the application and interpretation of statutory provisions. The provisions relevant to civil law in general and tort law include those that regard the right to compensation for damage,[22] the right to rehabilitation and compensation,[23] property rights,[24] personal rights,[25] marriage and family rights,[26] limitations on property rights,[27] and the freedom of economic initiative.[28]

55. In the RS, and previously in Yugoslavia, there were various ideas for the codification of civil law, but this did not come to fruition. The traditional disciplines of civil law, i.e., the general part of civil law, law of obligations, property law, family law, and inheritance law, are regulated in separate laws. These include the OZ[29] as the primary source of obligations and the general part of civil law, the Law of Property Code (LPC)[30] as the primary source of property law, the Family Code[31] as the primary source of family law, and the Inheritance Act[32] as the primary source

20. *See* Part III, Ch. 5, §2 for tortious provisions in sectoral laws.
21. Official Gazette RS, Nos 33/91-I, 42/97 – UZS68, 66/00 – UZ80, 24/03 – UZ3a, 47, 68, 69/04 – UZ14, 69/04 – UZ43, 69/04 – UZ50, 68/06 – UZ121, 140, 143, 47/13 – UZ148, 47/13 – UZ90, 97, 99, 75/16 – UZ70a, 92/21 – UZ62a.
22. Article 26 of the Constitution of the Republic of Slovenia.
23. Article 30 of the Constitution of the Republic of Slovenia.
24. Article 33 of the Constitution of the Republic of Slovenia.
25. Article 35 of the Constitution of the Republic of Slovenia.
26. Article 53 of the Constitution of the Republic of Slovenia.
27. Article 67 of the Constitution of the Republic of Slovenia.
28. Article 74 of the Constitution of the Republic of Slovenia.
29. Official Gazette RS, Nos 97/07 – official consolidated text, 64/16 – Constitutional Court decision, 20/18 – OROZ631.
30. Official Gazette RS, Nos 87/02, 91/13, 23/20.
31. Official Gazette RS, Nos 15/17, 21/18 – ZNOrg, 22/19, 67/19 – ZMatR-C, 200/20 – ZOOMTVI, 94/22 – Constitutional Court decision, 94/22 – Constitutional Court decision, 5/23.
32. Official Gazette SRS, No. 15/76, Official Gazette RS, Nos 13/94 – ZN, 40/94 – Constitutional Court decision, 117/00 – Constitutional Court decision, 67/01, 83/01 – OZ, 73/04 – ZN-C, 31/13 – Constitutional Court decision, 63/16.

of inheritance law. However, these laws do not constitute a comprehensive regulation of the traditional disciplines of civil law, as various issues in these areas are governed by numerous other laws, such as the Consumer Protection Act (ZVPot-1),[33] the Housing Act,[34] the Land Register Act,[35] the Inheritance of Agricultural Holdings Act[36] and many others.

56. The development of Slovenian civil law was significantly influenced by the Austrian *Allgemeines Bürgerliches Gesetzbuch* (ABGB) or General Civil Code (*Občni državljanski zakonik* – ODZ), which remained in force on the territory of the present RS until the end of the Second World War. It continued to be in use long after the establishment of socialist Yugoslavia and is still used in certain cases today (e.g., in the acquisition of property rights to real estate under the ODZ).[37] When the Yugoslav Obligations Act (Act on Obligation Relations (ZOR)),[38] a precursor of the Slovene OZ, was adopted in 1978, the legislator also followed the examples of the Swiss law on obligations and the Italian Civil Code. Additionally, it drew extensively from case law, the General Usages for Trade (*Splošne uzance za blagovni promet*),[39] and the so-called Hague Conventions.[40]

57. The ZOR was a highly modern law with remarkably contemporary solutions and closely comparable to the legislations of the Western countries of the time. For this reason, most of its provisions were incorporated into the OZ when it was adopted on 3 October 2001. As previously mentioned, the OZ is now the primary legal source for Slovenian law of obligations and tort law. In Article 10, it establishes one of its fundamental principles: the prohibition of causing harm (*neminem laedere*). Subsequently, in the second section, Articles 131 to 189 regulate liability for causing harm.

58. Other provisions of the OZ are also relevant to Slovenian tort law, including the provisions related to compensation for breach of contract (Articles 239 to 246 of the OZ), the statute of limitations for tort claims (Articles 352 to 354 and 357 of the OZ), the provisions on property insurance and more. In addition, various other laws regulate liability for compensation or address matters related to compensation, including the ZVPot-1, the Environmental Protection Act,[41] the Employment

33. Official Gazette RS, No. 130/22.
34. Official Gazette RS, Nos 69/03, 18/04 – ZVKSES, 47/06 – ZEN, 45/08 – ZVEtL, 57/08, 62/10 – ZUPJS, 56/11 – Constitutional Court decision, 87/11, 40/12 – ZUJF, 14/17 – Constitutional Court decision, 27/17, 59/19, 189/20 – ZFRO, 90/21, 18/23 – ZDU-1O, 77/23 – Constitutional Court decision.
35. Official Gazette RS, Nos 58/03, 37/08 – ZST-1, 45/08, 28/09, 25/11, 14/15 – ZUUJFO, 69/17, 11/18 – ZIZ-L, 16/19 – ZNP-1, 121/21.
36. Official Gazette RS, Nos 70/95, 54/99 – Constitutional Court decision, 30/13, 44/22 – ZKZ-G.
37. *See*, e.g., ECLI:SI:VSRS:2021:II.IPS.85.2020, ECLI:SI:VSKP:2020:I.CP.487.2019, etc.
38. Official Gazette RS, Nos 29/78, 39/85, 45/89 – Constitutional Court decision, 57/89, Official Gazette RS, Nos 88/99 – ZRTVS-B, 83/01 – OZ, 30/02 – ZPlaP, 87/02 – SPZ.
39. Official Gazette FLRJ, No. 15/54.
40. Cf. Damjan Možina, in Juhart et al., *Uvod v. civilno pravo* (2011), p. 39.
41. Official Gazette RS, Nos 44/22, 18/23 – ZDU-1O, 78/23 – ZUNPEOVE.

Relationships Act (ZDR-1),[42] the Game and Hunting Act (ZDLov-1),[43] the Copyright and Related Rights Act[44] and many others.

59. EU regulations also play a significant role in Slovenian civil and tort law. While the EU does not have general legislative authority in the field of civil law to enact a European civil code, it does have specific competences in areas such as consumer protection law, law of obligations, labour law, intellectual property law, private international law and more. As a result, the EU has adopted numerous acts (regulations and directives) that affect both civil law and tort law. For example, Directive 85/374/EEC[45] (*see more* in Part III, Chapter 2) has had a notable impact. In addition to the primary and secondary acts of EU law, the case law of the Court of Justice of the European Union (CJEU) is also significant in these areas, as its decisions on the interpretation of EU law within the framework of preliminary rulings are binding on all (*erga omnes*) and usually have a retroactive effect (*ex tunc*). CJEU case law is particularly important in cases such as determining compensation for non-pecuniary damage due to workplace discrimination or harassment under Article 8 of the ZDR-1. This is especially relevant in relation to the three principles: effectiveness, proportionality, and deterrence of compensation.[46]

60. Furthermore, an important source of Slovenian civil law includes customs as unwritten rules of conduct that arise spontaneously through repeated factual use by legal entities and are acknowledged by these entities.[47] Numerous legal rules explicitly refer to customs,[48] and Article 12 of the OZ explicitly elevates commercial customs – as behaviour expected between economic entities – to legal sources. A specific form of customs is usages (*Uzance*), which are codified business customs that are not adopted by the legislator but by associations of economic entities (e.g., chambers of commerce) or individual economic entities (e.g., exchanges, banks).[49]

61. Case law in the RS is not a formal source of law (with the exception of the fundamental legal opinions of the Supreme Court, which are binding on the Supreme Court senates and can only be changed in a new general session).[50] Nevertheless,

---

42. Official Gazette RS, Nos 21/13, 78/13 – corr., 47/15 – ZZSDT, 33/16 – PZ-F, 52/16, 15/17 – Constitutional Court decision, 22/19 – ZPosS, 81/19, 203/20 – ZIUPOPDVE, 119/21 – ZČmIS-A, 202/21 – Constitutional Court decision, 15/22, 54/22 – ZUPŠ-1.
43. Official Gazette RS, Nos 16/04, 120/06 – Constitutional Court decision, 17/08, 46/14 – ZON-C, 31/18, 65/20, 97/20 – corr., 44/22, 158/22.
44. Official Gazette RS, Nos 16/07 – official consolidated text, 68/08, 110/13, 56/15, 63/16 – ZKUASP, 59/19 and 130/22.
45. Council Directive 85/374/EEC of 25 Jul. 1985 on the approximation of the laws, regulations and administrative provisions of the Member States concerning liability for defective products (OJ L 210, 7.8.1985, p. 29–33).
46. *See* more in ECLI:SI:VSRS:2021:VIII.IPS.14.2021 and Petra Weingerl, *Nekompenzatorna povrnitev škode*, Pravni letopis (2022), p. 29–48.
47. Cf. Možina, *supra* n. 40, at 44.
48. *See*, e.g., Arts 23, 28, 32, etc. of the OZ.
49. *See more* in Vesna Kranjc, *Gospodarsko pogodbeno pravo* (2020), p. 59.
50. Cf. Art. 110 of the Courts Act (Official Gazette RS, Nos 94/07 – official consolidated text, 45/08, 96/09, 86/10 – ZJNepS, 33/11, 75/12 – ZSPDSLS-A, 63/13, 17/15, 23/17 – ZSSve, 22/18 – ZSICT, 16/19 – ZNP-1, 104/20, 203/20 – ZIUPOPDVE, 18/23 – ZDU-1O).

within the concept of established case law, court decisions have a kind of precedential effect, as courts are not allowed to deviate arbitrarily or without reasonable legal justification from the uniform and established case law.[51] Thus, established case law is a means of ensuring the uniform and equal application of formal legal sources. One can speak of established case law when there are several identical decisions on the same legal issue, although there are no mathematical formulas defining how many identical decisions are required to establish case law.[52] In the field of tort law, for example, case law is crucial in determining compensation for non-pecuniary damage, as the harmful consequences of a particular injured party are assessed in comparison to the harmful consequences of other injured parties in different scenarios from case law, thus ensuring consistent treatment and determination of compensation within appropriate frameworks (the principle of objective conditioning; *see more* in Part VI, Chapter 2, §3 and Chapter 4, §2).

62. The opinions of legal experts, usually expressed in scientific and professional publications, are not formal sources of law.[53] Nevertheless, courts and other competent authorities often refer to theoretical works when justifying their decisions if they contain persuasive arguments.

§3. Function of the Law of Torts

63. The fundamental function of Slovenian tort law is to remedy the unjust situation in which the injured party finds himself or herself, i.e., to redress his or her disadvantage.[54] This compensatory or reparative function of tort law is realised through the injured party's right to claim compensation for (actual and, under certain conditions, also future) damage and the tortfeasor's obligation to compensate for this damage.

64. The purpose of compensation for pecuniary damage is to restore the injured party financially to the position he or she would have been in if the tortious event had not occurred (principle of full compensation).[55] Pecuniary damage, on the one hand, can be compensated in kind (restitution) or in money (equivalence), and the injured party can choose between these two options unless the circumstances of the case dictate otherwise (*see* Part VI, Chapter 3, §2).[56] On the other hand, non-pecuniary loss cannot be discussed in terms of full compensation or reparation. Physical pain, mental suffering, and fear cannot be assessed in monetary terms. For this reason, the monetary compensation for non-pecuniary damage cannot conceptually aim to provide full compensation, as is the case with pecuniary damage, but

---

51. ECLI:SI:VSLJ:2016:V.CPG.276.2015, ECLI:SI:VSLJ:2017:V.CPG.939.2017, ECLI:SI:VSLJ:2019:V.CPG.37.2019, etc.
52. ECLI:SI:USRS:2019:U.I.56.17.
53. ECLI:SI:VSRS:2007:II.IPS.267.2005, ECLI:SI:VSLJ:2009:II.CP.4359.2008.
54. ECLI:SI:VSLJ:2016:I.CP.1397.2016, ECLI:SI:VSRS:2014:II.IPS.114.2012, ECLI:SI:VSRS:2015:II.IPS.59.2014, ECLI:SI:VSRS:2021:III.IPS.8.2020, etc.
55. Cf. Art. 169 of the OZ.
56. Cf. Art. 164 of the OZ.

it is intended to provide the injured party with adequate satisfaction for the harm caused. With the amount of money awarded, the injured party can afford comforts that he or she would not otherwise have, which in turn can contribute to the restoration of the disrupted psychological balance caused by physical pain, mental suffering, or fear.[57]

65. In addition to its compensatory function, Slovenian tort law also has a preventive or deterrent function. One of the fundamental principles of Slovenian obligations law, which is codified in Article 10 of the OZ,[58] is the principle of not harming anyone (*neminem laedere*). Everyone is thus obligated to refrain from (active and passive) actions that could potentially cause harm to another. Even though the intuitive aim of tort law is to restore, i.e., to remedy the negative consequences (damage) that occur in the victim's sphere, the aspect of prevention is also of paramount importance. Tort law or the threat of liability[59] therefore essentially also serves to encourage the specific offender and all potential wrongdoers to refrain from acts that could cause harm (specific and general prevention).

66. The preventive function of tort law is also realised through so-called prohibitory claims, which the affected party can assert even before damage occurs and request from the court or other competent authority a prohibition of specific conduct that violates or threatens his or her pecuniary or non-pecuniary rights or legally protected interests (*see* Part VI, Chapter 7, §2). These claims embody the principle of 'do no harm' in the sense that they enable the realisation of judicial protection even before the damage occurs or, if the damage has already occurred, facilitate the effective prevention of future harm.[60] In this regard, Article 134(2) of the OZ also stipulates that the court or other competent authority may order the infringer to cease the act that violates the personal rights of another, failing which he or she shall be obliged to pay the party concerned a specified sum of money, calculated either as a lump sum or per unit of time. This sum of money has the nature of a civil penalty intended to make the infringer cease behaviour that infringes upon personal rights, regardless of the damage.

67. The preventive or deterrent function must be distinguished from the punitive function of tort law in the strict sense, which is characteristic of countries with an Anglo-Saxon legal system. We refer to situations in which the court awards the injured party, in addition to the amount needed to restore his or her financial position to what it would have been had the injurious event not occurred or to the sum required for the subjective satisfaction (gratification) of the injured party, also an amount of damages intended to punish or avenge the wrongdoer. The fact that punitive damages are incompatible with the nature and purpose of Slovenian tort law follows from the aforementioned principle of full compensation, which requires that

---

57. ECLI:SI:VSKP:2015:I.CP.971.2014, ECLI:SI:VSRS:2012:II.IPS.59.2011, etc.
58. Official Gazette RS, Nos 97/07 – official consolidated text, 64/16 – Constitutional Court decision, and 20/18 – OROZ631.
59. Cf. Art. 131(1): 'Whoever causes harm to another is obligated to compensate for it … '.
60. Cf. Dunja Jadek Pensa, in Plavšak et al., *Obligacijski zakonik (OZ) (splošni del) s komentarjem, 1. knjiga* (2003), p. 763.

the liable party reimburses the injured party for the entire pecuniary loss and nothing more.[61] Similarly, the second paragraph of Article 179 of the OZ concerning non-pecuniary damages stipulates that the amount of compensation depends on the significance of the affected asset and the purpose of such damages, but should not support tendencies that are incompatible with its nature and intent. Both case law and theorists principally reject the punitive function of Slovenian tort law. However, there are mechanisms within Slovenian tort law and in broader civil law that contain elements of punishment (*see* Part VI, Chapter 7, §3).

§4. Relationship Between Torts and Criminal Law

68. In Slovenian law, there is a clear distinction between tort law and criminal law. Criminal law, as a branch of public law, comprises a set of legal rules and principles that regulate and at the same time limit the repressive power of the state. Thus, the provisions of criminal law define criminal offences, sanctions for these offences, and the conditions under which both natural and legal persons can be held accountable for criminal offences (substantive criminal law); the competencies of the authorities for detection, prosecution and adjudication; and the rights and obligations of the accused and other participants in criminal proceedings (procedural criminal law); the manner of enforcement of criminal sanctions (criminal enforcement law); and the organisation and position of the authorities responsible for detection, prosecution and adjudication in criminal legal matters, as well as their relationship to each other (organisational criminal law).[62]

69. The fundamental legislative sources of Slovenian criminal law are the Criminal Code (CC-1),[63] which is divided into a general[64] and a specific[65] part and represents the codification of the substantive criminal law of the RS, and the Criminal Procedure Act (ZKP),[66] which lays down procedural rules ensuring that no innocent person is convicted and that the perpetrator of a criminal offence is sentenced under the conditions stipulated by criminal law and following lawful proceedings.[67] In addition to these, the legislative sources of Slovenian criminal law also include the Liability of Legal Persons for Criminal Offences Act[68] and the Enforcement of

61. ECLI:SI:VSRS:1997:II.IPS.260.95.
62. *See* more in Liljana Selinšek, *Kazensko pravo, Splošni del in osnove posebnega dela* (GV Založba 2007), pp. 31–32.
63. Official Gazette RS, Nos 50/12 – official consolidated text, 6/16 – corr., 54/15, 38/16, 27/17, 23/20, 91/20, 95/21, 186/21, 105/22 – ZZNŠPP, 16/23.
64. The general part of the KZ-1 contains criminal law norms related to three fundamental concepts of criminal law: the general notion of a criminal offence, the concept of criminal liability, and the concept of punishment or criminal sanctions.
65. The specific part of the KZ-1 provides descriptions of individual criminal offences and the associated penalties.
66. Official Gazette RS, Nos 176/21 – official consolidated text, 96/22 – Constitutional Court decision, 2/23 – Constitutional Court decision, 89/23 – Constitutional Court decision.
67. Article 1(1) of the Criminal Procedure Act.
68. Official Gazette RS, Nos 98/04 – official consolidated text, 65/08, 57/12.

Criminal Sanctions Act.[69] Also relevant to criminal law are the legal regulations concerning the organisation of the courts, the public prosecution, and the police.[70]

70. Despite a clear distinction, criminal and tort law overlap in certain cases. The relationship between tort and criminal law is primarily reflected in the treatment of preliminary questions, the mutual reliance on final judgments, in dealing with identical factual situations, and in the adhesion procedure, i.e., when a criminal court deals with property rights claims arising from the commission of a criminal offence.

71. A preliminary question is a distinct legal issue, which the body conducting the procedure is not competent to resolve, but the resolution of which is crucial for the decision in the main matter, as it is part of the factual situation. In this context, a criminal offence is a preliminary question in tort proceedings, particularly in two cases: in the statute of limitations for damage claims and in a lawsuit for compensation due to a violation of human dignity. According to Article 352 of the OZ, a damage claim becomes statute-barred three years after the injured party has become aware of the damage and the person who caused it (subjective statute of limitations). However, in all cases, it becomes statute-barred within five years from the time when the damage occurred (objective statute of limitations). Nevertheless, if the damage was caused by a criminal act, and a longer statute of limitations is prescribed for the prosecution, the claim for damages against the responsible person expires when the period determined for the statute of limitations for the criminal prosecution expires. Similarly, the interruption or suspension of criminal prosecution also results in the interruption or suspension of the statute of limitations for the damage claim.[71] According to Article 181 of the OZ, a person who has been induced into criminal sexual intercourse or another sexual act by fraud, force, or abuse of a relationship of subordination or dependence as well as a person against whom any other criminal offence against personal dignity or morality has been committed, is entitled to fair financial compensation for mental anguish suffered. With the OZ, the commission of a criminal offence is no longer a preliminary issue in determining compensation based on the value the thing had for the injured party (*pretium affectionis*). It is sufficient that the thing was intentionally destroyed or damaged, not necessarily by a criminal act, as was provided for in the predecessor law, the ZOR.[72]

69. Official Gazette RS, Nos 110/06 – official consolidated text, 76/08, 40/09, 9/11 – ZP-1G, 96/12 – ZPIZ-2, 109/12, 54/15, 11/18, 200/20 – ZOOMTVI and 141/22.
70. *See* Courts Act (Official Gazette RS, Nos 94/07 – official consolidated text, 45/08, 96/09, 86/10 – ZJNepS, 33/11, 75/12 – ZSPDSLS-A, 63/13, 17/15, 23/17 – ZSSve, 22/18 – ZSICT, 16/19 – ZNP-1, 104/20, 203/20 – ZIUPOPDVE, 18/23 – ZDU-1O), State Prosecution Service Act (Official Gazette RS, Nos 58/11, 21/12 – ZDU1F, 47/12, 15/13 – ZODPol, 47/13 – ZDU-1G, 48/13 – ZSKZDČEU-1, 19/15, 23/17 – ZSSve, 36/19, 139/20, 54/21, 105/22 – ZZNŠPP), Organisation and Work of the Police Act (Official Gazette RS, Nos 15/13, 11/14, 86/15, 77/16, 77/17, 36/19, 66/19 – ZDZ, 200/20, 172/21, 105/22 – ZZNŠPP, 141/22).
71. Article 353 of the OZ.
72. Cf. Art. 168(4) of the OZ and Art. 189(4) of the ZOR.

72. According to the Civil Procedure Act (ZPP),[73] when a judgment in the main matter depends on the preliminary resolution of a certain issue and the latter has not yet been decided upon by the competent authority, the civil court may either resolve this issue itself unless otherwise specified by special regulations, or it may suspend the proceedings and await the resolution of this issue in the relevant domain. As far as the preliminary question of the existence of a criminal offence is concerned, there is no specific regulation expressly prohibiting its resolution in civil (compensation) proceedings.[74] However, according to Slovenian judicial practice, only in exceptional cases can the civil court itself decide whether the damage was caused by a criminal act. Thus, a civil court can only decide on the existence of a criminal offence as a preliminary question if it is clear that criminal proceedings can no longer take place (e.g., due to the offender's death, an amnesty or the withdrawal of the prosecutor's charges of which the injured party was not informed). However, if in the specific case, there are no obstacles to possible criminal proceedings against the perpetrator of the damage, preference should be given to the presumption of innocence under Article 27 of the URS, which generally prevents the civil court from deciding by itself on the existence of a criminal offence as a preliminary question.[75]

73. If the question of the existence of a criminal offence is resolved in a criminal procedure as the main issue, the civil court is bound by both the criminal conviction and the criminal acquittal.[76] As regards the binding effect of a rejection judgment (and the decisions concluding the criminal proceedings, i.e., the decision to discontinue the proceedings or to dismiss the indictment), the crucial factor is the reason for which the rejection judgment was issued. It is essential to consider that while some reasons leading to a rejection judgment (or the discontinuation of the criminal proceedings or the dismissal of the indictment) are essentially the same as the reasons for issuing an acquittal, the others are not (e.g., statute of limitations, amnesty, death of the offender).[77] Therefore, the civil court is also bound by the rejection of the criminal judgment if the reasons leading to the rejection of the judgment would also have resulted in a criminal acquittal (e.g., withdrawal of the indictment due to lack of evidence).[78]

---

73. Official Gazette RS, Nos 73/07 – official consolidated text, 45/08 – ZArbit, 45/08, 111/08 – Constitutional Court decision, 57/09 – Constitutional Court decision, 12/10 – Constitutional Court decision, 50/10 – Constitutional Court decision, 107/10 – Constitutional Court decision, 75/12 – Constitutional Court decision, 40/13 – Constitutional Court decision, 92/13 – Constitutional Court decision, 10/14 – Constitutional Court decision, 48/15 – Constitutional Court decision, 6/17 – Constitutional Court decision, 10/17, 16/19 – ZNP-1, 70/19 – Constitutional Court decision, 1/22 – Constitutional Court decision, 3/22 – ZDeb.
74. Cf. Arts 13(1) and 206(1) of the Civil Procedure Act.
75. ECLI:SI:VSRS:2003:II.IPS.548.2002 and ECLI:SI:VSRS:2013:II.IPS.381.2010.
76. In the past, the VSRS held that a civil court is not bound by an acquittal in criminal proceedings if it was issued due to a lack of evidence (*see* ECLI:SI:VSRS:2012:II.IPS.196.2011). This position was the subject of criticism in legal theory (*see* more in Aleš Galič, *Predhodno vprašanje in identična dejanska stanja v razmerju med kazenskim in pravdnim postopkom*, Pravni letopis (2016), pp. 132–135), it was also quickly surpassed in judicial practice (*see* ECLI:SI:VSRS:2016:II.IPS.149.2015 and ECLI:SI:VSRS:2019:II.IPS.347.2017).
77. Galič, *supra* n. 76, at 136.
78. ECLI:SI:VSRS:2012:II.IPS.196.2011 and ECLI:SI:VSLJ:2016:II.CP.35.2016.

74. One must distinguish between preliminary questions and cases in which a civil court examines the same factual circumstances or historical event from the perspective of the existence of a duty to compensate as a criminal court does regarding the existence of a criminal offence. In these cases, it is not about a preliminary question, as the existence of the obligation to compensate does not depend on the prior clarification of whether the damage was caused by a criminal act. Instead, it is simply a matter of both civil and criminal courts dealing with the same historical event, each from its own perspective. This situation is regulated by Article 14 of the ZPP, which states that when a lawsuit is based on the same factual situation that has already been decided in a criminal procedure, the civil court is bound by the final conviction issued in the criminal procedure, solely in terms of the existence of a criminal offence and the criminal liability of the perpetrator. Hence, the civil court is bound by the criminal court's findings regarding the illegality of the act, the occurrence of the prohibited consequence, and the causal link between the act and the outcome (existence of the criminal offence), as well as the findings on the perpetrator's mental competency and culpability (criminal liability). Therefore, a perpetrator of damage who has been definitively convicted in a criminal procedure cannot claim in a subsequent compensation lawsuit that the act was not committed, that it was not illegal, that there was no causal link between his or her action and the damage incurred, that no damage occurred, or that he or she was mentally incompetent or not guilty.[79] However, the civil court is not bound by other findings of the criminal court (e.g., determination of the extent of damage) unless they affect the existence of the criminal act.[80] As civil liability is stricter than criminal liability,[81] the civil court is not bound by a criminal acquittal in situations of identical factual circumstances, unlike in the case of a criminal act as a preliminary issue.[82] Even if a defendant is acquitted in a criminal procedure, the civil court may impose a compensation payment if it deems that all prerequisites for the compensation obligation have been met.

75. In the so-called adhesion proceedings, the criminal court decides on a claim which, due to its legal nature, bears the characteristics of a civil claim or lawsuit. This monetary claim or claim related to property damage/loss may relate to compensation for damage, the restitution of a thing, or the annulment of a specific legal transaction.[83] A criminal court can only decide on the monetary claim arising from a criminal offence if it delivers a conviction[84] but only if this would not unduly prolong the

79. ECLI:SI:VSCE:2007:CP.1311.2006.
80. *See* more in Galič, *supra* n. 76, at 124.
81. In civil law, strict liability is sometimes applied (*see* Part III, Ch. 5, §1), while strict liability is incompatible with modern criminal law. Certain offences are solely intentional (e.g., crimes against humanity and international law), whereas negligence always suffices for liability in tort. The age limit for tortious liability (*see* Part I, Ch. 1, §4) is lower than the age limit for criminal responsibility, etc. *See* Galič, *supra* n. 76, at 122.
82. ECLI:SI:VDSS:2019:PDP.544.2019, ECLI:SI:VDSS:2020:PDP.639.2019, ECLI:SI:VSKP:2017:I.CP.331.2017, etc.
83. Article 100(2) of the ZKP.
84. Cf. Art. 105(2) of the ZKP.

criminal proceedings.[85] In adhesion proceedings, the monetary claim can be asserted by anyone who is entitled to assert such a claim in a civil lawsuit.[86] The criminal court may grant the victim's monetary claim either in full or in part. In the latter case, it instructs the victim to pursue the remaining part of the monetary claim in a civil lawsuit. The criminal court shall instruct the victim to assert the entire monetary claim in a civil lawsuit if the data from the criminal proceedings do not provide a reliable basis for a full or partial judgment, and also in the event of a criminal acquittal, dismissal, or termination of the criminal proceedings.[87]

§5. Relationship Between Contractual and Delictual or Tortious Responsibility

76. In principle, in Slovenian law, one can speak of the unity of the institution of business/contractual responsibility and legal or delictual tortious responsibility,[88] even though delictual tort liability arises from the tortious conduct of the person causing the damage, who did not have a legal/business relationship with the injured party prior to the occurrence of the damage, in contrast to business liability, which arises from the breach of a legal/business obligation. Both forms of liability result in the tortfeasor's obligation to compensate the injured party for the damage for which he or she is responsible (tort obligation).[89]

77. The unity of the legal institution of tortious responsibility is also evidenced by the provisions of a special section in the OZ which regulates the specifics of contractual tort liability. Article 246 of the OZ provides that in the absence of a special provision, the provisions on compensation for non-contractual damages shall apply mutatis mutandis to compensation for damages resulting from a breach of a contractual obligation. Article 243(5) of the OZ extends the application of the two rules

85. Cf. Art. 100(1) of the ZKP.
86. Article 101 of the ZKP.
87. Cf. Art. 105 of the ZKP.
88. Already mentioned in earlier theory: Stojan Cigoj, *Teorija obligacij: splošni del obligacijskega prava* (2003), p. 169; Boris Strohsack, *Obligacijska razmerja I; Obligacijska razmerja II (odškodninsko pravo in druge neposlovne obveznosti)*, (1998), p. 15.
89. The prerequisites for non-contractual and contractual compensation obligations in Slovenian law are four: unlawfulness, impermissible damage, causation, and liability. However, the content of these prerequisites differs when considering their substance in non-contractual (tortious) contexts (for subjective liability *see* Part I, Ch. 1, §1; for strict liability *see* Part III, Ch. 5, §1) and in contractual contexts. In the latter case, the unlawfulness is manifested in a breach of contract (e.g., non-fulfilment or delay in performance) by the responsible party/counterparty, and this breach of contract is the cause of the damage (causation), unless the responsible party can exempt itself according to Art. 240 of the OZ ('A debtor is free from liability for damage if he proves that he could not fulfil his obligation or that he was delayed in fulfilling his obligation due to circumstances that arose after the conclusion of the contract, which he could not prevent, eliminate, or avoid.'). The question of the burden of proof is not among the differences, as there is a presumption of liability in both non-contractual and contractual obligations (reversed burden of proof). Similarly, the concept of legally recognised damage remains the same, although in the realm of contractual liability the principle of full compensation is significantly limited by the so-called principle of foreseeability (*see* Part VI, Ch. 2, §3).

contained in the section on contractual liability for damages (i.e., *duty to mitigate* and *compensatio lucri cum damno*) to delictual tort liability as well.

78. While case law has already indicated that the question of unity of the institution is more of a theoretical issue,[90] it is also true that recent literature[91] has shown that there are some important exceptions that help us understand the differences between contractual and delictual tortious liability. In particular, four features of business liability are important, namely: the limited possibility of exculpation of the injured party in business liability, where exculpation is not possible merely by proving that the injured party did not cause the damage (for more on exculpation *see* Part I, Chapters 1 & 2); limiting the extent of damage to the criterion of foreseeability (for more on limiting the compensation in business tort liability, *see* Part VI, Chapters 2 & 3); the possibility of pre-emption and extension of business liability (for more on exclusion clauses, *see* Part IV, Chapter 4); and a different limitation period for business tort liability (*see* Part IV, Chapter 1).

79. Although neither in Slovenian legislation nor in case law does the *non cumul* rule known from French law apply (even in the case of breach of contract, a tort lawsuit can be filed on the basis of law if the constituent elements of a civil wrong are met, as the court has repeatedly held in relation to the tortious liability of doctors),[92] under Slovenian law an injured party cannot claim compensation twice for the same damage by first claiming the full extent of the damage under one cause of action and then under another, even if the facts contain all the features of both causes of action. However, the injured party is free to choose the basis for the claim for damages.

80. The possibility of freely choosing the basis for damages is also evident in the case of pre-contractual liability (*culpa in contrahendo*). The only fact or form of pre-contractual liability explicitly regulated in the OZ is liability for unfair negotiations (Article 20 of the OZ).[93] All other forms of pre-contractual liability (obligation to

90. *See* ECLI:SI:VSRS:1999:II.IPS.70.98: The question of the monism or dualism of tort liability and tort obligations arising from contractual (business) and extra-contractual (non-business) grounds is a theoretical question. It is a question that has undergone a certain historical development, has been treated differently in different legal systems and has been dealt with by theorists, especially in comparative law.

91. Damjan Možina, *Pogodbena in nepogodbena odškodninska odgovornost: ODZ (1811) in Obligacijski zakonik (2001)*, in *Izročilo Občnega državljanskega zakonika* (2013), p. 356.

92. *See* ECLI:SI:VSLJ:2009:II.CP.2457.2009, where the court explicitly stated: Healthcare, the rights of patients, including the right to compensation, and the duties of health professionals are directly regulated by and derived from the law. The legal basis for compensation for the harm claimed by the complainant is thus established by the HSA (and not by the contract), while the conditions and forms of compensation recognised by law are regulated by the OZ in Arts 131 to 189.

It is clear from Slovenian case law that there are two types of medical liability for damages suffered by a patient, namely business or non-business liability, as the courts leave it up to the injured party to decide on which basis to claim damages (similar to the common law system) and do not reject claims based on one or the other (for more on this, *see* Part I, Ch. 2, §1 II).

93. The legal state of facts of unfair negotiations includes two forms: negotiations without the intention of concluding a contract (Art. 20(2) of the OZ) and unjustified withdrawal from negotiations (Art. 20(3) of the OZ).

make truthful statements before concluding the contract, obligation to disclose relevant facts, obligation to protect information obtained during negotiations) can be derived from general principles, in particular, the obligation to act diligently and in good faith when concluding legal transactions (Article 5(1) of the OZ).[94] Even if the two parties do not breach the contract by violating their pre-contractual obligations before the conclusion of the contract since it has not yet been concluded, the parties are not two 'strangers', as in the case of pure non-business tort liability (e.g., when a motorcycle driver runs over a pedestrian and injures the pedestrian's spine, causing damage),[95] and we are therefore approaching the views in case law and literature that define pre-contractual liability as a form of business tort liability.[96]

§6. Protected Interests

81. Slovenian law does not provide an exhaustive list of specific protected interests for which compensation can be sought, although some interests are explicitly highlighted in the OZ (e.g., loss of profits, loss of earnings). However, the rights defined in the URS are undoubtedly among the highest hierarchical rights (e.g., the right to inviolability of life, prohibition of torture, etc.).[97] Nevertheless, Slovenian tort law does not recognise a hierarchy of legally protected interests or legal goods.[98]

82. In Slovenian tort law, all interests (life, body, health, freedom, property, or other rights) are in principle legally protected if they can be subsumed under the concept of legally recognised pecuniary or non-pecuniary damage (*see* more on pecuniary and non-pecuniary loss in Part VI, Chapter 2, §3) and if the other three conditions (besides damage) for either non-contractual/tortious (subjective[99] or

94. Cf. Vesna Kranjc, *Gospodarsko pogodbeno pravo* (2020), p. 122.
95. Nevertheless, both case law (*see* ECLI:SI:VSLJ:2013: II.CP.1648.2012: Unfair negotiations condition tort liability, which is a special form of non-business tort liability.) as well as the literature; *see* Nina Plavšak, Miha Juhart & Renato Vrenčur, *Obligacijsko pravo: splošni del* (2009), p. 281, have held that pre-contractual liability is a special form of non-business tort liability.
96. Cf. Vesna Kranjc, in Plavšak et al., *Obligacijski zakonik (OZ) (splošni del) s komentarjem, 1. knjiga* (2003), p. 230; ECLI:SI:VSLJ:2011:I.CPG.1433.2010: The Court of First Instance correctly assessed the (un)fairness of the negotiations and, on that basis, drew its conclusions regarding the defendant's business tort liability; ECLI:SI:VSCE:2017:CP.462.2016: The Claimant did indeed claim damages under the provisions of Arts 239 and 243 of the OZ, but the Respondent did not violate the contents of the letter of intent or the contractual intent but executed the letter of intent as it read and therefore its conduct cannot be characterised as having the elements of tort liability under the rules on business liability, as explained above, as the Respondent's conduct at the negotiation stage was not unlawful, as it negotiated in good faith and performed all the obligations under the Letter of Intent as they stood therein.
97. Cf. Marijan Pavčnik, *Teorija prava* (2011), p. 157.
98. *See* more in Damjan Možina, *Obseg varstva pravnih dobrin v deliktnem pravu: kako generalna je generalna klavzula*, Pravni letopis (2022), pp. 9–28.
99. Article 131(1) of the OZ: 'Anyone who causes damage to another is obliged to compensate it unless they prove that the damage occurred without their fault.'

objective)[100] or contractual tortious obligations to arise are fulfilled. The result of these fulfilled conditions for all forms of tortious obligations is the obligation of the wrongdoer to compensate the injured party for the damage for which he or she is responsible.[101] This also stems from the general clauses for tortious obligations (subjective and objective) in Article 131 of the OZ and also for contractual tortious obligations in Article 239(2) of the OZ,[102] even though these general clauses do not explicitly enumerate the protected goods, unlike the German §823 *Bürgerliches Gesetzbuch* (Civil Code (BGB)). According to Slovenian law, a legally recognised pecuniary damage is not only an encroachment on the property rights of another (e.g., ownership), but there must also be a further consequence in the form of a reduction of the injured party's property or a prevention of its increase (lost profit).[103] Similarly, the mere interference with the physical or mental integrity of the injured party (primary consequence) is generally not sufficient to establish a tortious obligation of the responsible party, but there must also be a secondary consequence in the form of physical pain, mental anguish, or fear. The concept of legal interest is therefore not the same as legally recognised damage.

83. However, it should be emphasised that in Slovenian tort law, as in most legal systems, various interests are treated differently depending on the type of interest and the legal situation. It cannot be asserted that all interests are equally protected, as the level of protection may also vary depending on the specific circumstances of the case. For example, the right to a healthy living environment is ensured by Article 72(1) of the URS. The URS also mandates the state to take care of a healthy living

100. Article 131(2) of the OZ: 'For damage from things or activities that pose a greater risk of harm to the surroundings, one is liable regardless of fault.' Article 131(3) of the OZ: 'One is also liable for damages regardless of fault in other cases specified by law.'

101. In Slovenian law, the prerequisites for non-contractual and contractual compensation obligations are fourfold: unlawfulness, impermissible damage, causation, and liability. However, the content of these prerequisites differs in terms of their substance for non-contractual and contractual obligations. In non-contractual/delictual obligations, fault is the content of the fourth prerequisite, i.e., liability (*see* more in Part I, Ch. 1, §§1, 2). In the case of strict liability, fault is not a condition; instead, it is sufficient for the fourth prerequisite that the liable person cannot exempt himself or herself with the statutory reasons from Art. 153 of the OZ and is therefore liable. Also, the criterion of unlawfulness (or impermissibility) is not assessed in terms of the wrongdoer's unlawful act (as in fault-based liability) but manifests itself in the harmful fact of a dangerous thing or activity (*see* more in Part III, Ch. 5, §1). In contractual liability, the content of the unlawfulness prerequisite is a breach of contract (e.g., non-fulfilment or delay in fulfilment) by the responsible party/contractual partner, and this breach of contract is the cause of the damage (causal link) unless the wrongdoer/debtor can exempt himself or herself in accordance with Art. 240 of the OZ ('The debtor is free from liability for damage if they prove that they could not fulfil their obligation or that they delayed in fulfilling the obligation due to circumstances that arose after the conclusion of the contract, which they could not prevent, remedy, or avoid.'). Non-contractual and contractual liabilities do not differ in terms of the allocation of the burden of proof, as there is a presumption of liability in both non-contractual and contractual obligations (reversed burden of proof), and the concept of legally recognised damage is also the same, although the principle of full compensation in the field of contractual liability is significantly limited by the so-called foreseeability principle (*see more* in Part VI, Ch. 2, §3). For the relationship between contractual and delictual/tortious liability, *see supra* General Introduction, §5.

102. Article 239(2) of the OZ: 'If the debtor does not fulfil the obligation or delays its fulfilment, the creditor is entitled to demand compensation for the damage caused to him/her as a result.'

103. Cf. ECLI:SI:VSRS:2017:II.IPS.337.2016, ECLI:SI:VSLJ:2014:I.CPG.1460.2012.

environment, among other things, by setting conditions and methods for conducting economic and other activities (Article 72(2) of the URS). The court includes the right to a healthy living environment among personal rights,[104] which means that economic activities should not be conducted solely in the interest of achieving the highest profit, neglecting, among other things, the protection of the environment and thereby indirectly the interests of others. Therefore, the OZ provides preventive protection against interference with protected interests (e.g., personal rights) even before damage has occurred (*see* more in Part VI, Chapter 7, §2). However, in certain circumstances, liability is excluded despite interference with the legally protected interest of a particular person (e.g., the right to a healthy living environment); namely, under Article 133(3) of the OZ, if the damage was caused while performing a generally beneficial activity for which a competent body has granted permission. In such a case, compensation can only be claimed for the damage exceeding the customary limits (*see* more in Part VI, Chapter 7, §2). Similarly to the exclusion of unlawfulness in the case of performing a generally beneficial activity, even though it causes damage (but not exceeding the usual limit), the OZ specifies other exceptions to the principle of *neminem laedere*, stating that an act is not impermissible or the damage does not need to be compensated if the damage is a result of the injured party's consent,[105] necessity,[106] self-defence, or permitted self-help.[107] Moreover, other Slovenian legislation explicitly determines permissible acts that exclude unlawfulness. For example, one of the more significant exceptions prescribed outside the OZ is the exclusion of the unlawfulness of expropriation, which is defined even in the URS. Under certain conditions in accordance with Article 69 of the URS, property rights to real estate can be withdrawn or restricted in the public interest, even against the will of the owner, which constitutes a significant interference with a person's property (*see* more in Part VI, Chapter 5).

84. In all cases of interference with human life, physical integrity or health, both pecuniary and non-pecuniary damages are recognised for the direct victim and also for indirect victims (*see* more in Part VI, Chapter 2, §2, §3 and Part VI, Chapter 4). However, for some indirect victims, there are limitations regarding the reimbursement of pecuniary damages, e.g., for employers who must by law pay a compensation salary for a certain period of time to an employee (direct victim) who has been injured in a traffic accident by a third party (perpetrator), even if the employee is not working. Employers also suffer a loss as they have to pay other workers, but courts do not recognise the employer's subrogation claim against the perpetrator's insurance company[108] as this right is not recognised by any law (*see* more in Part VI, Chapter 6, §2).

104. ECLI:SI:VSRS:1993:II.IPS.507.92.
105. *See* Part IV, Ch. 2, §1.
106. *See* Part IV, Ch. 2, §2.
107. *See* Part IV, Ch. 2, §3.
108. ECLI:SI:VSKP:2009:CPG.129.2008. Institutions in the field of social insurance have a recourse claim against the responsible person (*see* more in Part VI, Ch. 6, §2).

85. Individual freedom (e.g., unjustified deprivation of liberty) is also protected by a claim for pecuniary and non-pecuniary damages under the OZ.[109] In judicial practice, compensation for unjustified deprivation of liberty is usually determined as a unified compensation for one form of damage, which means that the court will not award as much compensation for mental pain, as there are different circumstances that influenced its onset, but only one. A single compensation is awarded for the said damage, and the court considers all the circumstances of the case that influenced the nature, severity, and duration of the mental pain (e.g., the reputation the victim previously enjoyed in his or her environment, the attitude of the environment towards him or her after the conviction or after deprivation of liberty, the severity and nature of the crime, the duration of the deprivation of liberty, etc.). The courts in Slovenia do not acknowledge that there was a violation of the right to work under Article 49 of the URS and an interference with physical and mental integrity and personal dignity for those who did not comply with certain measures – such as testing at the employer's premises during the COVID-19 epidemic – and were therefore removed from their jobs by the employers. The courts recognised that the benefits that testing brought to the individual and the community (the functioning of all segments of society despite the prevalence of the SARS-CoV-2 virus among individuals, including the possibility of a functioning public life) outweighed the weight of the unpleasant consequences for the individual.[110]

86. The recognition of pure economic loss is limited in Slovenia according to the rules regarding the reimbursement of pecuniary losses in the business and non-business sphere (*see* Part VI, Chapter 2, §4). And for this, no such extensive protection is guaranteed as for the most important subjective rights of the individual, that is, when it comes to physical interference with life, health, physical integrity, freedom, or property.

109. *See* more in ECLI:SI:VSRS:2018:II.IPS.42.2016.

110. ECLI:SI:VDSS:2023:PDP.663.2022, ECLI:SI:VDSS:2022:PDP.389.2022 and ECLI:SI:VDSS:2022:PDP.260.2022.

Part I. Liability for One's Own Acts

Chapter 1. General Principles

§1. Unlawfulness and Fault

87. The unlawfulness of conduct is not expressly provided for in the OZ as a condition for fault-based tort liability. The OZ mentions only fault in Article 131(1),[111] but not unlawfulness. However, both theory and judicial practice have always considered unlawfulness as one of the four prerequisites for fault-based compensation obligation (the other three being: impermissible damage, causation, and fault). The injured party can only prove the first three conditions (unlawfulness of the conduct, occurrence of a legally recognised damage, and causal link between the two), but not fault, as the burden of proof is reversed in Article 131(1) of the OZ. If the injured party has successfully proven the first three conditions, the tortfeasor (the liable person) must exonerate himself or herself by proving that the fourth condition (fault) does not apply, i.e., that he or she is not at fault for the damage inflicted.

88. As regards the fulfilment of the element of wrongfulness, the older theory already tended towards the interpretation that any harm is unacceptable if the law or moral principles are violated and unlawfulness is not expressly excluded by law (e.g., self-defence).[112] It was also argued that any conduct (act or omission) that is generally impermissible, even if not necessarily expressly prohibited or commanded by a legal norm, is sufficient to give rise to tort liability.[113]

89. This point of view continues to be upheld by case law, which has repeatedly argued[114] that improper conduct, which is a condition of fault-based tort liability, is not only conduct that violates what is imposed on the individual by positive rules but also conduct that violates generally accepted rules (customs, moral principles)

111. 'Whoever causes damage to another shall be obliged to reimburse it, unless he proves that the damage occurred through no fault of his own.' Article 131(1) of the OZ.
112. Cf. Stojan Cigoj, *Komentar obligacijskih razmerij: veliki komentar zakona o obligacijskih razmerjih, I. knjiga* (1984), pp. 86 et seq.
113. Cf. Boris Strohsack, *Obligacijska razmerja I; Obligacijska razmerja II (odškodninsko pravo in druge neposlovne obveznosti)* (1998), p. 23.
114. *See* ECLI:SI:VSRS:2018:II.IPS.46.2016, ECLI:SI:VSRS:2016:II.IPS.129.2015 and ECLI:SI:VSRS:2015:II.IPS.224.2013.

of due care in certain relationships and situations. In the absence of a rule prescribing certain due care, unlawfulness is assessed according to the criterion of whether it was foreseeable that the omission of due care would lead to a harmful consequence (objective foreseeability of harm).[115] However, even this criterion of objective foreseeability is not absolute, so there is no tendency in case law to take into account the 'mere' objective foreseeability of the harm and thus automatically apply the presumption of unlawfulness, since this objective criterion is mitigated by observing the principle of justice[116] and all elements of civil wrong.[117] The question of unlawfulness is often intertwined with the question of fault, the fourth condition of non-business fault-based tort liability, which is assessed from the point of view of due care (for more on fault, *see* Part I, Chapter 1, §2). For example, the court denied the existence of unlawful conduct on the part of a house owner, who broke an oil bottle on the stairs in front of the house entrance and immediately picked up the broken glass, when a visitor slipped on the oil stain, fell, and injured himself before the owner could mop the floor (about twenty to thirty minutes later).[118]

90. The unlawfulness of conduct is a legal standard that is being complemented by case law in each individual case.[119] Take, for example, a manager of a multifamily residential home. Case law has held that he or she should be aware that the stairwell in such a building is used daily by many people (home owners, tenants, and others) and that omission of due care in maintaining the stairwell through repairs may result in injury to third parties who are not parties to the management contract, making the failure to properly maintain the stairwell unlawful.[120]

91. Case law also refers to the basic principle of tort law called *neminem laedere* (Article 10 of the OZ), which obliges everyone to refrain from conduct that may cause harm to another. For example, as regards the liability of organisers of sporting events, case law emphasises that when a person participates in a sporting activity, he or she basically assumes the risks involved, i.e., the risks that are typical and foreseeable for a particular sport. However, this does not exempt the operator from organising the activity in compliance with the standards of professional duty of care (Article 6(2) of the OZ), which is contained in the safety regulations, the professional rules, and the general principle of not causing harm (*neminem laedere*).[121] The content and scope of the standard of professional duty of care and

115. In Slovenia, case law has applied the criterion of objective foreseeability of damage on the basis of recent Slovenian theory, which introduced the criterion from the theory of economic analysis of law into the Slovenian sphere. *See* Nina Plavšak, in Plavšak et al., *Obligacijski zakonik (OZ) (splošni del) s komentarjem, 1. knjiga* (2003), pp. 702 et seq. The argumentation of the wrongfulness of conduct in the sense of any conduct (act or omission) that foreseeably leads to the occurrence of damage is justified from the point of view of the preventive function of tort law; Plavšak et al., *supra* n. 95, at p. 506.

116. *See* ECLI:SI:VSRS:2017:II.IPS.2.2016 and ECLI:SI:VSRS:2018:II.IPS.252.2016.

117. *See* ECLI:SI:VSRS:2018:II.IPS.197.2016.

118. *Ibid.*

119. *See* ECLI:SI:VSRS:2018:II.IPS.49.2017.

120. *See* ECLI:SI:VSRS:2007:II.IPS.526.2005.

121. *See* ECLI:SI:VSRS:2018:II.IPS.46.2016. Cf. ECLI:SI:VSRS:2014:II.IPS.291.2012 and ECLI:SI:VSRS:2011:II.IPS.690.2008.

avoidance of risks are thus determined by the legitimate expectations of safety in the sport in question. Accordingly, the operator must take care of those dangers that go beyond the normal risk associated with the practice of the respective sporting activity.

92. As we can see, the line between unlawfulness and fault in Slovenian tort law may sometimes be thin. This is all the more true because fault-based liability in civil law is also objectified by the criteria for assessing the abstract forms of fault, i.e., negligence (for more on these criteria, *see infra* Part I, Chapter 1, §2).

§2. CONCEPT OF FAULT

93. Fault is expressly provided for in Article 131(1) of the OZ as a prerequisite for subjective, non-business tort liability: 'Any person that inflicts damage on another shall be obliged to provide recompense for it, unless it is proved that the damage was incurred without the culpability of the former.' Subjective liability is a general rule, and strict liability or no-fault liability is an exception to this general rule; it is provided for particularly dangerous[122] things and activities as well as for other special cases established by law (e.g., parents are liable for children under 7 years of age without fault).[123]

94. The concept of fault is multidimensional, since, in addition to its various forms, it also encompasses the individual's capacity to recognise the unlawfulness of his or her voluntary act or omission, which is a prerequisite for his or her fault-based liability (*see* Part I, Chapter 1, §4 on the necessity of the tortfeasor's delictual capacity). There are two basic forms of fault, namely intent (or purpose)[124] and negligence, which are not defined in the OZ. Slight negligence (*culpa levis; plain or ordinary negligence*) on the part of the tortfeasor[125] is sufficient to give rise to tort liability since the basic function of damages in Slovenian law is reparation or compensation, which enables the injured party to obtain the full amount of the damage suffered (Article 169 of the OZ) and does not involve punishment of the tortfeasor.[126]

---

122. The fact that strict liability is an exception to the general rule of fault has been repeatedly confirmed by case law (*see* ECLI:SI:VSRS:2008:II.IPS.571.2005, ECLI:SI:VSRS:2009:II.IPS.949.2006, ECLI:SI:VSLJ:2009:III.CP.1039.2009, ECLI:SI:VSLJ:2015:II.CP.744.2015 and ECLI:SI:VSRS:2019:II.IPS.251.2018).
123. For rules on strict liability *see* Part III, Ch. 5, §1.
124. The OZ provides that fault exist when the tortfeasor causes the damage intentionally or negligently (Art. 135). Already in the older theory, at the time when Obligations Act was in force, the terms intent/intention/purpose were used as synonyms (*see* Cigoj, *supra* n. 88, at 184), and the same applies to the more recent theory (*see* Barbara Novak, in Juhart et al., *Uvod v civilno pravo* (2011), p. 241; Plavšak et al., *supra* n. 95, at 528).
125. The focus of tort law is on the injured party, who is entitled to compensation in the full amount of the damage, regardless of the type of fault inflicted by the causer (Jožef Salma, *Obligaciono pravo* (2005), p. 543).
126. On punitive damages in Slovenia *see* Part VI, Ch.7, §3.

95. Intentional conduct differs from negligent conduct in that the wrongdoer is aware that his or her conduct would lead to a harmful result.[127] Intent is always judged according to certain criteria. Civil law theory also distinguishes – following the criminal law model – between direct intent (*dolus directus*), where the tortfeasor intends the consequence, and conditional intent (*dolus eventualis*), where the tortfeasor considers the possibility that the consequence will occur but is indifferent to it because he thinks 'what will be, will be';[128] however, this distinction is not relevant in civil law and has not been shown to be relevant in case law.[129]

96. Although negligence is not defined in the OZ as it is in the German BGB,[130] the criterion used for the judgment in Slovenian civil law, as in German civil law, is objective and abstract (*culpa in abstracto*),[131] which is represented by reasonable care (for more on the forms of care, *see* Part I, Chapter 1, §3). A person who fails to exercise due care is negligent and culpable, provided that he or she is also capable of committing a tort (delictual capacity).

97. In civil law, we distinguish between two types of negligence: gross negligence (*culpa lata*) and plain or ordinary negligence (*culpa levis*).[132] However, the essence of these forms of negligence is not identical to that of conscious or unconscious negligence used in criminal law (Article 26 of the CC-1), since the question is not whether the causer is aware that he or she is about to commit an act (which will have harmful consequences), but whether he or she acts with due care.[133]

98. To determine the degree between the two forms of negligence, the court defines the abstract duty of care in the matter in question and compares this conduct with that of the specific perpetrator (e.g., parent, educator, driver, doctor; a distinction is made between laypersons and experts since the standard of care of each is to be judged according to the knowledge and skills applicable to the group to which the person belongs)[134] in order to assess whether he or she has acted with gross or ordinary negligence, if this is relevant to the decision.[135] Gross negligence means

127. Plavšak et al., *supra* n. 95, p. 528.
128. Cf. Jadek Pensa, *supra* n. 60, p. 797. It is a definition adopted from criminal law into the older theory (Cf. Art. 25 of the CC-1; *see also* ECLI:SI:VSRS:2017:II.IPS.237.2017).
129. *See* ECLI:SI:VSRS:2017:II.IPS.237.2017: It is therefore irrelevant whether the person who caused the damage intended it or not. In civil law, the damage is already intentional if the person causing the damage knew that damage would result from his or her conduct, regardless of whether he or she acted with the intention of causing that damage or whether the conduct was otherwise intended and the damage occurred as a result of such conduct.
130. *See* §276(2) BGB: 'A person acts negligently if he fails to exercise reasonable care.'
131. Thus already Cigoj, *supra* n. 88, at 185; Jadek Pensa, *supra* n. 60, at 798.
132. *See*, e.g., Arts 147(3), 148(2), 170(1), 242(1) and (2) of the OZ.
133. *See* ECLI:SI:VSMB:2012:I.CP.963.2012. For these reasons, a civil court cannot be bound by a criminal court's finding that the tortfeasor committed the act with unconscious negligence, since the definition of gross negligence is not the same as that of either conscious or unconscious negligence (for more on the relationship between tort and criminal law, *see* General Introduction, §4).
134. ECLI:SI:VSKP:2005:I.CP.842.2004.
135. Cf. ECLI:SI:VSCE:1999:CP.42.99.

that someone has not acted as an averagely diligent person/layperson or an averagely diligent expert would have acted in a comparable situation (breach of ordinary care).[136] For example, a parent who leaves their child unattended by a swimming pool is acting with gross negligence, as is a person who walks their dog in a crowd without a lead, or a surgeon who forgets an instrument in the patient's body during an operation. Ordinary negligence, however, occurs when a person merely acts contrary to the conduct of a particularly diligent person/layperson or expert but still acts as an averagely diligent person would act (breach of special care). For example, a customer of an online bank who does not read all the small print of the emails sent by the bank;[137] a doctor who fails to warn of a rather unlikely complication or consequence before a procedure, although he or she does warn of all serious and usual consequences. However, the criteria for assessing contractual tort liability are even stricter, since a party (layperson/expert) can only exempt himself or herself from liability on the grounds set out in Article 240 of the OZ and it is therefore not sufficient to prove that he or she did not cause the damage, i.e., that he or she acted with due care. In assessing due care of the party in case of damages arising from a breach of its business liability (e.g., delay in performance or improper performance of a contract), liability is also assessed according to subjective criteria,[138] as an upward adjustment, which means a lower probability of exculpation. The party must prove that it could not have foreseen, prevented, or avoided the circumstances that arose after the conclusion of the contract (Article 240 of the OZ). These circumstances do not include the reasons that fall within the scope of normal internal risks associated with the conclusion of legal transactions (e.g., in chain transactions, each party in the chain bears the risk associated with the choice of a contractual partner on the other side, so that claims for damages are chained in the same way as performance in the opposite direction and it is, therefore, irrelevant whether the intermediary is 'not at fault' for the breach of its contractual partner).[139] However, the OZ defines two cases of commercial liability (gratuitous contract of deposit and contract of partnership)[140] where fault is assessed according to a very specific criterion, namely the way the guilty party normally conducts its business (*diligentia quam suis*).

99. Although slight negligence on the part of the tortfeasor is sufficient to give rise to tort liability, the escalation of fault may in some cases be relevant in determining the amount of damages. In the case of lesser fault, damages may be reduced in some cases if certain other conditions are met (for more on this, *see* Part VI, Chapter 3, §4), while in the case of more serious fault, the court may also consider the affective value of the thing to the injured party when determining damages (for more on this, *see* Part VI, Chapter 3, §1). Similarly, recourse claims against tortfeasors (e.g., employees,[141] directors, and other members of organs)[142] in cases

136. ECLI:SI:VSLJ:2016:I.CP.1490.2016.
137. Cf. ECLI:SI:VSRS:2020:III.IPS.62.2019.
138. Cf. Cigoj, *supra* n. 112, at 100; *see also* ECLI:SI:VSKP:2005:I.CP.842.2004.
139. ECLI:SI:VSLJ:2010:I.CPG.129.2010. *See also* ECLI:SI:VSKP:2016:CPG.167.2016.
140. *See* Art. 731(1) and Art. 993(1) of the OZ.
141. Article 147(3) of the OZ.
142. Article 148(2) of the OZ.

where other persons are liable for their conduct (vicarious liability) presuppose greater fault on the part of the tortfeasor (*see* Part II, Chapter 1, §§1, 3); moreover, the possibility for the injured party to demand the reimbursement for damage directly from the employee also presupposes greater fault on the part of the latter (Article 147(2) of the OZ).

100. According to Article 131(1) of the OZ, the fault of the tortfeasor is presumed.[143] However, only the lowest level of fault – plain or ordinary negligence – is presumed. If a qualified form of fault is required (e.g., to claim the affective value of the thing), the burden of allegation and the burden of proof for such form of fault is on the injured party.[144] The injured party must prove the first three requirements of vicarious liability: the unlawfulness of the conduct, the legally recognised damage, and the causal connection between the two. As regards the presumption of fault, the burden of proof is reversed, and the tortfeasor must exonerate himself or herself by proving that there was no fault. However, because of the connection between the presumption of unlawfulness and the presumption of fault (*see* Part I, Chapter 1, §1), the burden of proof for the first presumption (unlawfulness) should be eased for the injured party, e.g., It is sufficient if the aggrieved patient, who is unable to gather all the documents relating to the medical intervention, at least makes allegations based on which the court can presume the existence of unlawfulness, whereupon the medical institution in question must provide arguments and evidence of due care (*see also* Part I, Chapter 2, §1 II).[145]

§3. Duty of Care

101. The principle of due diligence or duty of care, which is defined as a basic principle in Article 6 of the OZ, prescribes that the participants in obligational relationships must act with due care or diligence of a good manager (this applies to non-experts who are natural persons) or a good business person (this applies to non-experts who are legal persons), or with the diligence of a good expert when performing their obligations. The legal definition of the principle of due diligence thus defines three legal standards of due diligence in addition to the standard of value.

102. Everyone is expected to exercise duty of care in all their actions, in line with the general civil principle which defines that everyone must refrain from any conduct that could cause harm to another (the principle of *neminem laedere* – Article 10 of the OZ), which includes both active and passive conduct. Therefore, the principle of due diligence has always been interpreted broadly in theory, i.e., it

143. ECLI:SI:VSLJ:1994:I.CP.2288.93.
144. ECLI:SI:VSLJ:2007:I.CPG.975.2006 and ECLI:SI:VSMB:2008:I.CP.460.2008.
145. Case law emphasises that the assessment of the rules on the patient's burden of allegation and burden of proof must be based on reasonable and not excessive requirements (*see also* ECLI:SI:VSRS:2012:II.IPS.32.2012).

applies generally to the assessment of all conduct of individuals in business relationships (i.e., also when entering into obligations) as well as in non-business obligational relationships,[146] and has been used to assess conduct in all civil relationships.[147] Therefore, the duty of care (*skrbnost*) may be subsumed under the basic principle of Slovenian tort law and thus applied. The degrees of duty of care differ depending on whether the standard of care is that of a layperson (the standard of care of a good master or businessman) or that of an expert (the standard of a good expert – for more on the standard of care of experts, *see* Part I, Chapter 2, §1 I).[148]

103. The assessment of the standard of care for conduct (of the tortfeasor and the injured party) is of fundamental importance in all cases of (non-business and business) liability in Slovenian civil law, as the standard of care is used as a criterion for determining fault in non-business tort liability as well as for assessing relief of business tort liability (for more on the relationship between the degree of fault and the standard of care, *see* Part I, Chapter 1, §2), and also as a yardstick for the foreseeability of damage in the case of business tort liability under Article 243(1) of the OZ (for more on this, *see* Part VI, Chapter 2, §3, §4). Furthermore, the standard of care is also applied when assessing the conditions for the exclusion of strict liability (for more on this, *see* Part III, Chapter 1 and Chapter 5; Part II, Chapter 3), where the question is whether one should have foreseen or prevented a consequence in view of the standard of care to be expected of one.

104. The criterion for assessing the duty of care of a master or businessman in case law is objective. In order to determine whether the wrongdoer has acted properly (and can therefore be exempted from liability), his or her conduct is compared with that of a third party – a model conduct that does not exist in the specific case but is imagined. The standard of care required is thus the conduct expected of an abstract (but comparable) natural or legal person who is not an expert, in the face of a concrete real situation (the care of a good master or businessman). The common term *duty of care of a reasonable person* is also used in case law with reference to the duty of care of a good master or businessman, although stricter criteria are used for the duty of care of legal persons.[149] The court is interested in whether the tortfeasor acted with due care, i.e., with the care that is customary in relationships between persons comparable to him or her, or that is required in legal transactions for such relationships since each person must be judged according to the knowledge and skills that apply to the group of persons to which he or she belongs.

105. Under the standard of care of a good master (*skrbnost dobrega gospodarja*) or businessman (*skrbnost dobrega gospodarstvenika*), a distinction is made between ordinary and special care (the same applies to the standard of experts – *see* Part I, Chapter 2, §1 I). Gross negligence is most often recognised when there is a

146. Cigoj, *supra* n. 112, at 99.
147. Plavšak et al., *supra* n. 95, at 140. *See also* ECLI:SI:VSLJ:2013:I.CP.2348.2012 and ECLI:SI:VSLJ:2015:I.CP.3443.2014.
148. *See* ECLI:SI:VSKP:2005:I.CP.842.2004 and ECLI:SI:VSCE:2018:CP.411.2017.
149. ECLI:SI:VSLJ:2016:I.CP.1490.2016.

breach of ordinary care. This is because it presupposes a neglect of the precaution and care expected of any natural person (duty of care of a good master) or legal person (duty of care of a good businessman).[150] In contrast to gross negligence, ordinary negligence is the neglect of the precautions required of a particularly careful and diligent natural person or legal entity. It is therefore a breach of a higher standard of care or special care, but where the offender acted as a normally diligent person. The court must therefore always determine the abstract standard of care that is appropriate in the matter in question and compare the relevant conduct with that of the specific perpetrator (e.g., a parent, or a bank customer)[151] in order to assess whether the perpetrator acted with gross or ordinary negligence if this is relevant for the decision.[152] Gross negligence thus means that someone has not acted as an averagely diligent person/layperson would have done in a comparable situation (breach of ordinary care).[153] For example, a parent who leaves their child unattended by a swimming pool is acting with gross negligence, as is a person who walks their dog in a crowd without a lead. Ordinary negligence, however, is when someone merely acts contrary to the behaviour of a particularly careful person/layperson but still acts as an average person would (breach of special care). A good example is a customer of an online bank who does not read all the emails the bank sends in small print.[154]

§4. Capacity

106. In determining fault-based liability, the courts in Slovenia also take into account the question of delictual capacity, which the OZ does not explicitly define, but does state two criteria (age and capacity of discernment) that must be met in order for a person to be held liable in tort for unlawful conduct.

107. The capacity to commit a wrong (*delictual capacity*) is a precondition for fault-based liability. A person who does not have delictual capacity cannot be held liable for damages.[155] In the case of strict liability, delictual capacity is not required, as a valid legal relationship between the party causing the strict liability and the risk bearer is sufficient (for more on the regulation of strict liability, *see* Part III, Chapter 5, §1).

---

150. Cigoj, *supra* n. 112, at 600.
151. ECLI:SI:VSKP:2005:I.CP.842.2004.
152. Cf. ECLI:SI:VSCE:1999:CP.42.99.
153. ECLI:SI:VSLJ:2016:I.CP.1490.2016.
154. Cf. ECLI:SI:VSRS:2020:III.IPS.62.2019.
155. Legal entities are also recognised as possessing delictual capacity if their organs or their members commit a tortious act in their capacity as organs of the legal entity. The liability of a legal entity arises from the fact that its organs act as if they were it (ego) and not its alter ego or representative (*see* Cigoj, *supra* n. 88, at 183). We are dealing here with tortious acts of natural persons acting as members of the entity's organs or being otherwise connected with it (for more on the liability of legal entities for acts of their organs, *see* Part II, Ch. 1, §3).

108. The capacity of discernment is a factual capacity, which means that a natural person understands his or her conduct (has no impairment of intellectual faculties) and directs his or her voluntary actions according to this understanding (has no impairment of the capacity to control his or her actions).[156] Discernment (*razsodnost*) is a term from Slovenian civil law, while in criminal law the term sanity (*prištevnost*) is used. They are synonymous. A person who does not possess this capacity is therefore considered to be irrational or of unsound mind. The capacity of discernment is not equally pronounced in all people. It may well be lower in children and the mentally ill, as well as in people with other illnesses and disorders of consciousness (e.g., brain injuries).

109. An action in tort is subject to presumption of the injured party's capability of accounting for his or her actions or lack thereof. Depending on what is presumed, it is also necessary to consider who bears the burden of proving such capacity of discernment or lack thereof.[157] As far as the incapacity of discernment is concerned, there is an irrebuttable presumption (*praesumptio iuris et de iure*) that minors under the age of 7 are incapable of making a reasonable judgment and therefore lack delictual capacity (Article 137(1) of the OZ). As a rule, the parents (Article 142 of the OZ) or the persons charged with the supervision of the child are liable for the damage caused by the child (for more information on the liability of parents, teachers and instructors, *see* Part II, Chapter 2). However, for children between the ages of seven and fourteen, there is a rebuttable presumption (*praesumptio iuris*) of incapacity of discernment. This presumption must be rebutted by the injured party by proving that the minor in question was in fact of sound mind at the time the damage was caused (Article 137(2) of the OZ).

110. A minor who has reached the age of 14 is capable of committing a tort and is liable under the general rules of tort liability (Article 137(3) of the OZ). Until proven otherwise, such a person is presumed to be of sound mind (presumption of discernment) and thus capable of committing a tort. Therefore, persons with incapacity to contract may still have delictual capacity. Incapacity of discernment after the age of 14, which is either due to mental illness or the ingestion of certain substances (temporarily), must therefore be proven by the wrongdoer or his representative (Article 136(1) and 136(2) of the OZ). When trying to prove temporary incapacity of discernment (e.g., as a result of drug or alcohol consumption or refusal to accept hospital treatment), which must be done by the wrongdoer, the latter must also prove that he or she was not responsible for the state he or she was in (Article 136(2) of the OZ) or will be held accountable for the act otherwise (*acto libera in causa*).[158] We are dealing here with the case of stricter responsibility (*casus mixtus*). If it was another person who put the wrongdoer into a state of temporary incapacity of judgment, this person will be held liable (e.g., a person unnoticedly putting a drug mixture into another person's drinking glass; Article 136(3) of the OZ).

---

156. Cf. Cigoj, *supra* n. 112, at 608.
157. Cf. Novak, *supra* n. 124, at 88.
158. *See* ECLI:SI:VSLJ:2015:I.CP.1095.2015, ECLI:SI:VSLJ:2014:I.CP.1293.2014, ECLI:SI:VDSS:2019:PDP.689.2018 and ECLI:SI:VDSS:2020:PDP.767.2019.

111. Even people who are incapable of discernment due to mental illness can have a lucid moment (*lucida intervalla*) and be therefore held liable for damages. If a person had been completely deprived of the capacity to contract, which includes the capacity to discern, at the time the damage occurred, this is evidence of him or her being incapable of discernment. If the injured party claims that the person who caused the damage was of sound mind at the time the damage occurred, he or she must prove that the wrongdoer had a lucid moment or the capacity of discernment.[159]

112. In Slovenian law, there is also a provision that allows for so-called just liability of tortfeasors without delictual capacity, which applies in cases where compensation cannot be obtained from the person who has to supervise these persons (e.g., parents, school).[160] Thus, the court may order a tortfeasor without delictual capacity to compensate the injured party for all or part of the damage if justice so requires, especially in view of the financial situation of the tortfeasor and the injured party. The OZ also regulates the situations where the damage was caused by a minor who is capable of accounting for his or her actions but cannot provide recompense,[161] by stating that if justice so requires, particularly in view of the financial situation of the parents and the injured party, the court may order the parents to compensate all or part of the damage, even if they are not liable (*see also* Part VI, Chapter 3, §4).

159. *See* ECLI:SI:VSLJ:2005:II.CP.1627.2004.
160. Article 146(1) of the OZ.
161. Article 146(2) of the OZ.

Chapter 2. Specific Cases of Liability

§1. Liability of Professionals

I. In General

113. Experts are expected to have more knowledge than an average person (layperson). Since Slovenian law provides that everyone is judged according to the knowledge and skills of the group of people to which they belong, experts (doctors, lawyers, civil engineers, etc.)[162] are expected to have a higher standard of care (the standard of care of a good expert) and are therefore subject to stricter standards of liability if they have committed an act requiring their expertise. The standard of care of a good expert is therefore stricter than that of a good manager or businessman.[163]

114. The standard of care of a good expert is laid down in Article 6 of the OZ as one of the fundamental principles and applies to all relationships under the law of obligations (business and non-business), including cases where the damage was caused by wrongful conduct, in order to assess whether the party acted in such a way that it cannot be accused of fault.

115. The content of the standard of care for experts is objective or abstract. Article 6 of the OZ mentions only two of the most important criteria for the diligence of a good expert, namely: professional rules and customs. The professional rules comprise the knowledge of a narrow circle of experts, related to their respective professions (e.g., medicine, civil engineering, law, teaching),[164] but specialisations within the professions must also be taken into account. The benchmark for assessing the appropriate conduct of a particular expert is the average expert in the same field (e.g., a specialist in cardiology, a notary, etc.). The question that may arise in the court's assessment is what the relationship is – in terms of the standard of care – between the rules of professional conduct and customary practice if a conflict arises because in reality the customary conduct of experts usually deviates from the rules of their profession. The rules of the profession should in principle take precedence over customs, but if a certain practice has become established as customary, it can be potentially harmful (e.g., removing a healthy kidney without histological examination).[165] However, the application of professional rules can also

162. This applies to experts working in the liberal professions, in business entities, but also to civil servants, public bodies and other legal entities. A person who represents or acts on behalf of such a person shall also be deemed to be an expert.
163. For more information on the standard of care of a good expert *see* Part I, Ch. 1, §3.
164. These rules need not be expressly written down. In some cases, their mandatory application is prescribed by sectoral laws (e.g., HSA), or the sectoral laws explicitly set out professional rules of conduct (cf. ECLI:SI:VSRS:2013:III.IPS.79.2010).
165. Cf. ECLI:SI:VSMB:2009:I.CP.1046.2009: A doctor is bound by a higher standard of care in the exercise of his professional activity of healing (the care of a good expert within the meaning of Art. 6(2) of the OZ). However, in the case of a diagnosis requiring the removal of an important organ of the human body, a good expert is expected to ensure that such a diagnosis is correct, as it has far-reaching and irreversible consequences for the patient. If the treatment had been carried

lead to problems when it comes to which rules govern professional practice: domestic (the question already arises as to what counts as domestic professional practice if, for example, a certain operation is performed differently in two different hospitals in Slovenia) or international. And who can know all the rapidly changing rules or the changing profession, especially if the rules are not uniform. For more on this, *see supra* Chapter 2, §1, II. Medical Practitioners.

116. The court thus compares the concrete conduct of the expert with an abstract type of 'like' experts who are identical in their essential characteristics or belong to the same group. The criteria for determining the essential characteristics against which the conduct of experts is to be assessed are expertise, training, experience, age, skills, expected conduct, and special circumstances. Thus, the court must ask what conduct comparable experts most often engage in under the same circumstances,[166] or it must determine how a typical member of the narrow group would act or how the law would expect them to act under the circumstances.

117. In addition to the abstract criteria, stricter, subjective, or concrete criteria can also be considered when assessing the duty of care of experts, such as the criterion of upward correction (as a higher standard).[167] Thus, if a particular expert has more knowledge than (most of) his or her colleagues or has certain specific skills, it will be more difficult to exonerate him or her from liability.

118. The standard of care of a good expert is the standard for grading the fault of experts (especially their negligence) in non-business (as well as business) tort liability in Slovenian law (for more on the meaning of the standard and the principle of care in Slovenian tort law, *see* Part I, Chapter 1, §3). Professionals are liable for gross negligence if they do not act with ordinary care, i.e., with the care expected of any (normally careful) expert in a narrow group (e.g., if a doctor violates a very clear professional norm), and for slight negligence if they do not act with the utmost (special) care expected of a particularly careful expert.[168] The degree of fault (negligence) and the degree of care are inversely proportional (for more on the relationship between the degree of fault and due care, *see* Part I, Chapter 1, §2).

out with due care, in this particular case confirmation of the correctness of the diagnosis would have required further examinations, which the plaintiff did not undergo.

166. Cf. Plavšak et al., *supra* n. 95, at 144.

167. Cf. Strohsack, *supra* n. 88, at 77; Nataša Samec Berghaus & Rok Felicijan Pristovšek, *Nova dognanja o odškodninski odgovornosti zdravnika*, in *The patient – doctor relationship* (2016), p. 113.

168. Cf. Cigoj, *supra* n. 88, at 186. *See* ECLI:SI:VSLJ:2020:I.CP.1989.2019, ECLI:SI:VSLJ:2018:I.CP.2098.2017, ECLI:SI:VSCE:2017:CP.531.2016, ECLI:SI:VSLJ:2014:II.CPG.1254.2013, ECLI:SI:VSRS:2013:III.IPS.79.2010, ECLI:SI:VSKP:2012:CP.799.2011, ECLI:SI:VSRS:2009:II.IPS.51.2007, ECLI:SI:VSLJ:2009:II.CP.3162.2009, ECLI:SI:VSRS:2008:II.IPS.63.2007, ECLI:SI:VSRS:2000:II.IPS.106.2000 and ECLI:SI:VSRS:2000:II.IPS.89.2000.

II. Medical Practitioners

119. The liability of healthcare professionals is related to certain misconduct in the medical treatment of a patient (different malpractices in the procedure or choice of treatment, lack of informed consent or a failure to properly fulfil the duty to inform, inadequate organisation, non-compliance with instructions, inadequate supervision, etc.).

120. The central act regulating healthcare is the Health Services Act (HSA).[169] The Annex to the Order determining the uniform definition of key concepts in healthcare (Odredba o določitvi enotne definicije ključnih pojmov v zdravstvu)[170] stipulates that healthcare services that are intended for preventive, diagnostic, therapeutic, or rehabilitation purposes are provided by a doctor, a healthcare professional (nurses, midwives, clinical psychologists, etc.), or a related health professional (e.g., speech therapists, psychologists, biologists, etc.). Medical services provided by doctors (and dentists) as health professionals are further regulated by the Medical Services Act (MSA).[171] However, none of the aforementioned regulations regulates the liability of healthcare professionals, so the rules that apply to all healthcare professions listed above are general regulations on liability from the OZ (*see* Part I, Chapter 1). Furthermore, there are professional standards that apply to each healthcare profession and thus to all health professionals, which means that they are judged in accordance with stricter standards of professional diligence (*see* Part I, Chapter 2, §1, I).

121. An overview of Slovenian case law shows that most claims for damages (about 90%) are related to medical malpractice, with lawsuits directed against doctors and healthcare organisations or their insurance companies (Article 61 of the MSA), but not against other healthcare professionals (e.g., nurses, medical technicians, paramedics, etc.). This is a consequence of the fact that most damages in the healthcare system are due to problems in treatment (correct diagnosis and therapy), which is in the domain of doctors and therefore their responsibility.[172] The attending physicians are responsible for the work of their resident physicians (Article 15 of the MSA). The MSA expressly excludes the physician's responsibility for treatment if the patient provides false information about his or her state of health, does

---

169. Official Gazette RS, Nos 23/05 – UPB, 15/08 – ZPacP, 23/08, 58/08 – ZZdrS-E, 77/08 – ZDZdr, 40/12 – ZUJF, 14/13, 88/16 – ZdZPZD, 64/17, 1/19 – odl. US, 73/19, 82/20, 152/20 – ZZUOOP, 203/20 – ZIUPOPDVE, 112/21 – ZNUPZ and 196/21 – ZDOsk.
170. Official Gazette RS, No. 40/14.
171. Official Gazette RS, Nos 72/06 – UPB, 15/08 – ZPacP, 58/08, 107/10 – ZPPKZ, 40/12 – ZUJF, 88/16 – ZdZPZD, 40/17, 64/17 – ZZDej-K, 49/18, 66/19, 199/21.
172. In Slovenian case law, we can find only a smaller proportion of healthcare claims, relating to nurses' failure to act with due diligence, either in connection with doctors' liability (*see*, e.g., ECLI:SI:VSLJ:2021:I.CP.44.2021 and ECLI:SI:VSCE:2018:CP.180.2018) or their own misconduct in the care and protection of patients (*see*, e.g., ECLI:SI:VSLJ:2009:II.CP.2932.2009, ECLI:SI:VSLJ:2018:II.CP.1391.2018 and ECLI:SI:VSRS:2014:II.IPS.315.2013).

not follow the doctor's instructions, or does not participate in the protection, promotion and restoration of his or her own health (Article 48 of the MSA). The medical chamber may temporarily or permanently withdraw a doctor's license to practice medicine because of professional inadequacies or medical errors (Article 37 of the MSA). They are also criminally liable for failure to provide medical care (Article 178 of the CC-1),[173] negligent treatment (Article 179 of the CC-1), illegal transplantation of human body parts and alteration of the human genome (Article 181 of the CC-1), and for issuing a false medical certificate (Article 255(1) of the CC-1).

122. The number of claims for damages against physicians and healthcare organisations due to medical malpractice is increasing, as are the amounts of damages awarded by the courts. Pursuant to Article 147 of the OZ, liability for damage caused by an employee at work or in connection with work rests with the legal or natural person for whom the employee was working at the time the damage was caused, which means that compensation in medical cases usually falls on the shoulders of the medical institution where the physician or other healthcare worker is employed (for more on this, *see infra* Part II, Chapter 1, §1).

123. In Slovenian case law, two types of liability of doctors for damage to a patient can be identified, namely contractual and delictual liability, as the courts, which do not reject claims on either ground,[174] leave it up to the injured party on which basis to claim compensation (similar to the common law system). Therefore, there is no uniform position in case law regarding the legal nature of the doctor-patient relationship in Slovenia, so the legal relationship between a patient and a physician or a medical institution in Slovenian case law qualifies either as a contractual relationship, where medical malpractice (*zdravniška napaka*) is assessed as a contractual liability[175] or medical malpractice is assessed as a civil wrong or tort (*civilni delikt*) and as a delictual liability.[176] However, with regard to the conditions that must be met for liability – whether contractual or delictual – there is no difference, as we always ask ourselves the same question in both types of liability,

173. Official Gazette RS, Nos 50/12 – official consolidated text, 6/16 – corr., 54/15, 38/16, 27/17, 23/20, 91/20, 95/21, 186/21, 105/22 – ZZNŠPP and 16/23.

174. *See* more on the issue in Samec Berghaus & Felicijan Pristovšek, *supra* n. 167, at 116–118; Viktorija Žnidaršič Skubic, *Civilno medicinsko pravo, izbrane teme* (2018), pp. 83–84.

175. *See* ECLI:SI:VSRS:2016:II.IPS.207.2015, ECLI:SI:VSRS:2015:II.IPS.342.2014 and ECLI:SI:VSCE:2020:CP.412.2020.

176. *See* ECLI:SI:VSLJ:2009:II.CP.2457.2009, where the court explicitly stated that healthcare service, patients' rights, including the right to compensation for damages, and the obligations of healthcare professionals, were regulated directly by law and derived from it. The legal basis for the compensation for the damage alleged by the complainant was thus provided by the HSA (and not the contract), while the conditions and forms of legally recognised damages were regulated by the OZ in Arts 131 through 189.
See also: ECLI:SI:VSRS:2014:II.IPS.102.2014, ECLI:SI:VSLJ:2016:II.CP.1594.2016, ECLI:SI:VSRS:2012:II.IPS.32.2012, ECLI:SI:VSLJ:2016:II.CP.381.2016, ECLI:SI:VSMB:2011:I.CP.1115.2011 and ECLI:SI:VSLJ:2014:I.CP.60.2014.

namely whether the physician acted in accordance with his or her professional duty of care or whether his behaviour shows signs of *contra legem artis*.[177]

124. Although the doctor-patient relationship is also defined as a contractual relationship,[178] there is no special contract in Slovenia – as there is in Germany (*Behandlungsvertrag*) – however, the treatment contract can be subsumed under the regulations of the mandate contract, because it is an obligation of best effort, to which the physician or healthcare facility are obligated.[179]

125. The prerequisites for liability for damages that must be met for all healthcare professionals are as follows: Unlawfulness of the tortfeasors' act, inadmissible damage, causal link between the harmful act and the harmful consequence, and fault on the part of the tortfeasor (for more on the general prerequisites, *see* Part I, Chapters 1–2).

126. The unlawfulness of the physician's conduct is instigated when he or she did not act with due care and according to the rules of the medical profession, and the patient's state of health deteriorated (however, the physician is not responsible for complications[180] if these are not due to medical errors or are considered a natural deterioration).[181] Unlawfulness also exists if there was no informed consent (*privolitve*) of the patient for the procedure (exception: urgent cases) or if the consent was not adequate due to a breach of the duty to properly inform the patient.[182] As already explained, a stricter duty of care criterion is observed in the assessment of

177. This is also the position of other authors (*see* Žnidaršič Skubic, *supra* n. 174, at 84) and case law. A recent decision read that regardless of whether we assumed contractual or delictual liability, the analysis of the conditions that must be met for one or the other type of liability showed that in both cases, there was a breach of duty of care, and in that respect, both responsibilities merged and intertwined (*see* ECLI:SI.VSCE:2020:CP.412.2020).

178. If the patient's consent is not given, there is no contractual relationship. An example is when the physician carries out the procedure despite objections or consent cannot be obtained because the situation is urgent and requires immediate action. At this point, the physician is considered to be acting as a gestor, and even in this case, he or she has the same obligations as the contractor under the mandate contract (Art. 200(3) of the OZ). And if the patient later consents to the procedure, it is considered, according to the law, as if a mandate contract had been concluded from the beginning (*see* Art. 206 of the OZ).

179. *See* more in Samec Berghaus & Felicijan Pristovšek, *supra* n. 167, at 117.

180. *See* ECLI:SI:VSRS:2011:II.IPS.214.2008 and ECLI:SI:VSRS:2009:II.IPS.88.2009.

181. *See* ECLI:SI:VSRS:2012:II.IPS.334.2010.

182. Due to the breach of the duty to inform (*pojasnilna dolžnost*), the physician is liable if the patient has suffered a legally recognised damage resulting from any of the risks of which he or she should have been warned, but was not, even if the medical procedure was performed in accordance with medical doctrine or *lege artis*. The scope of the duty to inform depends on the circumstances of each individual case and therefore cannot be precisely defined in advance for an indefinite number of cases. In principle, the physician is not obliged to inform the patient of all possible side effects of the procedure, but in any case it is crucial that the physician informs the patient of the essential circumstances that enable him or her to understand the meaning of the consent, so that the patient has enough reasons to decide for or against a treatment in order not to be surprised by harmful consequences because he or she did not expect them. (ECLI:SI:VSRS:2012:II.IPS.72.2009, ECLI:SI:VSRS:2013:II.IPS.65.2012 and ECLI:SI:VSRS:2013:II.IPS.174.2012). The physician must appropriately explain to the patient the most important aspects of the situation, give a prognosis, and warn the patient of the usual, regular risk (ECLI:SI:VSRS:2008:II.IPS.99.2006). The

the medical standard of care, that is, the professional duty of care (Article 6(2) of the OZ). The content of the medical standard of care depends on the circumstances of each individual case and the established standards of behaviour and conduct, which are so diverse and dependent on variable circumstances that they cannot be determined precisely. The assessment of what is used as a medical standard is a legal issue that must be resolved by a court.[183] However, since the court lacks the necessary medical knowledge, the opinion is prepared by an expert – a specialist in the relevant medical field. Without an expert, a judge cannot set standards.[184] Of course, a judge can use his or her knowledge to review an expert's assessment, request additions, or even appoint another expert, as his or her independent and critical assessment is part of the judge's control, but in practice, this almost always results in a judge's assessment which is based on the presupposition that the expert's assessment is correct. Since we are dealing with experts, subjective criteria must also be used in addition to objective ones, but at best as an upward correction criterion (as a higher standard). So if a certain doctor has more knowledge than (most of) his or her colleagues or has certain special skills, it will be more difficult for him or her to be relieved of responsibility.[185]

127. The issue of determining the damage (pecuniary or non-pecuniary) in the case of medical errors does not differ significantly from other claims for damages (for more on these types of damages *see* Part VI, Chapter 2, §3).

128. In Slovenian case law, the standard of probative belief (clear and convincing evidence) is not used to determine the causal link in compensation cases where the burden of proof would be too high for the plaintiff (e.g., lack of evidence), especially when the cause of the damage cannot be determined with certainty. In these cases, the standard of persuasion (preponderance of the evidence) applies, which eases the burden of proof for the plaintiff.[186] The probability of a harmful consequence resulting from circumstances other than those that actually occurred is taken into account. The tortfeasor is liable for the entire damage caused by the harmful

scope of the duty to inform was defined by the Supreme Court of Slovenia in the case ECLI:SI:VSRS:2015:II.IPS.94.2015 with three principles.

183. Some cases from the jurisprudence of the Slovenian courts that were considered to be violations of medical standards: (1) due to the particular circumstances and indications surrounding a complication of cardiac arrest, the medical personnel involved should immediately suspect pneumothorax and react accordingly, in which case resuscitation would have been successful (ECLI:SI:VSRS:2015:II.IPS.342.2014); (2) treatment administered too late (ECLI:SI:VSLJ:2014:I.CP.60.2014); (3) a case of misjudgment of the size of the plaintiff's uterus by a gynaecologist and the consequent assumption that the pregnancy continued despite the abortion. In such a suspected case, an ultrasound examination should be performed to confirm or exclude the pregnancy. However, this was not done. Such actions by the gynaecologist during the said examination constitute negligent, careless and unprofessional conduct which is not in accordance with the standard rules of the profession or professional behaviour of a physician. (ECLI:SI:VSMB:2011:I.CP.1115.2011).

184. *See* ECLI:SI:VSRS:2015:II.IPS.342.2014, ECLI:SI:VSRS:2016:II.IPS.207.2015, ECLI:SI:VSCE:2020:CP.412.2020, ECLI:SI:VSLJ:2018:II.CP.1577.2018, ECLI:SI:VSCE:2016:CP.348.2016 and ECLI:SI:VSLJ:2020:I.CP.1512.2019.

185. Samec Berghaus & Felicijan Pristovšek, *supra* n. 167, at 113.

186. *See* ECLI:SI:VSRS:2010:II.IPS.402.2007.

act when the injured party can prove with a probability above the probability threshold (i.e., 50%) that the harmful act of the responsible person or the cause arising from his or her sphere caused the damage.[187]

129. Compensation disputes in the healthcare sector are in most cases no different from other compensation proceedings. Similarly, in medical malpractice disputes, the burden of proof for the first three assumptions (unlawfulness, damage, and causality) or facts justifying inferences of malpractice and the causal link between malpractice and damage also lies with the injured party, i.e., the patient.[188] Due to the reversed burden of proof with regard to the fourth assumption (fault), the burden of proof for the content of the legal standard of conscientious and medically correct treatment lies with the physician/healthcare facility, which allows for the exculpation of the liability of the physician/healthcare facility.

III. Legal Practitioners

130. Legal practitioners provide legal advice, represent clients, draw up documents, conduct negotiations, etc.[189] There is a confidential relationship (*intuitu personae*) between them and the client, and a client rightly expects their work to be done professionally. In addition, most clients are laypersons and even more need an appropriate professional approach. According to the general principle *neminem laedere*, legal practitioners are liable if damage occurs as a result of their wrongful conduct. Among legal practitioners, a distinction can be made between (independent) legal advisors and attorneys who, by virtue of their profession, enjoy special trust in their work and knowledge.

131. Legal advisor can be anyone who is (or is supposed to be) an expert in a particular field of law. Their position is not specifically regulated, but they should at least have legal education. Legal advisors as a rule cannot represent and defend clients in court and cannot file extraordinary legal remedies.

132. However, advocacy is a venerable profession that dates back to ancient times. The legal status of attorneys and the effective exercise of the freedom to provide

187. *See* ECLI:SI:VSLJ:2012:I.CP.2294.2012 and ECLI:SI:VSMB:2014:I.CP.1330.2013. *See* more on causation in Part V.

188. The assessment of the rules on the patient's burden of proof must be based on requirements that are reasonable and not too strict. The facts about the course of a particular procedure are best known to the healthcare institution. The patient is often in a situation where he or she is unable to collect (insure, keep for evidentiary purposes) all the necessary documentation about his or her health condition and the procedures performed. It is sufficient for the claim to present arguments on the basis of which the court can presume the existence of improper conduct. The health facility, which has all the documentation at its disposal, then makes substantiated claims of facts that refute the existence of the so-called professional errors (*see also* ECLI:SI:VSRS:2012:II.IPS.32.2012).

189. Legal practitioners are persons who practice law. For liability of other (legal) professions, such us notaries, judges, prosecutors, etc. *see infra* Part I, Ch. 2, §1, V–VI.

legal services are regulated by the Attorneys Act.[190] An attorney is a professional who can provide legal advice, represent and defend clients before courts and other state authorities, draft documents and represent clients in their legal relations. An attorney may be anyone who (among other things) meets the following conditions: having a legal education, passing the state legal exam,[191] having four years of practical experience, and being worthy of the trust required to practise the legal profession. The right to practise as an attorney is acquired by registration in the register of attorneys kept by the Bar Association of Slovenia.[192]

133. Due to the special nature of the relationship, Slovenian law lays down the rules on compulsory professional liability insurance for attorneys, which was even regulated as the first compulsory professional liability insurance in Slovenia as early as 1993.[193] Pursuant to Article 6 of the Attorneys Act currently in force, the Bar Association of Slovenia insures attorneys against liability for damages that may be incurred by the client in connection with the attorney's practice of the legal profession. The insurance covers damages caused by gross negligence, error or omission of the professional duties of attorneys and their employees. The purpose of compulsory professional liability insurance for attorneys is, on the one hand, to protect the attorney's property and, on the other hand, to protect the rights of clients. However, the Attorneys Act does not contain any further rules regarding liability for damages. Therefore, the general rules of the OZ apply.

134. The liability of legal practitioners can be classified under a broader institute of professional liability. According to Article 6 of the OZ, professionals must exercise greater diligence in the performance of the duties arising from their professional activity. They must also act in accordance with the rules and customs of their profession (the diligence of a good expert).[194] On the one hand, legal practitioners can be liable for the loss caused by professional errors, while on the other hand, they can also be liable for the loss caused by incorrect advice. This is particularly the case if such a practitioner is considered an expert who enjoys special trust and could foresee that the recipient of the advice will rely on the information (e.g., law professor, attorney).[195]

135. Since the law specifically regulates the legal profession, the due diligence of an independent legal advisor and that of an attorney differ. The liability of attorneys is generally stricter than the liability of independent legal advisors. Even though attorneys may carry out their activities in different organisational structures (e.g., law firm, entrepreneur under Companies Act (ZGD-1), private individual), this

190. Official Gazette RS, Nos 18/93, 24/96 – Constitutional Court decision, 24/01, 54/08, 35/09, 97/14, 8/16 – Constitutional Court decision, 46/16 and 36/19.
191. *See* State Legal Exam Act (Official Gazette RS, Nos 83/03 – official consolidated version, 111/07, 40/12 – ZUJF and 36/19 – ZOdv-F).
192. *See* Arts 1 and 25 of the Attorneys Act.
193. *See* Art. 9 of the Attorneys Act (Official Gazette RS, No. 18/93).
194. *See also* Part I, Ch. 1, §3.
195. Damjan Možina, *Odškodninska odgovornost za nasvet in informacije ter vprašanje zahtevkov tretjih oseb*, Podjetje in delo 2 (2015), p. 291.

has no influence on the content of their (contractual) relationship with the client and the assessment of liability. Since they perform their work as a profession (in accordance with the Attorneys Act), they must act with greater care, according to the rules of the profession and according to the standard of diligence of a good professional.

136. According to the diligence of a good professional (attorney), an attorney is expected to be familiar with national law, international legal acts directly applicable to national law (e.g., the United Nations Convention on Contracts for the International Sale of Goods), EU law, and to some extent even foreign law.[196] Additionally, an attorney must be familiar with (and refer the client to) the relevant case law, in particular, the relevant case law of the VSRS and the case law of the Constitutional Court of the Republic of Slovenia. In addition, attorneys must follow the client's instructions, taking into account professional standards and the client's interests.[197]

137. Attorneys usually have the authority to enter into a (contractual) agreement with a client. As a rule, the agreement is concluded as an obligation of efforts (contract of mandate).[198] In such cases, the attorney fulfils his or her obligation and is entitled to payment, which depends on diligence, irrespective of the success of the litigation. Exceptionally, the contract may also be concluded as an obligation of result (contract for work).[199]

138. According to Slovenian theory and case law, the rules of contractual liability generally apply.[200] The basis for the attorney's liability for damages is a breach of the contractual relationship. 'A breach of attorney's contractual obligation occurs in the case of his fault or conduct contrary to the diligence required of him in the performance of the lawyer's professional activity.'[201] Consequently, an attorney commits a breach of contract when he or she fails to act in accordance with the client's interests and expected professional standards. In such cases, the limitation period starts to run on the first day after the breach of contract.[202] Additionally, the time at which the plaintiff learns that the attorney has committed a professional error must be taken into account.[203] The content of the contractual obligation is the representation and conduct of the attorney according to the principle of due diligence (the diligence of a good expert). Consequently, there are various cases of breach of attorney's (contractual) obligation, such as failure to fill a response to the action,[204]

196. Špelca Mežnar, *Odgovornost pravnih poklicev – teorija in praksa*, Pravni letopis (2008), pp. 133–143.
197. ECLI:SI:VSCE:2017:CPG.120.2017.
198. *See* Arts 766–787 of the OZ.
199. *See* Arts 619–648 of the OZ; In accordance with the principle of contractual freedom in obligational relationships, the contracting parties may agree that a legal practitioner will be entitled to payment for his services only if the intended result is achieved, regardless of diligence. *See* ECLI:SI:VSLJ:2014:I.CP.656.2014.
200. Uroš Miklič, *Odškodninska odgovornost odvetnika in zavarovanje odgovornosti*, Odvetnik 96 (2020), pp. 13–16; ECLI:SI:VSLJ:2015:II.CP.568.2015 and ECLI:SI:VSLJ:2015:II.CP.1589.2015.
201. ECLI:SI:VSMB:2021:I.CP.285.2021.
202. ECLI:SI:VSLJ:2015:II.CP.1589.2015.
203. ECLI:SI:VSLJ:2016:II.CP.2922.2015 and ECLI:SI:VSLJ:2018:I.CPG.838.2017.
204. ECLI:SI:VSLJ:2021:I.CP.432.2021.

incorrect filing of a legal remedy,[205] failure to meet the appeal deadline,[206] failure to notify the client,[207] entering into a settlement without the client's consent,[208] etc. Exceptionally, attorneys (and independent legal advisors) are also subject to delictual liability towards third parties who are not entitled to contractual claims (e.g., in the case of publication of an incorrect legal opinion).

IV. Builders and Architects

139. Construction is complex and can lead to various forms of liability. Builders and architects are not only liable under contracts with their clients (contractual liability) but are also subject to delictual liability towards their clients and third parties who have no contractual claims. Damage may be caused to neighbouring buildings and to parked cars, and damage and injury may be caused to passers-by, contractual workers and other persons on the construction site (e.g., a building inspector), etc. The damage may be caused by direct (e.g., crane drop) or indirect activities (e.g., smoke, dust). The larger the construction site, the more damage can occur. Therefore, the legislation prescribes special rules to ensure safe construction (e.g., the construction site must be properly arranged and marked, etc.). The requirements for the construction process and other construction process-related issues are regulated in the Building Act (GZ-1).[209]

140. A special feature of the liability of builders and architects is that there are usually several persons (contractors) involved in any construction. These are: (1) the landowner; (2) the architect or a building designer who draws up the design documents; (3) the investor, who acquires a building permit that entitles him or her to proceed with the construction; (4) a builder (contractor) who (alone or with subcontractors) carries out the construction work on the site; and (5) a site manager who supervises the construction. All the above-mentioned persons may be natural persons or legal entities and may also be one and the same person.

141. Damage can be caused by different persons, at different levels of the construction and to different extents. Damage resulting from inadequate construction can occur even years after the construction work has been completed. The damage may be the result of an error in the design documents, improper construction, use of unsuitable materials, negligence or omission of safety measures, improper use and maintenance of the building, etc. In general, architects and building designers are liable for damage caused by inadequate planning; builders are liable for damage caused by inadequate construction, use of inadequate materials and failure to

205. ECLI:SI:VSLJ:2009:II.CP.4650.2008.
206. ECLI:SI:VSLJ:2000:II.CP.1139.2000.
207. ECLI:SI:VSLJ:2021:I.CP.1358.2020.
208. ECLI:SI:VSLJ:2010:II.CP.1303.2010.
209. Official Gazette RS, No. 199/21.

observe safety measures; landowners, investors and supervisors are liable for damage if they knew inadequate behaviour or could have recognised it but did nothing (or not enough) to prevent it.

142. Similar to legal practitioners, Slovenian legislation provides for compulsory professional liability insurance for builders and architects, as the nature of their work can cause great damage. According to Article 16 of the GZ-1, every contractor who wishes to carry out a construction activity shall be insured against liability for damages related to the performance of his or her activity. Liability insurance for damages includes liability for damages caused to the investor or a third party by the performance of the activity and covers damage caused by negligence, fault or omission on the part of the contractor and his or her employees.

143. According to Article 15 of the Architecture and Civil Engineering Act (ZAID),[210] professional liability insurance for architects must cover liability for negligence resulting in damage or material defects, which, in addition to direct material damage (damage and destruction), also includes the costs directly necessary to remedy or prevent damage without incurring direct damage.

144. Neither the GZ-1 nor the ZAID contain additional rules regarding liability for damages. Therefore, the general liability rules of the OZ apply. Persons involved in construction are liable for damage resulting from dangerous objects or dangerous activities[211] according to Article 131(2) and 131(3) of the OZ.

145. If more than one person is responsible for the damage, they are jointly and severally liable.[212] In addition, the OZ sets out a special rule for the (joint and several) liability of the contracting authority in Article 187. 'The contracting authority and the contractor for works on real estate shall be jointly and severally liable to a third person for damage they inflict in connection with the execution of such works.' This rule regulates a special form of liability, as the (joint and several) liability of a contracting authority (landowner or investor) is entirely dependent on the liability of the contractor (builder).[213] According to Article 187 of the OZ, the contracting authority is only liable if the contractor is liable for damage.[214] Consequently, the contractor is fully liable in the internal (recourse) relationship.[215] This is a special form of vicarious liability.[216]

146. Further provisions regarding the building contract are regulated in Articles 649–665 of the OZ. 'A building contract is a contract for work through which the contractor undertakes to build a specific structure on specific land according to a

210. Official Gazette RS, No. 61/17.
211. Part III, Ch. 5, §1.
212. *See* Art. 186 of the OZ; *see also* Part V.
213. ECLI:SI:VSLJ:2018:I.CPG.225.2018.
214. ECLI:SI:VSMB:2013:I.CP.432.2013.
215. Cf. Nina Plavšak, in Plavšak et al., *Obligacijski zakonik (OZ) (splošni del) s komentarjem, 1. knjiga* (2003), p. 1073.
216. Cf. Part II, Ch. 1.

specific plan by a specific deadline or to carry out any other construction work on such land or on an existing structure, and the ordering party undertakes to pay the contractor a specific fee for the work.'[217] Irrespective of fault, the contractor and the project designer are liable for defects and for the structural soundness of the construction.[218] Liability for defects in the execution of the construction in respect of its soundness may be enforced if such defects appear within ten years of delivery and acceptance of the work. In addition to contractual liability (irrespective of fault), builders and architects may also be subject to delictual liability if such a defect in the soundness of the construction is a cause of damage to the contracting party or a third party under the general rules of liability (*damnum extra rem*). For example, the building contractor and the project designer are (jointly and severally) liable in case of the demolition of a building if the damage was the result of inadequate planning and construction that could have been prevented.

V. Judges and State Prosecutors

147. The liability of judges and prosecutors can also be classified as part of a broader institute of liability of legal professionals for damage caused in the exercise of their profession. However, their position is a special one, as they do not enter into a private (contractual) relationship with their clients but perform their work on the basis of the law as official representatives in the exercise of public functions. Consequently, the state is generally held responsible for damages caused by their inadequate conduct. 'It is not possible to separate the activities of natural persons (state prosecutor, judge, etc.) from the activities of a state body or state, as their actions are at the same time the actions of a state body or state.'[219] Therefore, the state is generally liable for damages caused by judges and state prosecutors as representatives of a public authority.

148. It is very important that judges and state prosecutors are independent and impartial in their work. Therefore, the possibility of direct actions for damages must be significantly limited (or even excluded).[220] The rejection of direct (personal) responsibility of judges may also be justified by substantive judicial immunity, which ensures that a judge cannot be held accountable for an opinion expressed during decision-making in court.[221] However, immunity cannot apply to other improper conduct during the process (e.g., deliberate delay of a particular procedure, deliberate violation of procedural regulations, etc.). In such cases, judges and state prosecutors can be held liable under Article 148(2) of the OZ (the right of recourse of the legal person for damage inflicted by the body thereof).[222]

217. *See* Art. 649 of the OZ.
218. *See* Arts 634, 660 and 662 of the OZ.
219. ECLI:SI:VSRS:2015:II.IPS.74.2014.
220. Jan Zobec, *Odškodninska odgovornost sodnika in odgovornost države zanj*, Pravni letopis (2013), pp. 185–321.
221. *See* Art. 134(1) of the URS.
222. ECLI:SI:VSRS:2002:II.IPS.120.2002 and ECLI:SI:VSRS:2009:III.IPS.111.2009, *see also* Part I, Ch. 2, §2.

VI. Notaries

149. Notaries perform notarial service as a liberal profession. They serve the public in various non-contentious matters, usually involving general financial transactions, estates, deeds, powers of attorney, etc. The scope and powers of the notarial service are regulated in the Notariat Act (ZN).[223] Notaries may provide their services on the initiative and in the interest of one client (e.g., notarisation of signature) or in the interest of several unrelated clients (e.g., drafting public (notarial) deeds). If notaries do not represent a particular client, they must act impartially. In any case, however, they must act in accordance with applicable law and the public interest. In every case, the authorisation of the entitled person is required, as they cannot assume the role of judge or arbitrator in case of disagreement (e.g., to decide in favour of one or another client without the authorisation of the entitled person).[224]

150. An essential part of a notary's legal relationship with the clients of notarial services are statutory obligations. Although notaries exercise public authority, the state is not responsible for their inadequate conduct. Notaries are liable for damages resulting from violation of the (statutory) rules of the profession. The general rules for the liability of professionals apply.[225]

151. Irrespective of the basis of notarial liability (contractual or delictual), it is assumed that the notary is relieved of liability if he or she proves that he or she acted with due professional diligence in the fulfilment of his or her statutory duties (diligence of a good notary).[226] Any slightest omission or negligence is the basis for the notary's liability.[227] The relationship between the notary and the client may have some characteristics of a contractual relationship (e.g., preparation of private documents, and representation in non-contentious civil proceedings). In such cases, the (contractual) liability of notaries is similar to the (contractual) liability of attorneys.[228] Similar to attorneys, notaries conclude an insurance contract for damages for which they are liable to the parties according to the rules on obligations.[229]

§2. Liability of Public Authorities

152. Public authorities are all state or other public administrative bodies at national, regional, or local levels, as well as natural or legal persons performing public administrative functions based on state authorisation. In Slovenia, we relate

223. Official Gazette RS, Nos 2/07 – official consolidated version, 33/07 – ZSReg-B, 45/08, 91/13 and 189/20 – ZFRO.
224. ECLI:SI:VSRS:2018:II.IPS.175.2017.
225. For more *see* Bojan Podgoršek, *Odgovornost notarja*, Pravni letopis (2008), pp. 155–166.
226. *See also* Part I, Ch. 1, §3.
227. ECLI:SI:VSRS:2009:II.IPS.223.2008.
228. *See* Part I, Ch. 2, §1 III.
229. *See* Art. 14 of the ZN.

the liability of a public authority with the liability of the state, local self-government (municipalities) and other public-law entities.

153. The liability of public authorities is regulated at the constitutional level. According to Article 26 of the URS, everyone has the right to compensation for damage caused by unlawful acts in connection with the exercise of a function or other activity by a person or authority exercising such a function or activity within a state or local community authority or as a holder of public authority. However, the cited provision is not sufficient to comprehensively address the institute of liability for damages. Since the legislation does not provide any further rules for the liability of public authorities, the general rules of liability for damages of the OZ apply.

154. The liability of public authorities is primarily based on the rules regarding employer's liability (Article 147 of the OZ)[230] and the liability of a legal person for damage caused by its organs (Article 148 of the OZ).[231] According to Article 26 of the URS in conjunction with Article 147 of the OZ, the state, local self-government (municipalities), and holders of public authority are liable for the damage caused to a third person by an employee during or in connection with work, unless it is shown that the employee acted as was necessary under the circumstances. In addition, the Public Employees Act[232] stipulates in Article 135 that the employer is liable to third parties for damage unlawfully caused by public employees (individuals employed in the public sector) during or in connection with work.

155. According to Article 26 of the URS in conjunction with Article 148 of the OZ, the state is liable for the work and acts of state bodies, local self-government is responsible for the work and acts of local community bodies, and a holder of public authority is liable for his or her own work and acts. According to Article 148 of the OZ, a legal person is liable for damage inflicted on a third person by an organ of the legal person in the course of or in connection with the performance of its functions.[233] The state bodies (authorities) are: The President and representative bodies (e.g., the president of the Republic, the National Assembly, etc.), the state administration (e.g., the government, ministries, bodies within ministries (police, labour inspectorate, etc.), the judiciary (e.g., the Supreme Court, higher courts, etc.), agencies, and other public bodies (e.g., the bank of Slovenia, the Information Commissioner, the Office of the State Prosecutor General, etc.).[234] The organs of local self-government are the municipal council, the mayor, the local community, etc.

156. It is undisputed that the state, local self-government and a holder of public authority are liable for damages caused by unlawful acts in connection with the

230. *See also* Part II, Ch. 1, §1.
231. *See also* Part II, Ch. 1, §3.
232. Official Gazette RS, Nos 63/07 – official consolidated version, 65/08, 69/08 – ZTFI-A, 69/08 – ZZavar-E, 40/12 – ZUJF, 158/20 – ZIntPK-C, 203/20 – ZIUPOPDVE, 202/21 – Constitutional Court decision and 3/22 – ZDeb.
233. *See* Part II, Ch. 1, §3.
234. For more *see* central website of the state administration: https://www.gov.si/en/state-authorities/.

activities of their employees or bodies, according to the general rules of the OZ. However, the Supreme Court emphasised that the liability of public authorities is not classical but a special type of liability and that such special liability would require a special regulation.[235]

157. Although the courts apply the same (general) rules on liability, they do not treat the state (i.e., public authorities) in exactly the same way as private law entities. Among other things, one can see a tendency to socialise many common life risks by reference to the institute of state liability (e.g., too strict approach, unequal approach, excessive extension of liability, etc.).[236]

158. Recently, the question has been raised whether the state is liable for damages caused by holders of public authority (specifically for insolvency administrators) since the state delegates certain tasks for the exercise of sovereign right (*acta iure imperii*). According to recent case law, the state is not liable for the conduct of private entities to which the authority has been delegated, especially if these entities act in their own economic interest and are liable for their own work and actions, e.g., court experts, insolvency administrators, etc. Consequently, the state could only be held liable under the general liability rules for its own conduct, i.e., selection, lack of control over its work, etc. and not in the form of strict liability.[237]

§3. Abuse of Rights

159. Abuse of rights refers to the exercise of a right in a way that prevents other natural or legal persons from enjoying their own rights or that is contrary to the purpose for which it was established or recognised. In Slovenia, the abuse of rights is not regulated at the constitutional level. However, it is laid down in several statutory provisions, including the OZ and the ZPP.[238]

160. According to Article 7 of the OZ, the rights arising from obligational relationships are limited by the equal rights of others and must be exercised in accordance with the basic principles of the OZ and their purpose. Additionally, the participants must refrain from actions that would make it more difficult to fulfil the obligations of other participants. Any act whereby the holder of a right acts with the sole or clear intention of harming another shall be deemed to be a sham exercise of

---

235. ECLI:SI:VSRS:1999:II.IPS.387.97.
236. For more *see* Damjan Možina, *Odškodninska odgovornost države*, Pravni letopis (2013), pp. 141–165.
237. ECLI:SI:VSLJ:2021:I.CPG.456.2020 and ECLI:SI:VSRS:2021:III.IPS.33.2021.
238. Official Gazette RS, Nos 73/07 – official consolidated text, 45/08 – ZArbit, 45/08, 111/08 – Constitutional Court decision, 57/09 – Constitutional Court decision, 12/10 – Constitutional Court decision, 50/10 – Constitutional Court decision, 107/10 – Constitutional Court decision, 75/12 – Constitutional Court decision, 40/13 – Constitutional Court decision, 92/13 – Constitutional Court decision, 10/14 – Constitutional Court decision, 48/15 – Constitutional Court decision, 6/17 – Constitutional Court decision, 10/17, 16/19 – ZNP-1, 70/19 – Constitutional Court decision, 1/22 – Constitutional Court decision and 3/22 – ZDeb.

that right. The institute of abuse of rights is closely linked to the principle of conscientiousness and fairness, which is laid down in Article 5 of the OZ.[239]

161. According to Article 11 of the ZPP, the courts are obliged to prevent any form of abuse of the rights enjoyed by the parties and other participants in the proceedings. If the parties abuse their procedural rights with the intention of harming another person or with an aim which is contrary to good customs, conscientiousness, and fairness, the court may impose a fine or other sanctions provided for by law. In the case of abuse of rights, the court shall not uphold the plaintiff's claim.[240] A person who has abused the right may also be held liable for damages incurred as a result of such abuse.[241]

§4. Injury to Reputation and Privacy

162. Human rights and fundamental freedoms are covered at the constitutional level by Article 14 to Article 65 of the URS. These articles include the protection of human personality and dignity,[242] the protection of the rights to privacy and personality rights,[243] the protection of the privacy of correspondence and other means of communication,[244] and the protection of personal data.[245] The right to reputation and the right to privacy are interrelated and are granted (under different conditions and circumstances) to all natural and legal persons.

163. According to Article 134 of the OZ all persons (natural and legal persons)[246] have the right to request from a court or any other competent authority to order refrainment from, prevention or elimination of the consequences of acts that infringe the inviolability of the human person, personal and family life or any other personal right. This right is granted irrespective of whether or not the violation of the personal right causes legally recognised harm. The court or other competent authority may order the infringer to cease such an act. Otherwise, the person concerned is obliged to pay a sum of money to the person affected, determined as a total amount or per unit of time (e.g., for each day of the violation).[247]

164. Even though the right to reputation and the right to privacy are regulated by the URS, they are not absolute and are limited by (personal) rights of other persons, in particular by freedom of expression[248] and other permissible violations that are allowed by law (e.g., permissible video surveillance). The extent to which rights

239. *See also* Part I, Ch. 1.
240. ECLI:SI:VSRS:2012:II.IPS.281.2009.
241. ECLI:SI:VSLJ:2011:I.CP.2457.2011.
242. *See* Art. 21 of the URS.
243. *See* Art. 35 of the URS.
244. *See* Art. 37 of the URS.
245. *See* Art. 38 of the URS.
246. ECLI:SI:VSKP:2017:CPG.15.2017.
247. *See* Art. 134(2) of the OZ.
248. *See* Art. 35 of the URS.

are protected depends on the specific circumstances of each case (e.g., natural or legal person, public figure, etc.). Therefore, a weighing of the conflicting legally protected interests is required in each individual case.

165. In addition to the right to demand the cessation of the infringement, the person whose rights have been violated may claim his or her pecuniary (e.g., loss of job) and non-pecuniary (e.g., psychological distress) damage. According to Article 132 of the OZ, non-pecuniary damage to natural persons includes the infliction of physical or mental distress and fear. Consequently, a natural person is only entitled to monetary compensation if the violation of the personal right causes a further consequence in the form of mental pain or anxiety.[249] Legal persons, however, are entitled to just monetary compensation for defamation of reputation or good name, irrespective of the recovery of pecuniary loss, if the court finds that the circumstances justify it, even if there is no material damage.[250] In addition to monetary compensation, in any case of violation of a personal right (in the case of natural or legal persons), the court may order the publication of a judgment or rectification in order to eliminate or reduce the consequences of the violation.[251]

166. The right to reputation is a classic personal right. The right may be infringed, *inter alia*, by a statement of untrue facts that damage the honour or reputation of the victim.[252] The right is defined as the value that the (natural or legal) person has in society, as objective honour, as the external value of the individual in the eyes of society, and as his or her socially perceived value. Consequently, compensation is theoretically possible even when others are unaware of the improper conduct, i.e., when the person's reputation is not interfered with but only their honour is affected.[253]

167. The right to reputation is restricted by the freedom of expression in connection with the public's right to information (right to know), especially in the case of legal persons and public figures.[254] The right to be informed in matters of public interest is not limited to the one-time publication of a specific fact, but it is even desirable that it be published several times and in full.[255] The right can even be violated by anonymous postings in an online chat or forum.[256] However, the operator of the forum is not obliged to check the truthfulness of all posts but must react to the warning received and remove all offensive and illegal content.[257] It must be emphasised that the state as a public authority is not the holder of personal rights when it comes to the exercise of state authority (*acta iure imperii*).[258]

249. ECLI:SI:VSRS:2017:II.IPS.238.2015.
250. *See* Arts 132 and 183 of the OZ.
251. *See* Art. 178 of the OZ.
252. ECLI:SI:VSLJ:2020:II.CP.222.2020.
253. ECLI:SI:VSRS:2011:II.IPS.195.2010.
254. ECLI:SI:VSLJ:2017:II.CP.159.2017.
255. ECLI:SI:VSLJ:2015:I.CP.2214.2015.
256. ECLI:SI:VSLJ:2010:II.CP.4539.2010.
257. ECLI:SI:VSLJ:2017:I.CP.3097.2016.
258. ECLI:SI:VSLJ:2021:I.CPG.806.2019.

168. The content of the right to privacy depends on various circumstances, such as location of the violation (e.g., home, work, public place), injured person (e.g., public figures), expectation of privacy, extent of the violation, etc. For ordinary people, posting videos of their private lives[259] or publishing their personal information[260] without their consent may be considered an inadmissible infringement of the right to privacy. However, absolute public figures (e.g., the President, the Prime Minister, etc.) do not enjoy de facto privacy protection as long as their portrayal does not constitute an example of overt or convincingly justified malice aimed at satisfying people's curiosity.[261] In the case of legal persons, the right to privacy relates to the so-called communication privacy – the privacy of correspondence and other means of communication. In all cases of violation, the restriction of the right to privacy is assessed according to the criterion of the expected range of privacy.[262]

§5. Interference by a Third Person with Contractual Relations

169. The fundamental characteristic of contractual relations in Slovenian law is their relativity, which means that they are effective only between the contracting parties, *inter partes* (Article 125(1) of the OZ).[263] If the contractual relationship is not of a personal nature (*intuitu personae*), it also affects the universal legal successors of the contracting parties (Article 125(2) of the OZ). Therefore, for example, the contractual relationship may continue with the heir, who must assume the obligations to the other party under the deceased's contract until the contract is terminated (e.g., payment of the Netflix subscription).[264] Similarly, third parties may obtain a benefit and a direct claim (*actio directa*) from foreign contractual relationships (e.g., transport, insurance contracts) if they are contracts for the benefit of third parties (Article 125(3) of the OZ).[265]

170. The OZ also regulates the legal consequences of various forms of third-party interference in contractual relationships. The first group includes cases where one of the contracting parties 'involves' a third party in the contractual relationship, which is regulated in a special part of the OZ for individual types of contracts. An example is a contractor who entrusts part of the execution of the work to a subcontractor and is therefore responsible for it to the client.[266] Or cases where the lessor enters into a sales contract during the term of the lease contract (the OZ regulates

259. ECLI:SI:VSLJ:2015:I.CP.570.2015.
260. ECLI:SI:VSLJ:2018:II.CP.693.2018.
261. ECLI:SI:VSLJ:2012:II.CP.562.2012.
262. ECLI:SI:VSLJ:2013:II.CP.2201.2012.
263. *See* ECLI:SI:VSLJ:2008:I.CPG.490.2007.
264. Cf. ECLI:SI:VSCE:2022:CP.56.2022.
265. ECLI:SI:VSLJ:2010:I.CPG.27.2010.
266. *See* ECLI:SI:VSLJ:2008:I.CPG.490.2007 where the court concluded that given the relative nature of the obligation relationships in relation to the client, the entrepreneur was responsible for the correctness of the fulfilment (Art. 125(1) of the OZ). In this sense, the contractor was also responsible to the client for the work of his subcontractor (Art. 630 of the OZ). However, since the client and the subcontractor were not in a contractual relationship, the client could not assert claims from the subcontractor for the fulfilment of the contract, as well as civil law claims due to the breach of the

different consequences depending on whether the object of the lease has already been handed over to the tenant or not). Or cases of responsibility of the seller who sells someone else's thing.[267] The second group includes cases where a third party arbitrarily intervenes in a contractual relationship and causes damage (e.g., a third party causes a traffic accident and prevents the timely delivery of goods to another contracting party). The legal consequences of such arbitrary interventions of third parties in the contractual relationship, which result in the non-fulfilment of the contractual obligation of one of the contracting parties, are assessed in the relationship between the two contracting parties in accordance with the general rule on the relief of business liability under Article 240 of the OZ, assuming that the crooked conduct of the third party (the tortfeasor) was also unavoidable.[268] The assessment of the relationship between the third party and the injured party (contractor) is subject to the general rules on tort liability (*see* Part I, Chapter 1).

§6. Others

171. The OZ sets out several special cases of liability. Most of them can be interpreted within the general rules of contractual or delictual liability, but some special cases are regulated on the basis of certain characteristics. Even though the special cases of liability are grouped under the same title in Articles 156 to 163, they have almost nothing else in common.

172. Article 156 of the OZ deals with liability for acts of terrorism, public demonstrations, and events. The state or the person who should have prevented such acts according to regulations is liable for damage caused by death or bodily injury resulting from acts of terrorism or during public demonstrations and events. However, the injured party is only entitled to compensation for the damage suffered on the basis of this article in connection with acts directed against the state, its system or in its support, and not against the injured parties personally.[269]

173. According to Article 157, the organiser of an assembly of a large number of people (in an enclosed area or in the open air) is liable for damage caused by death or bodily injury caused by extraordinary circumstances that may arise in such situations, such as a mass movement and general unrest. In the case of an assembly

---

contract between the client and the contractor. Since the customer was not a party to the contractual relationship between the contractor and his subcontractor, he could not assert claims against the subcontractor due to the violation of the subcontractor's obligation to properly fulfil the contract from that relationship.

267. In accordance with Art. 420 of the OZ, the sale of foreign property also binds the contracting party; however, the buyer, who did not know and did not have to know that the property in question was a foreign item, may withdraw from the contract if he or she cannot achieve its purpose because of this, and claim compensation. *See also* ECLI:SI:VSLJ:2011:I.CP.809.2011.

268. *See also* ECLI:SI:VSKP:2016:CPG.140.2016, ECLI:SI:VSLJ:2020:II.CP.73.2020, ECLI:SI:VSKP:2007:I.CP.16.2006, ECLI:SI:VSLJ:2010:I.CPG.129.2010 and ECLI:SI:VSLJ:2010:II.CP.750.2010.

269. ECLI:SI:VSLJ:2010:II.CP.4463.2009.

of a large number of people, the greatest risk of damage is a crowd that can escape even the most careful supervision. In such cases, the organiser is liable for the damage irrespective of culpability.[270]

174. Articles 158 to 160 of the OZ regulate the liability of the keeper of an animal (dangerous or domestic) and the liability of the keeper of a building, which will be discussed in detail below.[271]

175. According to Article 161 of the OZ, a person who, without being at risk, fails to assist a person whose life or health is clearly endangered is liable for the damage caused thereby if the damage should have been foreseen in the circumstances of the case. The provision is based on the principle of solidarity, which imposes the duty to assist a person in danger.[272] However, the court may exempt such a person from compensation for the damage if justice so requires.[273]

176. Articles 162 and 163 refer to the breach of the obligation of the mandatory conclusion of a contract. If a specific act determines that a person must conclude a contract, a person with a legitimate interest may demand that this contract be concluded without delay.[274] Additionally, a person who is obliged by an act to conclude a contract must compensate the damage if he or she does not conclude the contract without delay at the request of the person concerned.[275] Furthermore, persons performing municipal or similar activities of general importance are also liable for damage if they discontinue the services or perform them irregularly without justifiable cause.[276]

270. ECLI:SI:VSLJ:2012:II.CP.549.2012.
271. For more *see* Part II, Ch. 3.
272. ECLI:SI:VSLJ:2016:I.CP.558.2016.
273. *See* Art. 161(2) of the OZ.
274. *See* Art. 17 of the OZ.
275. *See* Art. 162 of the OZ.
276. *See* Art. 163 of the OZ.

Part II. Liability for Acts of Others

Chapter 1. Vicarious Liability

§1. Employee/Employer

177. Article 147 of the OZ lays down a special rule on liability for damage caused by an employee at work or in connection with work. This is a form of liability for the conduct of another person, which is based on the fact that the worker performs work on behalf of and in the name of the employer. The employee's acts in relation to third parties are therefore regarded as the employer's own acts. Also, any risks and rewards associated with the result of the work are in the interest of the employer. The employer is liable for damages for the conduct of the employee and not for his or her own conduct. Consequently, it is the appropriateness of the worker's conduct that is assessed and not a possible fault on the part of the employer regarding the choice of the worker (*culpa in eligendo*), the giving of incorrect instructions (*culpa in instruendo*) or the failure to supervise (*culpa custodiendo*).[277]

178. The existence of an employee-employer relationship is a prerequisite for the employer's liability under Article 147 of the OZ. The existence of such a relationship is the least ambiguous where the worker performs work on the basis of an employment contract or where the relationship shows the elements of an employment relationship.[278] An employment relationship exists where the worker voluntarily engages in the employer's work process and, in return for remuneration, personally and continuously performs work under the direction and supervision of the employer.[279] In addition, an employee-employer relationship under Article 147 of the OZ also exists in all other cases where a natural person in a subordinate position performs certain work under the direction and supervision of the employer, irrespective of the legal basis and duration of the relationship. It is important that the work is done for someone else and completed in person rather than through assistants in performance. In addition, such a person does not assume any risks and rewards related to the work performed.

277. Cf. Jadek Pensa, *supra* n. 60, at 836.
278. Even if the parties do not conclude an employment contract, an employment relationship shall be assumed if the elements of employment relationship are present (Art. 18 of the ZDR-1).
279. *See* Art. 4 of the ZDR-1.

179. Even if there exists an employee-employer relationship under Article 147 of the OZ, the employer is not liable for every act of the employees. The employer can be relieved of his or her liability in two ways, either by proving that the damage did not arise out of or in connection with the work, or by proving that the worker acted as was supposed in the given circumstances.[280] However, it follows therefrom that the employer is also liable if the worker intentionally causes damage, in so far as the conduct is causally connected with the performance of the work imposed.

180. An act is deemed committed during work or in connection with work if it is done within the scope of the functions performed by a person who has been entrusted with the respective functions as an employee. If the damage occurs during working hours and at the workplace, the damage is generally considered to have occurred during work or in connection with work. However, it is necessary to establish in each specific case the substantial link between the work imposed and the conduct of the employee. If the employee's conduct is not related to the work that he or she is supposed to perform, the employer is not liable, even if the damage occurs at the workplace and during working hours. For example, an employer would not be liable if a cashier in a clothing shop shot his ex-wife's partner with a gun for personal reasons during working hours. However, the situation would be different, for instance, if the employee's work position enabled or substantially facilitated the commission of the tort. In such a case, the employer would be liable also in the event of personal motives and manifest abuse of power, especially if the employee would not have been able to commit the tort in the first place without such a position.[281] This would be the case, for example, if the same act had been committed by a shop security guard, where the right (and also the obligation) to keep and bear arms arises out of a specific employment relationship and is also in the interest and for the benefit of the employer.

181. However, the employer can also relieve himself or herself of tort liability by proving that in the given circumstances, the employee acted as he or she should have acted. The employer's liability therefore depends on the conduct of the employee and the specific circumstances of each individual case. Since any conduct of the employee is to be regarded as the employer's own conduct, the appropriateness of the employee's conduct must be assessed in the same way as if the employer had performed the act himself or herself.[282] This distinction is highly important because in most cases, the employer will be regarded as the expert. As a result, stricter criteria will have to be applied in assessing the appropriateness of the employee's conduct in such a case. Also, the employer will not be able to relieve himself or herself of liability by merely proving that the employee acted with due diligence of a good master but will have to prove that the employee acted in accordance with a higher degree of

280. *See* Art. 147(1) of the OZ.
281. ECLI:SI:VSRS:2012:II.IPS.257.2011.
282. Plavšak et al., *supra* n. 95, at 569.

diligence[283] (i.e., the diligence of a good expert), which includes compliance with the rules of the profession and the customs applicable to the employer.[284]

182. Although the employee does the work for the employer and does not assume the risks and rewards of the result, this does not mean that he or she is completely free from tort liability. In certain examples, the employer has the right to a compensation under the internal (recourse) relationship. The employer may claim reimbursement of the sum paid to the injured party if the damage was inflicted by the employee intentionally or out of gross negligence. This right of the employer becomes statute-barred within six months from the date on which the compensation was paid.[285] In case of damage inflicted by the employee intentionally, the injured party may demand the reimbursement of damage directly from the employee.[286]

183. These rules, however, shall not prejudice the rules on (strict) tort liability originating from dangerous objects or dangerous activities. If damage to a third party arises from a dangerous object or occurs in connection with the pursuit of a dangerous activity, the liability (of the employer) is assessed according to the rules of strict liability.[287] This would be the case, for example, if an employee was transporting cargo in a lorry under the direction, supervision and on behalf of the employer, and in the process injured a pedestrian crossing the road. In such a case, the employer could only be relieved of liability for the damage caused by proving the existence of one of the grounds for exemption from strict liability set out in Article 153 of the OZ.

§2. Independent Contractors

184. In addition to the employee-employer relationship referred to in Article 147 of the OZ, a natural or legal entity may also perform contractual obligations through independent contractors or assistants. An example is a contractor who undertakes to build a house. Most of the work is carried out by the contractor's own employees, but the contractor may hire another (sub)contractor for specific services (e.g., installation of windows). This type of relationship differs from an employment relationship under Article 147 of the OZ, particularly with regard to the independent contractor (subcontractor) being independent in carrying out the work and not being bound by instructions and supervision as regards the performance of the work. The subcontractor also assumes any risks and rewards relating to the results of the work carried out.[288]

283. *See more* Part I, Ch. 1, §§2–3.
284. *See* Art. 6(2) of the OZ.
285. *See* Art. 147(3) and 147(4) of the OZ.
286. *See* Art. 147(2) of the OZ.
287. *See* Tittle II s. 2 subs 5 of the OZ.
288. *See* Title XI of the OZ: Contract for Work.

185. If the independent contractor causes damage to third-party property during work, the question arises as to who is liable (main contractor or assistant in performance) and under what conditions. The OZ does not lay down a specific rule governing the issue of liability for the conduct of independent contractors in general. However, specific rules are laid down in the context of individual contracts. There are different types of contracts a contractor may conclude with assistants, with the most common types being contract for work and contract of mandate. It should be noted that it must be assessed on a case-by-case basis whether the relationship is that of employee-employer as referred to in Article 147 of the OZ or whether it is an independent contractual relationship. If the relationship is dependent and non-independent in substance, the rules of Article 147 of the OZ must be complied with, even if the contractor concluded a contract for work or another civil law contract with the subcontractor.[289]

186. A contract for work is a contract with which a subcontractor undertakes to carry out a specific business in return for payment. It is an obligation of result. The subcontractor undertakes to achieve a certain result and only then is he or she entitled to payment for the work done. Unless the parties agree otherwise (or it proceeds from the nature of the transaction), the subcontractor is not obliged to perform the transaction personally.[290] In such a case, the sub-contractor may achieve the necessary result through assistants. This creates two independent contractual relationships with the same object of the obligation, namely the ordering party-contractor relationship and the contractor-subcontractor relationship. If the subcontractor causes damage to the ordering party in the performance of the work (e.g., causes a fire during the performance of the work, which destroys part of the building), the question is from whom the ordering party can demand reimbursement for the damage caused.

187. It can be established that the ordering party can claim damages directly from the tortfeasor (the subcontractor) as well as from the contractor, as both are jointly and severally liable for the damage caused by the performance of the works. According to Article 630 of the OZ, the contractor is liable for persons who worked on the accepted transaction under the contractor's orders as if the contractor had done the work in person. This is a special (accessory) form of liability for the conduct of others. The liability of the contractor is dependent on the liability of the subcontractor. If there is no liability of the subcontractor, there is no liability of the contractor.[291] Joint and several liability also arises from Article 187 of the OZ, which stipulates that the contracting authority (contractor) and the contractor for works (subcontractor) on real estate are jointly and severally liable to a third person (the ordering party) for any damage inflicted by them in connection with the execution of the works. It should be pointed out that the rules on joint and several liability apply only to reimbursement of non-business damages. Since the ordering party and the subcontractor are not in a contractual obligational relationship, the ordering

289. *See* Part II, Ch.1, §1.
290. *See* Art. 629 of the OZ.
291. ECLI:SI:VSRS:2013:III.IPS.50.2011.

party cannot exercise claims for non-performance and improper performance of (contractual) obligations directly from the subcontractor.

188. Unlike a contract for work, a contract of mandate is considered an obligation of means. In a contract of mandate, the mandatary undertakes to perform a specific task for the ordering party (mandator) and is deemed to have performed the obligation agreed upon if reasonable diligence to fulfil the obligation has been exercised. Typical examples of a contract of mandate are a medical treatment contract and a contract for the provision of legal services.[292] The mandatary must fulfil the contract in person and may only engage assistants if the mandator has given permission or if the mandatary is compelled to do so by circumstances. If the mandatary is a company or a legal entity, then this legal entity shall be the party to the contract of mandate.[293] In such a case, the personal execution of the contract shall be deemed to be the execution by any of the employees of the legal entity, unless the mandator expresses interest in having the transaction executed by a specific natural person.

189. If the mandator agrees to the inclusion of an assistant in performance or if circumstances compel it, the mandatary shall be liable only for the choice of the substitute *(culpa in eligendo)* and for the instructions provided thereto (*culpa in instruendo*).[294] Consequently, the mandatary shall be liable for the damage caused by the assistant in performance only if the substitute has not been chosen with due diligence of a good manager or professional or if the mandatary has not given the substitute adequate instructions. *A contrario*, if the mandatary has acted with due diligence, he or she shall not be liable for the damage inflicted, even in case the assistant in performance has caused the damage intentionally or due to gross negligence. The situation would be different if the mandatary had engaged an assistant in performance without the consent of the mandator and without other valid reasons. In that case, the mandatary is liable not only for the choice of the substitute and the instructions given but also for the work and conduct of the assistant in performance. The liability of the mandatary is even stricter than if he had completed the work in person, since in this case, he or she is also liable for the accidental destruction of or damage to the thing with the assistant in performance.[295]

190. However, unlike in the case of a contract for work, the mandator can, by virtue of a special rule, in any event (whether or not the mandatary was allowed to engage an assistant to perform the transaction) exercise a direct claim for performance also against the assistant in performance.[296] If the first mandatary is also liable for the correct performance, the liability towards the mandator is joint and

292. If the subject of a medical or legal services contract is a result (e.g., cosmetic surgery or winning a lawsuit), such a contract is judged according to the rules of a contract for services.
293. Nina Plavšak, in Plavšak et al., *Obligacijski zakonik (OZ) (posebni del) s komentarjem, 4. knjiga* (2004), p. 247.
294. *See* Art. 770(3) of the OZ.
295. *See* Art. 770(4) of the OZ.
296. *See* Art. 770(5) of the OZ.

several, since both mandatary parties are responsible for the same exercise behaviour (performance of the transaction) and the obligation is therefore indivisible.[297]

§3. Liability of Legal Entities for Acts of Their Organs

191. In addition to the liability for employees under Article 147 of the OZ, Article 148 of the OZ lays down a special rule regarding the liability of a legal entity for damage inflicted by its organs. A legal entity is an artificial creation which formulates its intention within organs composed of natural persons. In legal transactions, a legal entity declares its intention through organs as its own intention. Consequently, a legal entity is liable for any damage inflicted by its organs to a third party during or in connection with the performance of their functions.

192. The conduct of an organ is therefore considered an act of the legal entity itself. Since the organ is part of the legal entity, it is not the case of liability for the acts of another but rather the case of liability for one's own acts. If the law does not provide for strict liability in a particular case, the legal entity is liable under the general rules of fault-based liability. As a result, the legal entity may be exonerated from liability for damages providing it proves that the members of the organ acted with due diligence expected in concluding that particular type of transactions or related conduct. It should be pointed out that in any case, diligence is judged according to the criteria of due diligence for legal entities, but if a particular matter concerns gainful activities of the legal entity, the members of its organs are required to exercise a higher degree of diligence (the diligence of a good professional),[298] which includes observance of the rules of the profession and of custom.[299]

193. If the members of the organ caused the damage intentionally or out of gross negligence, the legal entity is entitled to recourse. It may claim reimbursement of the amount paid within six months of the payment of compensation.[300] The members of the organ shall be jointly and severally liable for the damage.[301] However, if the damage originates from a collegial body, the legal entity may seek the right of recourse only against those members who (out)voted the decision at issue.[302]

194. In addition to liability for damage caused by its body, a legal entity is also liable, in certain cases, for the conduct of its representatives. These are persons who are not part of the legal entity, but who act actively and passively in the name and on behalf of the legal entity in legal transactions. If the representative's conduct is not independent and is subject to the (employer's) direction and supervision, it is judged under Article 147 of the OZ.[303] In such a case, the legal entity is deemed

297. ECLI:SI:VSLJ:2016:III.CP.2494.2016.
298. *See* Part I, Ch. 1, §§2 and 3.
299. *See* Art. 6 of the OZ.
300. *See* Art. 148(2) and 148(4) of the OZ.
301. *See* Art. 186 of the OZ.
302. Jadek Pensa, *supra* n. 60, at 847.
303. *See* Part II, Ch. 1, §1.

liable if the representative has caused damage during or in connection with their work, not having acted in the manner required (e.g., apparent authority, procurator). However, if the representative acts in an independent capacity (e.g., an external authorised person), the legal entity is liable for the conduct of this person only in the event of transgression of authorisation.[304] If a person does not hold a (valid) authorisation, or if his or her actions are not in accordance with the given authorisation, such person is considered a *falsus procurator*. In such a case, a joint and several liability of the legal entity is not established.

195. These rules of the OZ fall under the general provisions of tort liability regarding legal entities. However, the special rules regulate certain issues differently. For example, special rules apply to the liability of members of a management or supervisory body, which are laid out in Article 263 of the ZGD-1. Two differences, in particular, are worth noting with regard to the OZ, namely the question of the responsibility of members of bodies towards third persons and the question of due diligence assessment.

196. Under the general rules of the OZ, a natural person who is a member of a body of a legal entity is not liable to third parties for damage caused while performing his or her duties.[305] The reason why a natural person who is a member of a body of a legal entity is not directly liable is that their conduct is considered to be the conduct of the legal entity itself.[306] In consequence, a third party does not have a direct claim for damages against a member of a body of a legal entity (e.g., the president of an association) under the rules of the OZ, even if the damage was caused intentionally.[307] However, due to the nature of commercial legal relationships, the ZGD-1 provides for a special direct claim by the company's creditors, which is only applicable if the creditors cannot be repaid out of the company's assets.[308]

197. For members of corporate bodies, the ZGD-1 also lays down special rules for assessing the due diligence of their conduct. In the performance of their duties, they must act for the benefit of the company with due diligence of a conscientious and good businessman, safeguarding the company's business secrets. They shall be jointly and severally liable for damages resulting from a breach of their duties unless they prove that they performed their duties honestly and conscientiously. If the act which inflicted damage to the company was based on a lawful decision of the assembly, the company shall have no right of recourse. Due to the nature of business, a special business judgment rule applies to the assessment of the due diligence

304. *See* Art. 72(5) of the OZ.
305. ECLI:SI:VSLJ:2015:I.CP.1186.2015, ECLI:SI:VSRS:2015:II.IPS.101.2013 and ECLI:SI:VSRS:2012:II.IPS.111.2009.
306. ECLI:SI:VSRS:2014:III.IPS.72.2014.
307. Given that in certain cases the injured party has a direct claim for damages against the employee, it is necessary to assess in each specific case whether the person has caused the damage as a member of the body of the legal entity (Art. 148 of the OZ) or as an employee, in which case tort liability is judged according to the provisions regarding the employer's liability (Art. 147 of the OZ).
308. *See* Art. 263(3) of the ZGD-1.

of the members of bodies, which, although not enacted in the Slovenian legal order, is taken into consideration by case law in assessing the appropriateness of the conduct.[309] This rule provides that any business decision that is harmful does not necessarily constitute conduct that is contrary to the standard of due diligence.[310]

309. ECLI:SI:VSRS:2015:III.IPS.97.2015.

310. Nataša Samec Berghaus, *Odškodninska odgovornost članov organov vodenja in nadzora gospodarskih družb in pravilo podjetniške presoje (business judgement rule),* (2016).

Chapter 2. Liability of Parents, Teachers & Instructors

198. The liability of parents, teachers and instructors is regulated in Articles 141 to 146 of the OZ. It is a special form of liability for another, which is based on the duty to exercise supervision over persons who, because of their age or medical condition, are incapable of sound judgment and control over their actions. Unlike with liability for the conduct of employees, independent contractors and members of the legal entity's bodies, what is assessed in this case, is the appropriateness of the conduct of persons whose duty is to supervise a specific natural person (*culpa in inspiciendo*) rather than the appropriateness of the conduct of the persons who caused the damage.

199. Any damage caused by a person who for reason of mental development disabilities or mental health problems or for any other reason is not capable of accounting for his or her actions is the responsibility of the person who is obliged to supervise him or her according to an Act, according to a ruling by the relevant authority or according to a contract.[311] This is a form of fault-based liability, as the person liable may be released from liability if it is proven that he or she conducted the obligatory supervision or that the damage would have occurred even under careful supervision.[312] The adequacy of the supervision exercised is assessed on a case-by-case basis and depends, *inter alia*, on the status of the obliged person. If the supervision of a specific natural person is the obligation of another natural person, his or her conduct will be assessed in accordance with the due diligence of a good manager. This, however, does not apply to e.g., a public institution, which is a professional organisation for the education and care of persons. In conducting supervision, the personnel of such an institution must exercise professional care and, owing to their professional competence, expect unpredictable reactions from the wards.[313] Regardless of this, the responsibility of the institution is not strict, as the behaviour of the mentally disabled is often unpredictable and the institution (even as a good professional) cannot prevent or avoid every unlawful conduct of a ward.[314]

200. Under Article 142 of the OZ, the liability for damage caused by a minor to another person lies with the child's parents, or they are jointly and severally liable if the child is also liable for damage.[315] The type of parental liability depends on the age of the child, as the law provides for strict liability for children up to the age of 7, and for fault-based liability of parents for children aged over 7. Therefore, if the damage is inflicted by a child under the age of 7, the parents cannot be released from liability by proving that they exercised the necessary supervision. In such a case, exclusion of parental liability is only possible based on Article 153 of the OZ. If the cause of the damage is the child's conduct (and not, for instance, the conduct of a

311. *See* Art. 62 of the OZ.
312. *See* Art. 62(2) of the OZ.
313. ECLI:SI:VSCE:2008:CPG.170.2008.
314. ECLI:SI:VSMB:2015:I.CP.1275.2014.
315. *See* Art. 143 of the OZ.

third party or the injured party), this is by rule not considered an external event, so release from parental liability is not possible.[316]

201. The situation is different if the damage is inflicted by a minor above seven years of age. In this case, the parents can be released from liability for damage if they can prove that the damage was caused without their fault, i.e., that they did not fail to exercise due care. Parental due care is defined within parental rights. While with younger children, the fault of the parents is established mainly in relation to their failure to provide care and supervision, poor or improper upbringing is at issue with older children. For example, it is unreasonable to request or expect the parents of a 16-year-old unproblematic adolescent to constantly exercise direct control over their child's movement and actions. Nevertheless, parental education must focus on guiding the child's behaviour in situations that parents should and could expect.[317] Situations in which children are on their own, e.g., when playing with friends, on their way to school, etc. are particularly important. A higher degree of diligence is required from parents of children with aggressive behavioural outbursts because in such cases, they can only be released from liability if they have sought appropriate professional help in time.[318]

202. However, parents are not generally liable for the damage caused by their minor child while under the care and supervision of another.[319] In such a case, the duty of supervision effectively passes on to the custodian, kindergarten, school, or other organisation, which are liable for the inflicted damage under the rules of fault-based liability. They may be released from liability if they can prove that they acted with due diligence while exercising supervision or that the damage would have occurred despite diligent supervision.[320] However, Article 145 of the OZ also stipulates special parental liability based on the poor upbringing of the minor, poor example, or bad habits set by the parents. If the damage is caused as a result of poor upbringing, the injured party has the right to demand compensation from the parents. If case the person who is responsible for supervision in a particular case pays compensation to the injured party, he or she has the right to demand that the parents reimburse the sum paid.

203. The obligatory supervision of the school extends from the moment pupils enter the school premises to the time they go home.[321] A continuous presence of a custodian, teacher or tutor is particularly important with younger children (e.g., in kindergarten). By the age of 8 to 9, children are already able to comprehend the importance of house rules and are mature enough to make a constant supervision of

316. ECLI:SI:VSLJ:2014:III.CP.2686.2014.
317. ECLI:SI:VSLJ:2014:I.CP.3003.2013.
318. ECLI:SI:VSLJ:2017:I.CP.2114.2016.
319. In such a case, the parents are liable for damages only if the tortious conduct of their minor is due to inadequate upbringing or other circumstances of which they did not give adequate warning, and if the liability of the person to whom the child was entrusted is not established (Art. 142(3) of the OZ).
320. *See* Art. 144 of the OZ.
321. ECLI:SI:VSRS:2012:II.IPS.413.2009.

a teacher in the short time before school starts unnecessary.[322] Children aged thirteen should already be aware of the fact that playing catch and tripping classmates might lead to harmful consequences, so a constant supervision of pupils of this age is not necessary.[323] Furthermore, exercising constant supervision is practically impossible, so the mere fact that the teacher was facing away from the pupils at the precise moment of the harmful event does not mean that he or she thereby failed to exercise the required obligatory supervision.[324] Just as a child may be accidentally injured while under the parent's care, he or she may also be accidentally injured at school. Liability for another does not apply only to kindergartens, schools, and other public institutions, but to all situations in which a minor child is entrusted to another custodian. Consequently, grandparents, neighbours, friends, babysitters, coaches, cultural and sports associations and other natural persons or legal entities who (explicitly or implicitly) take care of minor children may also be liable for damages under Article 144 of the OZ.

204. In addition to liability for damage caused by minors, the law also prescribes other responsibilities to parents. One of the more important ones is the responsibility for mandatory vaccination of children, which is laid down in Article 22 of the Communicable Diseases Act (ZNB).[325] As vaccination against communicable diseases is a legal obligation which can only be omitted if the prescribed conditions are met, a health inspector can order parents to take their child to mandatory vaccination.[326] The objective of making some vaccinations mandatory is to prevent the spread of certain serious infectious diseases, so the legislator has the right and even the duty to take appropriate measures. Based on the mandatory nature of vaccinations, it can be concluded that an unvaccinated child poses a risk to the environment and particularly to persons who, for legitimate medical reasons, cannot be vaccinated. Since any medical procedure on children under 15 years of age (including vaccination) requires the consent of their parents or guardians,[327] it can be concluded that parents are obliged to ensure that their children are vaccinated. It follows that the parents of a child who has not been vaccinated (but should have been according to the law) are liable for any damages if, for example, their unvaccinated child infects a person who could not be vaccinated for medical reasons.

322. ECLI:SI:VSLJ:2014:II.CP.2202.2014.
323. ECLI:SI:VSLJ:2019:I.CP.1897.2018.
324. ECLI:SI:VSRS:2011:II.IPS.696.2009.
325. Official Gazette RS, Nos 33/06 – official consolidated version, 49/20 – ZIUZEOP, 142/20, 175/20 – ZIUOPDVE and 15/21 – ZDUOP.
326. ECLI:SI:VSRS:2003:I.UP.413.2003.
327. *See* Art. 35 of the Patients' Rights Act (Official Gazette RS, Nos 15/08, 55/17 and 177/20).

Chapter 3. Liability for Things and Animals

205. The OZ sets out specific rules regarding liability for damage occurring in connection with (immovable and movable) property and for damage caused by animals. Liability for property and animals is regulated in various articles of the OZ, and certain issues are also regulated by other Acts. Liability for damage from a dangerous thing (or dangerous activity) is regulated in Articles 149 to 153 of the OZ, liability of holder of building is regulated in Articles 159 and 160 of the OZ, and liability of keeper of animal is regulated in Article 158 of the OZ. As regards liability for property and animals, special reference should be made to liability in the event of accidents caused by moving motor vehicles,[328] liability of the producer for the product,[329] and liability for damage caused by wild animals.[330]

206. The OZ lays down specific rules on liability for damage caused in connection with a dangerous object or activity. In several aspects, these rules differ from general (fault-based) tort liability, the key distinction, however, regards causal link and the presumption of fault. If the damage arises in connection with a dangerous object (e.g., a car, a machine, a weapon), it is deemed to originate from the dangerous object, where the person liable (the keeper of the object) cannot be released from liability by proving that he or she was not at fault for the damage, regardless of how diligent he or she was in trying to prevent the damage from occurring.[331] However careful the supervision or however exact the rules of use, they cannot prevent a dangerous thing from getting out of control, 'slipping', thereby causing damage.[332] The harmful consequence is therefore inherent in the very possession of the dangerous object, as a pre-existing risk of damage.[333]

207. Damage caused by a dangerous object is the responsibility of the keeper of the object.[334] This is normally the owner of the object, but not necessarily, as the legal title, based on which a person actually handles the dangerous object is irrelevant.[335] The risk of increased danger should be borne by the person who uses the dangerous object for his or her own benefit, who has it at his or her disposal, who manipulates and maintains it for his or her own use, or who has placed it in a position where it could endanger others and cause damage.[336] In case the dangerous object was removed unlawfully from its keeper, the person who took it shall be liable for the damage, unless the holder is liable.[337] For example, parents are deemed liable for the (unlawful) removal of their car and thus for a car accident

328. For more, *see* Part III, Ch. 1.
329. For more, *see* Part III, Ch. 2.
330. *See* Art. 54 of the Wild Game and Hunting Act (Official Gazette RS, Nos 16/04, 120/06 – Constitutional Court decision, 17/08, 46/14 – ZON-C, 31/18, 65/20 and 97/20 – corr.).
331. *See* Arts 149 and 150 of the OZ.
332. Jadek Pensa, *supra* n. 60, at 848.
333. ECLI:SI:VSRS:2019:II.IPS.251.2018.
334. *See* Art. 150 of the OZ.
335. Cigoj, *supra* n. 88, at 206.
336. ECLI:SI:VSRS:2017:II.IPS.341.2016.
337. *See* Art. 151 of the OZ.

caused by a minor child because the child had access to the spare keys of the car.[338] If the keeper entrusts the use of a dangerous object to another person (e.g., lending a log splitter to a friend),[339] the liability risk for the damage is transferred to the latter, while the holder is jointly and severally liable if the damage was the result of a concealed defect or an attribute of the object to which the keeper drew no attention.[340] However, the keeper of the object shall also be liable if he or she entrusted the dangerous object to a person who was not qualified or entitled to handle it.[341]

208. As regards tort liability under Article 150 of the OZ, it is particularly important to define what is considered a dangerous object (dangerous activity). It should be noted that an object itself, without human action, rarely causes damage. Even in case of a collapse, explosion, fire, etc. these instances are usually a result of people failing to provide proper maintenance, storage, or some other activities. The definition which has emerged in legal theory and case law describes a dangerous object as an object which, by its purpose, characteristics, position, location, and manner of use, or in some other way constitutes a heightened degree of danger to its surroundings and must therefore be supervised with particular care.[342]

209. In principle, an object is not inherently dangerous but is or becomes so only in relation to the circumstances of a specific case.[343] Even if an object (e.g., a forklift truck) is generally considered dangerous, its keeper is objectively liable only if the circumstances of the case give rise to an increased risk. For example, a stationary forklift truck is not a dangerous object because it does not in itself pose a threat to anyone.[344] In the event of damage (e.g., injury while dismounting a forklift), the liability of the keeper will be assessed according to the rules of fault-based liability. However, in certain circumstances, even a vehicle at rest may be considered a dangerous object. For example, if the damage is caused by the vehicle catching fire, the keeper of the vehicle is strictly liable even if the vehicle was stationary and the engine was turned off. In such a case, the vehicle is deemed to be a dangerous object, as its characteristics (its weight or the fact it contains flammable substances and electronic components) imply an increased risk to human health and property.[345] Therefore, strict liability is only involved when, taking into consideration the circumstances of the case, the object is so dangerous that it cannot be kept completely under control, despite considerable amount of diligence.

210. Similarly, the rules on strict liability do not apply if the increased risk is the result of mere impermissible or wrongful conduct. Objects which become dangerous only when used in an improper manner are not considered dangerous.[346] For

338. ECLI:SI:VSRS:2003:II.IPS.498.2002.
339. ECLI:SI:VSLJ:2020:II.CP.2227.2019.
340. *See* Art. 152 of the OZ.
341. *See* Art. 152(4) of the OZ.
342. ECLI:SI:VSRS:2008:II.IPS.198.2006.
343. ECLI:SI:VSRS:2001:VIII.IPS.263.2000.
344. ECLI:SI:VSLJ:2014:II.CP.1473.2014.
345. ECLI:SI:VSLJ:2014:II.CP.1992.2014.
346. ECLI:SI:VSRS:2002:II.IPS.475.2001 and ECLI:SI:VSRS:2006:II.IPS.659.2004.

example, a badminton racket cannot constitute a dangerous object, either by its size, weight, or other attributes (metal ring), even if a player might hit a teammate instead of a shuttlecock in a doubles game.[347]

211. The conditions for release from liability for damage arising in connection with a dangerous object (dangerous activity) are laid down in Article 153 of the OZ.[348] In the case of strict liability, the obligor cannot be relieved of liability by proving that he or she is not at fault, but only by proving the existence of one of the statutory grounds for exoneration. Under Article 153 of the OZ, the keeper of a dangerous object is exempt from liability if he or she proves that the damage did not originate from the object in question but rather from an external cause which could not have been foreseen, avoided, or averted.[349] These are the so-called elements of qualified coincidence linked to the exteriority of the cause, which theory and case law refer to as force majeure, although the OZ does not use this term.[350] In addition to force majeure, the OZ specifically references two other exculpatory grounds, namely the act of the injured party and the act of a third party, where the elements of qualified coincidence must also be present. When the damage is caused solely by the act of the injured party or a third party, the keeper of the dangerous object is not liable, although the keeper must prove, in this case also, that the act could not have been foreseen and its outcome not prevented or avoided.[351] In the case of an exculpatory reason for the injured party's conduct, the mere fact that the injured party assumed the risk of damage by having used the dangerous object (*volenti non fit iniuria*) is not sufficient.[352] Merely by using a dangerous object (e.g., escalators in a department store), one does not assume the risk of harm, since when using the respective object, one does not think of the possible risks, let alone wish to shoulder them. The situation would be different, for instance, if an individual wanted to engage in activities that were obviously dangerous and risky, but in such a case, the said individual must show willingness and awareness to take the risk.[353]

212. An exoneration from strict liability of a keeper of a dangerous object can be illustrated with a case of a road accident involving a car driver and a cyclist. Tort liability of the car driver (in relation to the cyclist) is a strict liability because a moving motor vehicle is a dangerous object.[354] The keeper of the vehicle (the driver) can only be relieved of liability based on an external cause, which does not include, for example, a flat tyre, a defect in the vehicle, etc. Even when the accident results from an external cause (e.g., stones on the road, wild animals, etc.), from the conduct of a third party or from the injured party, the keeper of the vehicle must still prove that he or she could not have avoided, prevented, or averted (elements of qualified casus) the consequences of this act.

---

347. ECLI:SI:VSLJ:2009:I.CP.908.2009.
348. This article is used also for other cases for which the law prescribes strict liability.
349. *See* Art. 153(1) of the OZ.
350. Cigoj, *supra* n. 88, at 189.
351. *See* Art. 153(2) of the OZ.
352. *See also* Part IV, Ch. 1.
353. Stojan Cigoj, *Odškodninsko pravo Jugoslavije* (1972), p. 302.
354. ECLI:SI:VSLJ:2012:II.CP.3921.2011.

213. There are different ways in which damage to real estate can occur. In some cases, the property itself is a source of increased risk, e.g., a precipice, a cave, a sinkhole, etc. According to Article 150 of the OZ, the owner of the real estate is not necessarily the one liable for the damage caused in such cases, but rather the person who is actively involved in a particular activity related to the (dangerous) real estate, or who caused the danger. For example, a construction contractor is strictly liable for damage caused by an unprotected construction pit,[355] while an organisation that built the path to a dangerous lookout and advertised it is strictly liable for any damage caused due to the dangerous lookout instead of the real estate owner,[356] etc.

214. Similarly, damage to real estate can be caused due to various buildings collapsing or objects falling from them. Under Article 159 of the OZ, the holder of a building is liable for damage caused by a dangerously placed object falling or being thrown from the building. The rule only applies to objects that are (were) not part of the immovable property, being irrelevant whether the object falls on its own or is thrown, pushed, or poured by someone. Examples of such harmful acts are the falling of a flowerpot, the falling or spilling of a pot of boiling water, etc. This is a special form of strict liability, as the OZ does not require the existence of fault as a condition for liability. Although strict liability is based on an increased risk due to a dangerously placed (thrown) object, it is sufficient for the injured party to prove that the damage was caused by a falling object. Since things fall due to gravity, it follows from the very falling of the object that it was positioned dangerously (irrespective of the actual cause of the fall, e.g., clumsiness, gust of wind, etc.).[357] The holder of the building can only be exonerated from liability based on exculpatory grounds set out in Article 153 of the OZ.[358]

215. However, should the damage be caused by the fall of an object that was previously built into the building (a component of the immovable property), the owner of the building is liable under Article 160 of the OZ, which defines liability for the demolition of a building. Examples of liability for damage under Article 160 of the OZ are falling bricks, roof tiles, windowsills, loose plaster, etc. Unlike liability for dangerously positioned or discarded objects, the liability under Article 160 of the OZ is fault-based liability, as the holder of the building may be exonerated by proving that the event was not caused by a defect in the quality of the building and that he or she took all reasonable steps to avert the danger. The building holder is thus (jointly and severally) liable for damages resulting from a fault in the construction of the building, in which case he or she may demand reimbursement of the amount paid from the building contractor. Even if the immediate cause of the harmful event is an external incidence (e.g., a storm), causing a part of the building to collapse, the holder of the building will only be relieved of liability if he or she can

355. ECLI:SI:VSLJ:1999:I.CP.2158.98.
356. ECLI:SI:VSLJ:2014:II.CP.1579.2014.
357. Plavšak et al., *supra* n. 95, at 910.
358. *See* Part III, Ch. 5, §1.

prove that the building was constructed in accordance with relevant technical standards and that it has been professionally and diligently maintained.[359]

216. A case often seen in practice is the issue of tort liability caused by snow sliding off the roof of a building. Although there exist cases where the Court judged liability for damage caused by snow sliding off the roof based on Article 159 of the OZ,[360] the liability of the building holder must in such a case be assessed under the general rules of civil (tort) law, i.e., according to Article 131 of the OZ.[361] Snow is not an element of the building, nor is it an object that would be (dangerously) positioned or thrown/discarded by the building holder.

217. Tort liability of an animal keeper is regulated in a specific article of the OZ, although the same rules could reasonably be derived from Article 150 of the OZ. Under Article 158 of the OZ, the keeper of a dangerous animal is (strictly) liable for any damage inflicted by such animal, while the keeper of a domestic animal is culpably liable for any damage inflicted by the respective animal. In the latter case, the keeper may be relieved of liability by proving that he or she has ensured the necessary care and supervision of the (domestic) animal. The wording of the legal rule is not the most appropriate, since a domestic animal may also be considered dangerous if its characteristics make it obvious that even very careful supervision is not necessarily sufficient to ensure adequate safety for persons and property. For example, the Court considered both a raging bull[362] and a restless mare in the breeding season[363] to be dangerous animals, while the same judgment was not made of a frightened horse intended for recreational riding which, due to an exceptional event, got startled and fell into a powerful trot.[364]

218. Cases of tort liability due to dog bites are a particularly common occurrence. As dogs are considered domestic animals, the keeper of a dog generally bears culpable liability. He or she can be relieved of liability by proving that he or she provided the necessary care and supervision to effectively prevent the dog from injuring someone.[365] But the keeper's care does not end with confining the dog to a kennel. He or she must also ensure that the kennel cannot be easily opened or that persons (especially children) do not have access to it.[366] However, if the dog's character or its past behaviour indicates an increased risk, the keeper's liability is assessed under the first paragraph of Article 158 of the OZ. Although certain breeds of dogs tend to be more aggressive, the dangerousness of a dog must be assessed on

359. ECLI:SI:VSLJ:2020:II.CP.48.2020.
360. ECLI:SI:VSCE:2007:CP.1624.2006.
361. ECLI:SI:VSLJ:2015:II.CPG.1030.2015, Cf. ECLI:SI:VSRS:2002:II.IPS.635.2001, ECLI:SI:VSLJ:2010:II.CP.3610.2009 and ECLI:SI:VSLJ:2015:II.CP.500.2015.
362. ECLI:SI:VSRS:2004:II.IPS.175.2003.
363. ECLI:SI:VSLJ:2013:II.CP.2890.2012.
364. ECLI:SI:VSRS:2004:II.IPS.175.2003.
365. ECLI:SI:VSCE:2005:CP.288.2004.
366. ECLI:SI:VSLJ:2018:II.CP.2279.2017.

a case-by-case basis. If the dog meets the legal standard of a dangerous animal, its keeper cannot be relieved of liability, irrespective of the level of care employed, except on the basis of the exculpatory grounds set out in Article 153 of the OZ.

Part III. Forms of Strict Liability

Chapter 1. Road and Traffic Accidents

219. Road accidents are a relatively common cause of property and non-property damage, owing to increasing traffic density, different types of motorised vehicles, and other circumstances. The legislation of the RS includes a number of regulations governing road traffic rules and defining terms, such as road accident, vehicle, motor vehicle, etc.[367] As the purpose of these (public law) acts differs from the purpose of tort law, these rules cannot be automatically followed, so individual concepts and rules must be interpreted in accordance with the purpose and the fundamental principles of the OZ. Thus, the term 'traffic accident' will be used in this chapter to refer to all forms of accidents on roads, streets, pavements, or other places which are in any way associated with traffic.

220. In assessing the type and existence of tort liability in the event of a road accident various factors need to be considered. Initially, it is important to establish whether motor vehicles were involved in the accident and whether the damage was caused solely to the keepers of the motor vehicles or other road users as well. Three different types of road accidents will be analysed further on, namely: (1) a road accident not involving a motor vehicle; (2) a road accident involving a motor vehicle and damage being inflicted to a third party; and (3) a road accident involving several moving motor vehicles.

221. The most common road accidents not involving a motor vehicle are collisions between cyclists and pedestrians, collisions between cyclists, or collisions with other road users using non-motorised transport (horse-drawn carriage, scooter, skateboard, roller skates, etc.). If damage occurs in such cases, the liability of the parties involved in the accident is generally assessed in line with the general rule of subjective liability set out in Article 131 of the OZ. The party who caused the accident is liable for the damage unless it is proved that the damage occurred without fault on his or her part.

367. *See* Road Traffic Rules Act (Official Gazette RS, Nos 156/21 – official consolidated version and 161/21 – corr.), Roads Act (Official Gazette RS, Nos 109/10, 48/12, 36/14 – Constitutional Court decision, 46/15, 10/18 and 123/21 – ZPrCP-F), Motor Vehicles Act (Official Gazette RS, Nos 75/17 and 92/20 – ZPrCP-E), etc.

222. However, when a motor vehicle is involved in an accident, tort liability is usually assessed according to stricter criteria. Motor vehicles are considered to have the characteristic of operating with an increased risk of tort, as they cannot always be fully controlled due to the characteristics of the engine and the speed at which they are driven. Due to the increased risk of motor vehicle use, the multitude of motor vehicles used, and the frequency of road accidents, the legislation of the RS makes motor vehicle insurance compulsory. The obligation to take out insurance before using the vehicle on the road is prescribed for the protection of motor vehicle drivers as well as injured parties, since in the event of a road accident, the insurance company with which the person who caused the accident has taken out liability insurance shall pay the damage up to the amount of the insured sum.[368]

223. However, the obligation to take out compulsory insurance does not affect the assessment of the liability of the driver of the motor vehicle. Since motor vehicles are considered to have the characteristic of operating with an increased risk of tort, the liability of the driver of a motor vehicle is assessed according to the general rule on liability for dangerous objects and dangerous activities.[369] Consequently, the definition of the term 'motor vehicle' in Slovenian tort law is not even that relevant, since the answer to the question of whether or not strict liability applies in a particular case does not depend on the answer to the question of whether the damage was caused in connection with the motor vehicle, but on whether the damage was caused in connection with the use of a dangerous object.[370] Liability is stricter in the case of the use of a dangerous object since the keeper (i.e., the driver of the motor vehicle) must bear part of the risk for the increased danger caused.

224. Liability for dangerous objects is dealt with in detail in Part II Chapter 3, so only some highlights that are directly related to the use of motor vehicles are showcased here. Since strict liability applies only to cases of increased danger, the rules of strict liability are not applied to stationary motor vehicles, which do not normally endanger anyone per se.[371] It is therefore necessary to assess per each specific case involving a motor vehicle, whether the increased risk of the vehicle originates from the specific case. In addition to conventional moving motorised vehicles (cars, lorries, etc.), various modern moving vehicles, such as electric bicycles, electric scooters, electric skateboards, and other motorised vehicles, are also considered to be dangerous objects (i.e., an object that poses a greater risk of harm to the surroundings). However, various consequences of the operation of moving vehicles, such as the loss of cargo,[372] a burst tyre left on the road,[373] a stone ejected from under the wheels of the vehicle,[374] etc. are considered by case law as accidents involving a moving motorised vehicle.

---

368. Compulsory Motor Third-Party Liability Insurance Act (Official Gazette RS, Nos 93/07 – official consolidated version, 40/12 – ZUJF, 33/16 – PZ-F and 41/17 – PZ-G).
369. *See* Art. 150 of the OZ.
370. Jadek Pensa, *supra* n. 60, at 879.
371. ECLI:SI:VSLJ:2014:II.CP.1473.2014.
372. ECLI:SI:VSLJ:2013:I.CPG.1400.2011.
373. ECLI:SI:VSLJ:2013:II.CP.301.2013.
374. ECLI:SI:VSRS:2004:II.IPS.569.200.

225. According to the general rules of strict liability, the keeper of a motor vehicle may be exempted from liability only based on the grounds for exoneration set forth in Article 153 of the OZ. The driver shall be exonerated from liability if he or she proves that the damage originates from a cause external to the object, the effects of which could not have been foreseen, avoided or averted, or if the damage was caused exclusively by an act of the injured party or a third party which could not have been foreseen by the driver and the consequences of which could not have been avoided or averted. It is the very requirement of the elements of qualified casus (unexpectedness, unavoidability and unpreventability) that makes it impossible in most cases to completely exempt the driver of the motor vehicle from liability. The unexpectedness of an act is judged by the strictest criterion, i.e., the criterion of utmost care. Drivers must therefore expect all possible obstacles in traffic or transport (e.g., an oil stain on the road,[375] the possibility of a riding horse startling,[376] etc.), especially in residential areas (e.g., a child dashing into the road,[377] a pedestrian crossing the road at an unmarked place,[378] a cyclist committing several serious traffic offences,[379] etc.). Regardless of this, a driver of a motor vehicle may be partially relieved of liability had the injured party or a third party contributed to the damage (e.g., by violating traffic regulations).[380]

226. The most common road accident is one involving multiple moving motorised vehicles. In such a case, we are dealing with a competition of strict liability of the keepers of the dangerous objects (the vehicles with the increased risk of damage), and the keepers are usually also the injured parties. Since in this specific case, all the keepers of dangerous objects involved in the accident (the drivers of the vehicles) should bear part of the risk (higher degree of liability) for contributing to increased danger, this situation requires a special regulation.

227. Liability in the event of an accident involving several moving motorised vehicles is assessed according to the special rules established in Article 154 of the OZ. If the damage is inflicted only on the keepers of the said vehicles, the liability between them will be judged according to the rules of strict liability, since in such a case, they all contributed to the increased risk (by using the dangerous object). If the damage was caused by the exclusive fault of one of the keepers of the motorised vehicles, the latter shall be fully liable, since the other keeper(s) did not contribute in any way to the occurrence of the tortious event.[381] However, if the fault of the accident lies with several drivers of the involved motor vehicles (mutual fault), each driver shall be liable in proportion to the degree of fault (shared liability).[382]

---

375. ECLI:SI:VSRS:2006:II.IPS.55.2005.
376. ECLI:SI:VSCE:2020:CP.464.2019.
377. ECLI:SI:VSLJ:2014:I.CP.246.2014.
378. ECLI:SI:VSRS:2015:II.IPS.207.2012.
379. ECLI:SI:VSRS:2020:II.IPS.133.2019.
380. *See* Art. 150(3) and 150(4) of the OZ.
381. ECLI:SI:VSLJ:2014:I.CP.2373.2014.
382. *See* Art. 154(1) and 154(2) of the OZ.

228. Fault exists if the tortfeasor causes the damage intentionally or out of negligence.[383] The appropriateness of the conduct (the driver of the vehicle is neither negligent nor reckless and thus bears no fault), however, is assessed according to the principle of diligence established in Article 6 of the OZ. In the case of road traffic accidents, the (non-)observance of the public-law road traffic regulations is crucial for the assessment of the appropriateness of one's conduct. However, if multiple motor vehicle drivers are culpably liable for the damage, the shares of their liability (degrees of fault) are determined on the basis of their individual contributions to the damage, which are assessed taking into account all the circumstances of the case, giving due weight to the one circumstance that was the decisive cause of the damage, and taking into account the seriousness of the traffic violation committed by both motor vehicle keepers and the degree of risk arising from the operation of each motor vehicle.[384] Although the use of any moving motor vehicle contributes to increased risk, and although any traffic violation can be considered at least minor negligence on the part of the driver of the motor vehicle, the actual state of accidents can vary widely.

229. Drivers of different motor vehicles contribute to increased risk to varying degrees. Take, for example, the drivers of a tanker lorry, a lorry, a car, or a motorcycle. The driver of a tanker lorry carrying flammable materials contributes much more to increased risk than a motorcycle driver. The motorcycle is in an inferior position compared to the heavy and dangerous cargo vehicle. If the fault of the keepers of motor vehicles is mutual, their shares in the fault are also assessed based on the contribution of each of them to the increased risk, taking into consideration, in particular, the type of vehicle and its hazard due to its weight and speed.[385] However, this rule does not apply if the damage is caused by the exclusive fault of one of the drivers.[386]

230. Similarly, individual traffic offences (e.g., (minimal) speeding, failure to stop at a red light, etc.) contribute differently to increased risk. Therefore, it must be established in each specific case which offence contributed more to the increase in risk and is therefore more burdensome. In the case law of the VSRS, the principle has been established that in the case of simultaneous speeding offence and violation of the right-of-way rule, the driver who violated the right-of-way rule generally bears a greater share of the liability.[387] However, in special circumstances (e.g., poor visibility, vehicle on an emergency run, etc.) the decision may be different.

231. If none of the drivers of moving motor vehicles can be blamed for the accident, the keepers of the motor vehicles are equally liable for the damage, unless justice demands otherwise.[388] Equal-share liability occurs when none of the drivers of the moving motor vehicles is at fault for the accident (e.g., an unexpected obstacle

383. *See* Art. 135 of the OZ.
384. ECLI:SI:VSRS:2015:II.IPS.128.2013.
385. Jadek Pensa, *supra* n. 60, at 883–888.
386. ECLI:SI:VSRS:1995:II.IPS.71.94.
387. ECLI:SI:VSRS:2013:II.IPS.238.2009.
388. *See* Art. 154(3) of the OZ.

in the road)[389] or when no one can be shown to be at fault (e.g., an unknown vehicle drives into the driver's lane).[390] If liability for the damage in equal shares is not appropriate in a specific case, the court may establish a different ratio, taking into account the principle of justice. This is particularly appropriate not only in the case of drivers whose contributions to the occurrence of a danger differ but also, for instance, in the case of a significant difference in the value of the vehicles involved. For example, in an accident between a newer, higher-value car and a lower-value car that is 10 or more years old, it is certainly fairer and more appropriate for the two drivers, if neither of them was at fault for the accident, to bear different shares of the damage (e.g., each driver bears his or her own share of the damage), rather than dividing the total damage into two equal shares.

232. Lastly, we will look at an accident involving several moving motor vehicles, where the damage is inflicted also to other road users (e.g., a cyclist, a pedestrian, etc.). The general rule laid down in Article 186 of the OZ is that all persons involved are jointly and severally liable for damage caused by several persons together. In the relationship between keepers of motor vehicles and other participants, the liability of the former is assessed according to the rules of liability for dangerous objects, while in the internal (recourse) relationship, the rules of fault-based liability apply.

233. In addition to the general rule of joint and several liability laid down in Article 186 of the OZ, Article 154 of the OZ establishes a special rule regarding accidents caused by moving motor vehicles. '*If the two keepers of the motor vehicles are partly or fully liable for damage suffered by others, the liability shall be joint and several.*'[391] This rule raises various questions in Slovenian theory and case law, but the key question is whether a keeper of a moving motorised vehicle may be exonerated from liability for damages to others (e.g., a pedestrian) based on this rule if it is proved that he or she was not at fault for the accident or that the damage was the exclusive fault of the other driver.

234. Some theoreticians emphasise that all drivers of moving motor vehicles are jointly and severally liable in the external relationship, that is, regardless of whether or not they are liable in the internal (recourse) relationship, since they contribute to an increased risk of damage simply by using the vehicle (dangerous object), even if they are not at fault for the accident.[392] This is intended to provide better legal protection for other road users, who generally do not contribute to an increased risk of damage, and to avoid burdening the litigation procedures against others by establishing fault shares of motor vehicle drivers in the internal (recourse) relationship.

235. Other theoreticians, however, argue that it should be possible for a faultless driver of a moving motor vehicle to be fully exonerated from liability in an existing

389. ECLI:SI:VSLJ:2009:I.CP.2140.2009.
390. ECLI:SI:VSLJ:2019:II.CP.1889.2018.
391. *See* Art. 154(4) of the OZ.
392. Jadek Pensa, *supra* n. 60, at 883–885.

(not only in a subsequent recourse) litigation if it is clear that he or she did not contribute in any way to the cause of the accident. Such a rule is considered more appropriate in traffic accidents also because of the legal regulation of compulsory insurance, which has significantly strengthened and improved the position of injured parties. It is undisputed that the keeper of a motor vehicle cannot (only) partially relieve himself or herself from liability, as this would contradict the essence of joint and several liability. The situation is different in the case of exclusive fault. If, in a specific case, the court finds that only one of the drivers of the moving motor vehicles involved in the accident is exclusively at fault, then, according to the advocates of this theory, only that driver is liable while the others can be exculpated. If exclusive fault does not exist, the shares of liability are not established, and all drivers are jointly and severally liable.[393]

236. Although the VSRS has not yet ruled on this issue, it should be noted that in recent years a largely uniform case law of the higher courts has emerged. According to the case law, the plea of exclusive liability of the other driver of the motor vehicle must in principle be admissible, but in a very limited form.[394] The driver of a motor vehicle can be exonerated in this way only on condition that he or she proves that the other keeper of the moving motor vehicle is exclusively and strictly liable for the tortious event, to the (evidentiary) extent that the presumed basis (causality) of his or her strict liability is contested.[395] The plea is therefore not applicable if the accident is due to the dangerous operation of all motor vehicles involved, even if in the internal relationship only one keeper of the motor vehicle shall be held liable.

393. Tomaž Pavčnik, *(Ne)dopustnost ugovora, da je za nesrečo izključno odgovoren le en voznik: (člen 154/4 OZ)*, Pravni letopis (2014), p. 113; Igor Strnad, *Kako OZ ureja odgovornost imetnikov motornih vozil nasproti drugim?*, Pravna praksa 12 (2004), pp. 22–25.

394. ECLI:SI:VSLJ:2013:II.CP.301.2013, ECLI:SI:VSLJ:2015:II.CP.1366.2015, ECLI:SI:VSLJ:2010:I.CP.103.2010, ECLI:SI:VSLJ:2010:II.CP.451.2010, ECLI:SI:VSLJ:2011:II.CP.3812.2010, ECLI:SI:VSLJ:2017:II.CP.334.2017 and ECLI:SI:VSLJ:2013:II.CP.1555.2012.

395. ECLI:SI:VSLJ:2020:II.CP.62.2020.

Chapter 2. Product Liability

237. Product liability or producer's liability for a product is a special form of strict liability in Slovenian law, which was already regulated in Slovenia in the predecessor of the OZ, namely in the ZOR (the ZOR from 1978),[396] which was a modern law for its time.[397] Therefore, the continuity of the regulation of Article 179 of the ZOR regarding the liability of the manufacturer of a faulty product has been maintained in Article 155 of the OZ.

238. Directive 85/374/EEC[398] (with the last amendment by Directive 1999/34/EC;[399] hereinafter referred to as Directive 85/374/EEC) was transposed into the ZVPot-1,[400] Articles 58 to 65 of the ZVPot-1. The ZVPot-1, which came into effect on 26 January 2023, only transposed the substantively identical provisions of the previously applicable Consumer Protection Act (ZVPot)[401] on producer liability, which fully implemented Directive 85/374/EEC with the amendment ZVPot-G[402] in 2015.[403]

239. Slovenia still maintains a two-tier product liability regime,[404] which in the past has led to various interpretations in the literature regarding the possibility of simultaneous application of both regulations.[405] However, recent judicial practice[406] has taken the position that the ZVPot transposed Directive 85/374/EEC into

396. Official Gazette SFRY, Nos 29/78, 39/85, 45/89 – Constitutional Court decision, 57/89; Official Gazette RS, Nos 88/99 – ZRTVS-B, 83/01 – OZ, 30/02 – ZPlaP and 87/02 – SPZ.
397. *See* more about ZOR in General Introduction, §2, IV.
398. Council Directive 85/374/EEC of 25 Jul. 1985 on the approximation of the laws, regulations and administrative provisions of the Member States concerning liability for defective products (85/374/ES), OJ L 210, 7.8.1985, pp. 29–33.
399. Directive 1999/34/EC of the European Parliament and of the Council of 10 May 1999 amending Council Directive 85/374/EEC on the approximation of the laws, regulations and administrative provisions of the Member States concerning liability for defective products, OJ L 141, 4.6.1999, pp. 20–21.
400. Official Gazette RS, No. 130/22. It came into effect on 26 Oct. 2022, but has been in use since 26 Jan. 2023 (Art. 249 of the ZVPot-1).
401. Official Gazette RS, Nos 98/04 – official consolidated text, 114/06 – ZUE, 126/07, 86/09, 78/11, 38/14, 19/15, 55/17 – ZKolT, 31/18 and 130/22 – ZVPot-1.
402. Official Gazette RS, No. 19/2015.
403. The previously applicable Consumer Protection Act (Official Gazette RS, Nos 98/04 – official consolidated text, 114/06 – ZUE, 126/07, 86/09, 78/11, 38/14, 19/15, 55/17 – ZKolT, 31/18 and 130/22 – ZVPot-1) regulated product liability in Arts 4–11a.
404. Article 13 of the Directive 85/374/ES states: 'This Directive shall not affect any rights which an injured person may have according to the rules of the law of contractual or non-contractual liability or a special liability system existing at the moment when this Directive is notified.' Therefore, Art. 58(1) of the ZVPot-1 also specifies that 'in accordance with the general rules on liability for damage and the rule on the liability of the producer of a faulty product, the producer compensates for the damage caused...', thus explaining that the producer is also liable based on the OZ.
405. Before EU accession, some interpreted the parallel regulation as an optional right of the injured party to decide on which legal basis (the OZ or the ZVPot) he or she would enforce his or her claim (Igor Strnad, *Odgovornost za izdelek*, Podjetje in delo 6–7 (1999), p. 1281); others did not specifically address the issue of the simultaneous existence of both regulations, but merely pointed to the peculiarities in the ZVPot and used its provisions to 'clarify' the provisions from the OZ (cf. Peter Grilc, in Plavšak et al., *Obligacijski zakonik (OZ) (splošni del) s komentarjem, 1. knjiga* (2003),

the legal order of the RS. Therefore, the legislation in RS (Article 155(1) of the OZ), which additionally regulates the area of liability for product defects, should be interpreted in line with Directive 85/374/EEC. This is consistent with the already established principle of loyal interpretation, as Directive 85/374/EEC establishes full harmonisation, preventing different rules on the legal status of victims or responsible entities in national laws. It aims to establish consistent criteria for protection and liability in relation to product defects in all Member States. Directive 85/374/EEC and the current ZVPot-1 only regulate the producer's strict liability for damage caused by a product defect, but not fault-based liability. According to this judicial stance, it is not permissible to grant a victim rights arising from the producer's strict liability for defects in goods in a way that is in conflict with Directive 85/374/EEC, e.g., in line with Article 155(1) of the OZ.[407] The subsidiary application of the OZ provisions for relationships not regulated in consumer legislation has also been determined by the new ZVPot-1 in Article 3(1).

240. This means that, according to Slovenian case law, the choice of injured parties on the basis of strict liability is limited when it comes to the area of product liability as regulated in Directive 85/374/EEC and implemented in the ZVPot-1. However, since Directive 85/374/EEC harmonised (and the ZVPot-1 in turn implemented) the manufacturer's liability for damage to another thing (so-called consequential damage) caused by a defective product, if the damaged thing is typically intended for private use and was predominantly used privately by the injured party (where the injured party's share of the damage is EUR 500), Article 155(1) of the OZ can be applied in cases where the damaged thing is intended for business use.[408] This article stipulates that anyone who puts into circulation a thing manufactured by them which, due to a defect, poses a danger to persons or property, is liable for the damage caused by that defect.[409] In line with this provision of the OZ, which is rather concise and leaves a wide scope for judicial interpretation, it is sufficient for the manufacturer's liability for damage that his or her defective product exists and that this product has caused personal injury or damage to property to a customer or a third party, regardless of the manufacturer's fault.[410] The regulation in the OZ is thus more favourable to injured parties than in Directive 85/374/EEC

---

pp. 891 et seq.). After Slovenia's accession to the EU, the theory has leaned towards mandatory application of the regulation in the ZVPot, where the Directive was transposed, and since it is a measure of full harmonisation, this consequently means that the retention of national systems that conflict with the Directive is not permissible (Damjan Možina, *Odgovornost proizvajalca za proizvod z napako: evropsko obligacijsko pravo izpodriva nacionalno pravo*, Podjetje in delo 1 (2007), p. 84; Kevin Rihtar, *Odgovornost proizvajalca za proizvod: aktualna vprašanja*, Podjetje in delo 5 (2015), p. 863).

406. *See* ECLI:SI:VSLJ:2016:I.CP.1397.2016, ECLI:SI:VSLJ:2017:I.CPG.664.2017 and ECLI:SI:VSLJ:2019:I.CPG.287.2017.

407. Cf. ECLI:SI:VSLJ:2016:I.CP.1397.2016, ECLI:SI:VSLJ:2017:I.CPG.664.2017 and ECLI:SI:VSLJ:2019:I.CPG.287.2017.

408. *See also* ECLI:SI:VSLJ:2015:I.CPG.663.2015.1, ECLI:SI:VSLJ:2021:I.CPG.80.2020 and ECLI:SI:VSMB:2018:I.CPG.51.2018.

409. Cf. Rihtar, *supra* n. 405, at 863; Judgment of the EU Court in the case *of Moteurs Leroy Somer v. Dalkia France* (C-285/08) dated 4 Jun. 2009.

410. Grilc, *supra* n. 405, at 894.

and the ZVPot-1,[411] as it does not provide for the manufacturer's liability only in cases of private use of the (other) damaged thing, nor does it contain a threshold for the amount of damage to be compensated or the required contribution of the injured party up to an amount of EUR 500, as set out in Article 58(2) of the ZVPot-1. Moreover, the compensation for damage to the product itself is not excluded, as set out in Article 58(1)(2) of the ZVPot-1. Additionally, as it concerns strict liability under the OZ, causality is presumed, so the injured party does not need to prove it (*see* more on strict liability in Part III, Chapter 5, §1).[412]

241. Article 155(2) of the OZ provides for fault-based liability of the manufacturer for the hazardous properties of a thing (not for a defect)[413] if the manufacturer did not take all necessary measures to prevent the damage which he or she could have foreseen by use of warnings, safe packaging, or other appropriate measures. On this basis, it cannot, of course, be required that the manufacturer also takes into account any careless (imprudent and incorrect) actions of the consumer (who disregards clear instructions for use without reason) and warns the latter that failure to follow the instructions for use may lead to damage. For example, it is sufficient if the instructions for heating milk state that the milk should be stirred while heating, without explicitly warning of the possible consequence of not following these instructions, namely that in very rare cases, the milk may overheat and splash, causing burns and other damage.[414]

242. The product liability rules from the ZVPot-1 set out the manufacturer's obligation to compensate for damage if the defective product causes death, bodily injury, or impairment to a person's health, or if the defect in the product[415] causes damage to another thing (Article 58(1) of the ZVPot-1). The ZVPot-1 does not utilise the possibility of limiting the total damage (death or bodily injury) provided for in Article 16 of Directive 85/374/ES. Just as under the general provisions, the manufacturer is liable for such damage without limitation. Article 9 of Directive 85/374/

---

411. Cf. Možina, *supra* n 405, at 84; Rihtar, *supra* n 405, at 863.

412. *See* ECLI:SI:VSMB:2014:I.CPG.326.2013: The legal basis of the claim is defined by Art. 155 of the OZ (liability of the producer for a defective product). It refers to strict liability (liability based on causality) of the producer who puts a defective product on the market. Based on the quoted provision of Art. 155 of the OZ, it is incumbent on the plaintiff as the injured party to assert and prove facts that establish the legal presumption of the existence of causation (presumed basis), that is, that the defendant (manufacturer of the product) placed a defective product on the market that caused damage to the plaintiff. If the presumed basis is established, causation is assumed.

Since the plaintiff managed to prove the presumed basis (that the defendant, the manufacturer of the product, placed a defective product on the market that caused damage to the plaintiff), causation is assumed. However, a strictly liable manufacturer of a defective product may be relieved of its responsibility if it demonstrates that the damage occurred exclusively due to the actions (fault is generally not decisive) of the injured party. This may be the case, for example, if the product was not used in a typical and appropriate manner or if the person using it did not follow instructions or protocols. Partial exoneration from liability is of course also possible.

413. Since this is not a case of the manufacturer's strict liability, there is no doubt that this provision can be applied in Slovenian law.

414. *See* ECLI:SI:VSLJ:2013:I.CP.1145.2013 and ECLI:SI:VSRS:2014:II.DOR.1.2014.

415. The term 'product' refers to any movable property, even if it is part of another movable thing or is associated with immovable property, including electricity.

ES stipulates that this provision is without prejudice to the rules of the national legal systems (of the Member States) regarding non-material damage. The ZVPot-1 also refers to the application of the general rules on liability for damage and the rule on the liability of the manufacturer for a defective product. It can thus be concluded that the scope of the legally recognised forms of pecuniary damage and especially non-pecuniary damage is determined by these rules (*see* more in Part VI, Chapter 2, §3). As regards compensation for damage to another thing, the injured party's contribution to the damage is set at EUR 500 and the manufacturer will only compensate the damage if the damaged thing was generally intended for private use and the victim used it predominantly for private purposes. So, for instance, if a car that is typically used for private purposes is damaged while it was being used for a business trip, this will not affect the obligation to compensate the damage.

243. It is important to note that the manufacturer has these obligations towards all injured parties, not only towards consumers (Article 65 of the ZVPot-1) and that the manufacturer cannot limit or exclude its obligations by contract. If the manufacturer of the goods or the importer cannot be identified, any supplier of the goods is considered the manufacturer, unless he or she informs the injured party within a reasonable time who the manufacturer or importer is or who supplied him or her with the goods (Article 58(3) of the ZVPot-1).

244. A product is considered defective if its safety does not correspond to what a consumer can reasonably expect. In assessing what level of safety a consumer can reasonably expect, particular attention should be paid to the presentation of the product according to its intended purpose, the predictable use of the product in a 'reasonable' manner, and the time when the product was placed on the market. This emphasises that it is still about the appropriate use of a product, even if it is not used entirely according to its defined purpose. For example, using a chair as a ladder when the chair breaks, or 'chewing' a pen leading to poisoning, is still considered 'predictable' use. However, if, for example, a microwave is used to dry a cat or a cleaning product is used as a drug (sniffing), the product is not considered defective. Similarly, a product is not considered defective just because a better product was later put on the market (Article 60(2) of the ZVPot-1).

245. The manufacturer is liable for damage caused by a defective product if the damage occurred within ten years from the date the defective product was put on the market (objective period). A product is deemed to be put on the market at the moment the manufacturer, regardless of the legal title, makes it available, makes it available for use, or dispatches it. According to the OZ, there is a subjective limitation period of three years for compensation claims (*see* more on this in Part IV, Chapter 1), which is applicable since the ZVPot-1 does not specify a specific period.

246. According to Article 61 of the ZVPot-1, the injured party must prove the defect, the damage, and the causal link between the two. According to case law, the concept of proving a defect and the resulting causation should not be interpreted in a way that imposes an unreasonable burden of proof on the injured party. This is because the purpose of Directive 85/374/ES is to strike a balance between the position of the injured party and the (strict liability of the) manufacturer, taking into account the due protection of the consumer, who reasonably expects to be protected from harm caused by a defective product. To prove a defect within the scope of causation, the injured party must prove a physical defect in the product that led to insufficient safety. The injured party does not bear the burden of proving all the details of the origin of the defect or the precise nature of the defect in the product.[416]

247. A fair distribution of risk between the injured party and the manufacturer means that the manufacturer can be exempted from liability if it proves the existence of exonerating circumstances, which the ZVPot-1 lists exhaustively (Article 64(1) of the ZVPot-1). Consumer protection requires the liability of all manufacturers involved in the production process if the finished product, component, or raw material supplied by them is defective. It is clearly stipulated that the seller's liability is excluded if it did not put the goods on the market, if the circumstances indicate that the defect did not exist at the time the goods were put on the market, or if the defect results from the fact that the goods complied with mandatory regulations. This also applies if they only produced a component or an ingredient of the goods and the defect arose due to the design or manufacture of the goods into which the component was incorporated, or for which the primary or additional raw material or additive was used, or that the defect arose due to instructions given by the manufacturer of those goods. Liability is also excluded if the global state of science and technical progress at the time when they put the goods on the market was not such that it would have been possible to detect a defect in the goods (e.g., by means of known methods and analyses) and if they did not produce the goods for sale or for any other form of economic distribution, nor did they manufacture them or put them on the market as part of their business.

248. If damage is caused by multiple manufacturers, Article 186(1) of the OZ should be applied, which stipulates joint and several liability when several parties jointly cause damage, as the ZVPot-1 does not have a specific provision for this.

249. However, it is important to note that injured parties also have other legal grounds under Slovenian law to claim compensation for their damage in relation to a defective product, provided that the prerequisites for doing so are met. For instance, due to a breach of contract because of material defects, any buyer can pursue legal remedies and claim compensation from the seller not only for material defects as per Article 468(1) of the OZ and the related damages[417] but also for

416. ECLI:SI:VSLJ:2021:I.CP.1240.2020.

417. *See* ECLI:SI:VSLJ:2020:I.CPG.217.2019: The provision of Art. 468(1) of the OZ grants the buyer the right to make a claim against the seller. Liability for material defects is a relationship under the law of obligations in which the party whose object of performance has material defects is bound to eliminate the negative consequences of these defects in the legally protected sphere of the other (contractually faithful) party; the latter (i.e., the contractually faithful party) has the right to demand the elimination of these negative consequences. Considering the principle of relativity of obligation relationships from Art. 125 of the OZ, it follows that a buyer can only enforce such a claim against the seller. With regard to the plaintiff, the decisive factor is whom the sales contract was

so-called consequential[418] damage that occurs to other goods (e.g., an oil leakage from a defective car engine, polluting a pond and killing all the fish in it; an explosion of a microwave oven causing severe injuries and material damage in an apartment, etc.). In addition, injured parties can also seek compensation from the perpetrator based on the grounds of tort liability for non-contractual damages (*see* more on fault liability in Part I, Chapter 1, §2).

concluded with (Art. 435(1) of the OZ). The appellate position that – in the context of the provisions of the OZ concerning liability claims for material defects in connection with sales contracts – the importer or supplier should also be regarded as the seller, therefore lacks a legal basis.

418. *See* Art. 468(3) of the OZ.

Chapter 3. Liability for Service

250. Non-commercial and commercial damages arising in connection with the provision of services must be assessed through the prism of the type of service provided by the contractor (e.g., legal, medical, construction, etc.; *see* Part I, Chapter 2 for liability related to the type of service). In the case of professionals (e.g., lawyers, doctors, builders), the objective standard of care in assessing the appropriateness of their conduct (professional diligence) leads to an objectification of liability (for more on liability of professionals, *see* Part I, Chapter 2, §1 I), which is also related to the grounds for exculpation with respect to their professional tort liability (Article 240 of the OZ), yet this remains an aggravated subjective or at most subjective-strict liability rather than a special form of strict liability.

251. The general rules on strict liability from the OZ apply only in the case of the provision of services, where the court finds that the conditions for the application of the legal standard of 'dangerous activity' are fulfilled. In case law, this is reserved for those activities which, despite due care, entail above-average risks to the safety of persons and property (e.g., transport activities, work with explosives or with weapons, work at height, work underground).[419] However, strict liability is also provided for in certain sectoral laws for services involving greater danger (e.g., rail and air transport, environmental pollution); *see more* on these sectoral laws in Part III, Chapter 5, §2.

252. A specific provision on strict liability in rendering services is established in the OZ for anyone organising mass gatherings in an enclosed space or in the open air. In particular, organisers who organise events as part of their commercial undertaking (or organise a meeting on any other basis) shall be liable for damage caused by death or physical injury resulting from extraordinary circumstances which may arise in such situations, such as mass movement, general disorder, and similar (Article 157 of the OZ).[420] Strict liability under Article 157 of the OZ is expressly conditional on the extraordinary circumstances that can be created by a crowd of people. Therefore, gathering of a mass of people at a certain venue is not sufficient for liability to exist.[421] The provisions of Article 157 of the OZ apply to both contractual and non-contractual legal bases. While there may exist a contractual relationship between the organiser of 'an assembly of a large number of people' and the participants, such a relationship is not a legal requirement.[422]

253. Producer's liability, which is a strict liability (for more on this, *see* Part III, Chapter 2), may apply to the provision of certain services if the harm is caused by

419. *See* ECLI:SI:VSMB:2021:I.CP.584.2021, ECLI:SI:VSLJ:2021:II.CP.1991.2020, ECLI:SI:VSLJ:2020:II.CP.756.2020, ECLI:SI:VSLJ:2014:II.CP.2591.2014, ECLI:SI:VSRS:2000:II.IPS.600.99, ECLI:SI:VSRS:2000:II.IPS.295.99, etc. For more information on general rules of strict liability and the definition of the legal terms 'dangerous activity' and 'dangerous object' *see* Part III, Ch. 5.

420. *See* ECLI:SI:VSLJ:2012:II.CP.549.2012.

421. *See* ECLI:SI:VSCE:2019:CP.112.2019.

422. *See* ECLI:SI:VSMB:2018:I.CP.767.2017.

a defect in a product that someone placed on the market. For example, in a case of food-borne infection (from Olivier salad), the court held that the caterer was strictly liable under the producer's liability provisions, even though the harm was due to contaminated eggs from another producer.[423]

423. *See* ECLI:SI:VSLJ:1999:I.CP.49.99.

Chapter 4. Environmental Liability

254. Environmental protection and liability for pollution or damage to the environment were first introduced in Slovenia through the right to a healthy living environment under Article 72 of the URS, though all cases constituted an indirect environmental protection, i.e., protection through civil law claims for damage caused to people or their property, because it was not until 2008 that Slovenia complied with the constitutional requirement from 1991, which stipulated that the law should establish the conditions and the extent of compensation for damage caused by a person to the living environment (Article 72(3) of the URS).

255. Slovenia has a dual-track system of liability under environmental law, one pertaining to civil law and the other to administrative law, which covers different types of environmental damage.[424]

256. The dual-track liability regime of today was influenced by the implementation of Directive 2004/35/EC of the European Parliament and of the Council of 21 April 2004[425] on environmental liability with regard to the prevention and remedying of environmental damage, through the amendment to the Environmental Protection Act (EPA-1B).[426] Thus, it is necessary to distinguish the liability regime for traditional damages to which the injured party is entitled under civil law and which are caused to a person or to his or her property, from the concept of liability for environmental damage under the Environmental Protection Act (Article 3 of the EPA-2),[427] which is an autonomous concept of administrative law. Prior to the amendment to the EPA-1B,[428]

---

424. Liability and sanctions for infringements are also provided for as criminal offences in Ch. 32 of the Criminal Code (Official Gazette RS, Nos 50/12 – UPB, 6/16 – corr., 54/15, 38/16, 27/17, 23/20, 91/20, 95/21 and 186/21 – CC-1), which defines offences against the environment, space, and natural assets.
425. Official Journal EU, No. 143 of 30.4.2004, p. 56.
426. The deadline for the Directive to be incorporated into the national laws of the Member States was 30 Apr. 2007. Slovenia was considerably late with its implementation of the requirements from the Directive, so the European Commission brought action before the Court of Justice, which ruled on 12 Mar. 2009 that in the case C-402/08, Slovenia failed to fulfil its obligations. Most obligations under the Directive, except for Annexes I and II, were implemented with the Act Amending the Environmental Protection Act (Official Gazette RS, No. 70/08; EPA-1B). Annexes I and II were incorporated with the Rules on the content defining environmental damage (Official Gazette RS, No. 46/09) and the Decree on types of measures for remediation of environmental damage (Official Gazette RS, No. 55/09), respectively.
427. Official Gazette of the RS, Nos 44/22, 18/23 – ZDU-1O and 78/23 – ZUNPEOVE. With the EPA-2, the remaining irregularities have finally been addressed, and solutions have been introduced due to the reminders and preliminary procedures initiated by the European Commission. Key administrative procedures are now more clearly and transparently regulated, including the preliminary procedure, the environmental impact assessment process, procedures for issuing environmental permits, the procedures for determining the immediate threat to environmental damage, and the procedures for determining environmental damage. Following existing practice, the right of the public to participate and the legal protection of this right are also regulated within this framework. The EPA-2 entered into force on 13 Apr. 2022 (*see* Art. 321(1) of the EPA-2).
428. Official Gazette RS, No. 70/08.

which introduced the concept of environmental damage, EPA-1[429] included only a general provision stating that the person responsible for causing an excessive burden shall be held criminally responsible and liable for damages in accordance with the Act (Article 9 of the EPA-1), i.e., in accordance with the general rules of civil and criminal law.

257. Environmental damage includes damage caused to special components of the environment (i.e., protected species, their habitats and habitat types, water, and soil) if it reaches a certain level of intensity.[430]

258. The liability of the person causing a threat of environmental damage does not depend on whether the damaged asset (e.g., soil, habitats) is the property of a natural or legal person.

259. Of course, an activity affecting the living environment, such as the destruction of natural habitats, the release of harmful substances, etc. can lead to both traditional and environmental damage. Thus, if the same event causes both traditional damage and environmental damage, claims for damages can be made for both. The main difference between the two types of damage, in addition to the content of the presumptions in making claims, is the method of compensation, since the EPA-2 contains *lex specialis* provisions (focusing on liability for prevention and remediation of damage under the polluter-pays principle) in relation to the general civil law rules on compensation for traditional (property and non-property) damage (for more on these types of compensation, *see* Part VI, Chapter 3).[431]

260. Strict liability for environmental damage is provided in the EPA-2 for exhaustively defined entities causing a threat of environmental damage (Article 161(2) of EPA-2), which are engaged in particularly hazardous activities, such as the operation of a facility that may cause industrial emissions; the handling of waste; the release of hazardous substances through the discharge of wastewater into surface waters or groundwater; the manufacture, use, storage, processing, filling, discharge into the environment, or transportation of hazardous substances or mixtures within a facility; the handling of certain mining wastes; the transportation of hazardous goods or pollutants by road, rail, inland waterways, sea, or air; and the

429. Official Gazette RS, No. 39/06 – official consolidated text, 49/06 – ZMetD, 66/06 – odl. US, 33/07 – ZPNačrt, 57/08 – ZFO-1A, 70/08, 108/09, 108/09 – ZPNačrt-A, 48/12, 57/12, 92/13, 56/15, 102/15, 30/16, 61/17 – GZ, 21/18 – ZNOrg, 84/18 – ZIURKOE, 158/20 and 44/22 – ZVO-2.

430. The definition of environmental damage under the EPA-2 excludes minor environmental effects, as damage is defined only as a major measurable adverse change to a specific component of the environment (*see* Art. 162 of the EPA-2). Thus, the question of the legal recognition of environmental damage depends on the ability of science and technology to measure the alteration of a specific component of the environment.

431. The Court has already clarified for the precursor to EPA-2 (for EPA-1) that EPA-1 applies to damage to fauna, flora and their respective environments, but not to damage inflicted to humans. The OZ, including its provisions on limitation, is used for compensation claims for non-pecuniary damage in cases of mental anguish that results from the violation of a person's right to a healthy living environment (*see* ECLI:SI:VSMB:2011:I.CP.1888.2010).

work with genetically modified organisms.[432] All other persons causing a threat of environmental damage are responsible under fault-based liability, though this does not apply to all forms of environmental damage, but only to environmental damage affecting protected species and habitat types.[433] Persons causing a threat of environmental damage must take precautionary and preventive measures as soon as there is an imminent threat of environmental damage (Article 164 of the EPA-2), and they must remediate the environmental damage when it occurs (Article 165 of the EPA-2). If there are multiple entities causing environmental damage and it is not possible to determine the liability of each, they are jointly and severally liable (Article 161(5) of the EPA-2). The competent ministry may require the parties to carry out these measures on its own initiative or on the initiative of third parties who may have been harmed, but also on the initiative of non-governmental organisations and civil initiatives (Article 168 of the EPA-2). If no entity is liable for the environmental damage or if the consequences of the environmental damage cannot be remedied in any other way, subsidiary liability of the country or municipality (in the case of consequences of environmental damage caused by municipal waste management) is provided for.[434] In this case, the country or municipality shall bear the entire cost of remedying the environmental damage (Article 13 of the EPA-2).[435]

261. Since traditional damage to natural and legal persons may occur together with environmental damage to nature, as also provided for in Article 161(6) of the EPA-2, the person causing such damage shall be held strictly liable under the rules of strict liability from the OZ (*see* Part III, Chapter 5, §1).[436]

262. According to Article 2(1)(6) of the Collective Actions Act (CAA),[437] it is also possible to bring a collective action for tort liability for an environmental accident as defined in the EPA-2.[438] An environmental accident can cause both environmental and

---

432. *See* ECLI:SI:VSMB:2019:I.CP.748.2018: With regard to remedying the consequences of excessive pollution, including tort liability, the EPA-1 provides strict liability for entities causing it.
ECLI:SI:UPRS:2016:I.U.1652.2015: Environmental damage is not only damage to protected species, their habitats and habitat types, but also damage to water and environmental damage to soil.
433. Article 161(3) of the EPA-2.
434. *See* Art. 61 of the EPA-2.
435. *See* ECLI:SI:UPRS:2016:I.U.1711.2015.15: If no other entity claims ownership of illegally deposited (non-municipal) waste on state-owned land, the owner of the land (the RS) cannot successfully avoid the obligation to pay for the costs of illegally deposited waste on its land by pleading that it has never exercised any actual control over the waste, since, in accordance with the principle of subsidiarity, the RS must also bear the costs of eliminating the consequences of such waste, unless the costs can be allocated to specific or identifiable responsible entities.
436. *See* ECLI:SI:VSLJ:2019:II.CP.1914.2018: The motor oil stored by the defendant and used for heating purposes is hazardous waste for which the law imposes strict criteria and conditions for collection, storage, and further processing, precisely because of its potential danger to humans and the environment. Therefore, the Court of Appeal agrees that it is a hazardous substance and that its collection, storage, and use constitute a hazardous activity within the meaning of Art. 131(2) of the OZ and that the defendant, who used the waste oil for heating purposes, is therefore liable without fault for the damage caused due to its spillage.
437. Official Gazette RS, No. 55/17 – hereinafter CAA.
438. An environmental accident is an uncontrolled or unforeseen event related to an intervention in the environment, which due to the environmental impact, sooner or later results in a direct or indirect

traditional damage. The CAA can also be applied retroactively (Article 65), for cases of mass damage that occurred before its entry into force in 2017 (for more information on the CAA, *see* Part VI, Chapter 2, §1).

263. In cases where an activity does not (yet) cause direct traditional or environmental damage (or at least it is difficult to prove this because, for example, the emissions are generated by industrial activities, and the harmful effects of air pollution are dispersed),[439] but could potentially harm the natural environment or does already, certain measures can be taken against the polluter preventively by means of prohibitory civil injunctions under Article 231 of the EPA-2 and Articles 133 and 134 of the OZ, which are also based on the strict liability of the person responsible for the activity affecting the environment.[440]

264. Article 231 of the EPA-2 explicitly defines the right to a healthy living environment and also further regulates its legal protection. To exercise the right to a healthy living environment, an individual, a non-governmental organisation, or a civil initiative may request in court that the operator of the planned environmental intervention or the manager cease the implementation of the planned intervention, its operation, or the operation of the facility or activity, if the operator has not obtained a relevant decision or environmental permit, or if the implementation or operation violates these, or if the operation of the facility or activity causes excessive environmental pollution or poses a direct threat to human life or health, providing that a high probability of such consequences is demonstrated (Article 231(3) of the EPA-2). Additionally, in the case of excessive environmental pollution (or imminent threat of its occurrence), anyone may request a competent environmental inspectorate to prohibit the activities of the party causing the excessive pollution

threat to human life or health, or the quality of the environment (Art. 3(4.7) of the EPA-2). A major accident is an environmental disaster resulting from uncontrolled events during the operation of a high-risk facility (Art. 3(4.8) of the EPA-2).

439. *See* ECLI:SI:UPRS:2016:I.U.1652.2015.

440. Also, Art. 75 of the LPC (Official Gazette RS, Nos 87/02, 91/13 and 23/20 – LPC), provides for the possibility of prohibitory injunction or negatory claim against an owner of an immovable property for the prohibited nuisance (e.g., smoke, noise), for which he or she is strictly liable, and for the potential damage resulting from it, according to the OZ. This is a preventive measure unrelated to potential tort liability, as the latter is merely an alternative presumption for establishing liability for nuisance. In order for the owner to be held liable, there does not have to be an unlawful act, as it is sufficient that the prohibited nuisance result from the intentional conduct on the part of the owner arising from the use of the property. *See* ECLI:SI:VSRS:2013:III.IPS.12.2011: In the case of requesting compensation for prohibited nuisance in a lawsuit, the criterion of unlawful conduct is the provision of Art. 75(1) of the LPC, which stipulates that in his or her use of an immovable property, the property owner must refrain from actions and eliminate causes which stem from the said immovable property and which impede the use of other immovable property beyond the extent that is normal in view of the nature and purpose of the immovable property and the local conditions, or which cause substantial damage. The foregoing means that nuisance which is normal with regards to the nature and purpose of the immovable property and the local conditions must be tolerated, even though it may be disturbing.

An analysis of the case law shows that while in most cases, the courts tend to examine whether the locally considered normal level has been exceeded, they rarely examine the existence of significant harm. Civil law protection against emissions is provided by a negatory action under Art. 99 of the LPC.

(Article 231(5) of the EPA-2). In such a case, the competent inspector conducts an unannounced inspection of the polluter to determine the actual situation. If excessive environmental pollution is found, the inspector shall prohibit the polluter from carrying out the activity until lawful conditions are restored. However, such measures are not required if the event is a short-term exceptional occurrence, of which the intervention proponent or manager notifies the inspector in charge, explaining the reasons and outlining the measures required to remedy the effects, if any have occurred (Article 231(7) of the EPA-2). The Human Rights Ombudsman is also responsible for protecting this right to a healthy living environment in accordance with the law. Already under Article 14 of EPA-1, in order to exercise the right to a healthy living environment, citizens could, as individuals, or through associations, societies and organisations, file a request with a court that the person responsible for an activity affecting the environment ceases the activity if the latter would cause or is causing an excessive environmental burden, or if it would present or is presenting an imminent threat to human life or health, or that the person at issue is prohibited from starting the activity if the probability of it causing such consequences is high. Although strict liability was provided for under Article 14, there is practically no case law on this basis,[441] which is probably due to a challenging burden of proof, since the claimant had to prove one of the otherwise alternatively specified legal conditions (either that the person's conduct causes or threatens to cause an excessive environmental burden or that the person's conduct causes or threatens to cause an imminent danger to human life or health), which possessed a problem for the claimant in terms of proving both the fault of the person responsible for the environmental burden (e.g., dispersed pollution) and the resulting consequence.[442] For this reason, the relevance of this popular action under Article 14 of EPA-1 can be assessed as low.

265. Even before the EPA-1, the law of obligations provided protection against the source of danger to all persons at risk and to the environment in general (unlike the protection against nuisance in the LPC, observing the good neighbour principle, which only protects the owners or the users of neighbouring properties).[443] In theory, the provisions of Article 133 of the OZ have been interpreted as one of the legal mechanisms for the exercise of the right to a healthy living environment and the implementation of the principle of preservation of natural and cultural heritage as laid down in Article 72 of the URS.[444] Under Article 133 of the OZ, anyone may require another person to remove a source of danger that poses a serious risk to him

---

441. There have only been two court decisions, both of which have rejected the preventive claim of potentially vulnerable parties on this basis (*see* ECLI:SI:VSRS:2018:I.UP.15.2018 and ECLI:SI:VSKP:2010:CPG.162.2009).
442. Apart from the fact that in case of the summation of highly dispersed emissions, delayed effects of pollution (e.g., air pollution leading to cancer), and insufficient information on the state of the environment, we are talking about *probatio diabolis*, such evidence involves high financial costs for experts, as the issues are complex and require a large number of experts to be involved (*see* Dušan Pichler et al., *Komentar Zakona o varstvu okolja* (2010), p. 201).
443. The legislation providing protection under civil law (OZ, LPC, EPA-2) is complementary. *See more* on the issue: Matija Damjan, *Množični zahtevki zaradi posegov v zdravo življenjsko okolje*, Pravni letopis (2011), pp. 243 et seq.
444. Cf. Jadek Pensa, *supra* n. 60, pp. 761–762.

or her, or an indeterminate number of persons (mandatory injunction) and to refrain from an activity that causes a disturbance or risk of damage (prohibitory injunction) if the occurrence of the disturbance or harm cannot be prevented by appropriate measures. This means that the mandatory and the prohibitory injunctions are subsidiary, as the prohibition of such an activity or the removal of the source of damage can only be requested if the nuisance or damage cannot be prevented by appropriate measures. However, as it is not possible to require the prohibition of activities in the public interest (e.g., the operation of roads, railways, and airports),[445] the relevance of this provision is also reduced with regard to major polluters and the potential damage resulting from their activities. In such cases, the affected parties must tolerate the disturbance at issue, as they cannot resort to mandatory or prohibitory injunctions. However, if the impact (e.g., of polluters) exceeds the 'customary boundaries' (Article 133(3) of the OZ), those affected can seek compensation for the damage that exceeds these boundaries, as such damage is unlawful.[446] This is also a case where strict liability applies. In addition, it is possible to demand that reasonable measures be taken to prevent or reduce the damage (Article 133(4) of the OZ).

266. The possibility of bringing a preventive action against any environmental damage (traditional and environmental) on the basis of the strict liability of the infringer also derives from Article 134 of the OZ, which allows any person whose 'any' personal right is infringed to seek a mandatory or prohibitory injunction against the infringer. It is clear from the case law that the courts uniformly recognise the right to a healthy living environment as a personal right, the violation of which gives rise to compensation for non-material damage under Article 179 of the OZ for the mental anguish resulting from the impairment of this personal right.[447] However, we cannot find any court decision recognising preventive protection on the basis of Article 134 of the OZ in the event of a violation of the right to a healthy living environment. This is apparently due to the courts' understanding that the constitutional provisions regarding the protection of the environment are already concretised by the claims under Article 133 of the OZ.[448] For more on the claims under Articles 133 and 134 of the OZ and the related assumptions, *see* Part VI, Chapter 7, §2.

---

445. More on the issue: Miha Juhart, *Zahtevki zaradi opravljanja splošno koristne dejavnosti*, Podjetje in delo 6–7 (2009), pp. 1302–1311.
446. *See* ECLI:SI:VSLJ:2016:II.CP.511.2016.
447. *See* ECLI:SI:VSRS:2010:II.IPS.409.2009, ECLI:SI:VSRS:2012:II.IPS.417.2011 and ECLI:SI:VSLJ:2014:III.CP. 729.2014: Living in an urban environment requires one to adapt and tolerate emissions, but only within 'normal' limits. However, when these emissions exceed the limit values, the impact on the individual's personal right to a healthy living environment is such that his or her damage is legally recognised and subject to tort liability.
448. *See* ECLI:SI:VSKP:2010:CPG.162.2009.

Chapter 5. Others

§1. Strict Liability under the Civil Code

267. Slovenia does not have a civil code as is the case in Germany and Austria, for example, so our OZ is also the codification of the general part of civil law (for more on this *see supra* General Introduction, §2 IV). Strict liability is provided for in the OZ only as an exception to the general rule of fault-based liability,[449] namely for particularly dangerous objects and activities (Article 131(2) of the OZ).[450] It is therefore a liability for the cause (not for the act or omission).

268. In strict liability, fault is not defined as a prerequisite for tort liability.[451] Nor is the presumption of unlawfulness (or wrongfulness) assessed from the point of view of the wrongful conduct on the part of the tortfeasor (as is the case with fault-based liability). Instead, the wrongfulness (the harmful fact) manifests itself in the dangerous object or activity (Article 131(2) of the OZ).[452] Furthermore, the OZ established the potentially liable persons (tortfeasors) as follows: the keeper of a dangerous object is liable for the damage from such object, and the person involved in a dangerous activity is liable for the damage resulting from that activity (Article 150 of the OZ).[453] The burden of proof on the injured party is eased by the fact that he or she only has to prove the first two presumptions for strict tort liability, namely the use or operation of a dangerous object or activity, and impermissible damage resulting therefrom. In strict liability, the third prerequisite, causation, is presumed, since Article 149 of the OZ states that any damage occurring in connection with a dangerous object or activity is presumed to have been caused by that object or activity unless it is proved that it was not the cause.[454] It is therefore a rebuttable presumption that the dangerous object or activity was the cause of the damage. The presumption of causation is based on the abstract concept of danger. In order to be relieved of liability, the liable person can either rebut the presumption of causation (by proving that the damage did not result from the operation of the dangerous object or activity)[455] or prove one of the three exculpatory grounds set out in Article

---

449. For more on fault-based liability *see* Part I, Ch. 1, §2.
450. Case law has confirmed time and again that strict liability is an exception to the general rule of fault-based liability (Cf.: ECLI:SI:VSRS:2008:II.IPS.571.2005, ECLI:SI:VSRS:2009:II.IPS.949.2006, ECLI:SI:VSLJ:2009:III.CP.1039.2009, ECLI:SI:VSLJ:2015:II.CP.744.2015 and ECLI:SI:VSRS:2019:II.IPS.251.2018).
451. *See* Cigoj, *supra* n. 112, at 514.
452. *See* ECLI:SI:VSKP:2006:I.CP.850.2006: In the event of a collision between a car and a bicycle, the rules of strict liability apply. In applying these rules, however, fault is not a presumption of tort liability since strict liability is based on responsibility for the cause and not for the unlawful conduct.
453. There are certain exceptions to this, e.g., when the keeper did not use the object but entrusted another person with its use, or when the object was unlawfully removed from its keeper (Art. 151 of the OZ). Read more on this in Part II, Ch. 3.
454. More on causation and proof of causation *see infra* Part V.
455. For example, if mining was performed under a house for the purpose of building a tunnel and the owner of the house claimed compensation for cracks after the mining was completed, the person

153(1)(b) of the OZ.[456] However, these only allow for exoneration if the responsible person proves that the cause of the damage was beyond his or her control, with elements of qualified casus (meaning that it was an unexpected, irrevocable, or unavoidable cause), e.g., force majeure. Not every natural event therefore meets the criteria of force majeure. Even if flooding is a natural event, it can be foreseen, and with due diligence appropriate precautionary and preventive measures can be taken.[457] In addition to natural events that cannot be prevented (e.g., earthquakes, tornadoes), culpable actions, whether of the injured party or third parties, can also be considered causes beyond the sphere of the liable party, but they must be objectively unexpected and unavoidable. For example, the conditions for a full exemption of the keeper of a motor vehicle are not fulfilled even if a cyclist rides the bicycle through the pedestrian crossing instead of walking beside it, thereby causing a violation that leads to an accident. This is because the keeper of the motor vehicle has to act with diligence or pay special attention, which could have prevented the accident.[458]

269. The OZ does not define dangerous objects and dangerous activities that lead to strict liability. These are legal standards to be interpreted according to the circumstances of each individual case, but restrictively, i.e., limited to cases where the damage occurs despite due care, or where the 'danger' (from an object or activity) cannot be eliminated by any precautionary measure.[459] In case law, the standard of 'danger' is assessed through the prism of two characteristics: (1) the probability of damage must be statistically greater than normal, and (2) the extent of the threatening damage is potentially greater.[460] Since strict liability is an exception in Slovenian legislation, the general rule of interpretation dictates that exceptions must be interpreted narrowly. More specifically, modern case law regarding torts generally limits the scope of strict liability primarily to objects and activities that pose an increased risk either in themselves or, to a lesser extent, in light of the circumstances of each case. If an object or activity does not in itself pose an above-normal risk, and the activity only becomes dangerous due to certain circumstances, the creation of these circumstances can in most cases be attributed to the actions (including omissions) of certain persons. A similar but opposite situation exists where an object or activity is inherently dangerous but can be neutralised by reasonable care.[461] Again, this does not fall under the legal standard of a dangerous object or activity from which strict liability is derived. According to case law, strict liability

---

performing the mining could challenge the presumption of causation by proving that the cracks had been there before. *See also* ECLI:SI:VSRS:2009:II.IPS.849.2008.

456. Cf. Jadek Pensa, *supra* n. 60, at 849; Plavšak et al., *supra* n. 95, at 577.

457. *See* ECLI:SI:VSLJ:2019:II.CP.1914.2018 and ECLI:SI:VSKP:2017:CPG.33.2017.

458. *See* ECLI:SI:VSRS:2020:II.IPS.133.2019, ECLI:SI:VSLJ:2011:III.CP.3026.2010 and ECLI:SI:VSLJ:2016:II.CP.2046.2015.

459. Cf. Vesna Bergant Rakočević, *Nepogodbeno odškodninsko pravo v Sloveniji – nekatere razvojne tendence v praksi sodišč*, in Razvojne tendence v obligacijskem pravu: ob 40-letnici Zakona o obligacijskih razmerjih (2019), pp. 213–216.

460. *See* ECLI:SI:VSLJ:2015:II.CP.744.2015.

461. More on this *supra* in Part II, Ch. 3.

is reserved for the treatment of activities which, despite due care, involve above-average risks to the safety of persons and property (e.g., means of transport, explosives, working machines, weapons, work at height, work underground).[462]

270. In addition to the general rule of strict liability for dangerous objects and dangerous activities, the OZ also provides that strict liability may be imposed in other cases set forth by law (Article 131(3) of the OZ). Such cases are defined in the OZ and in sectoral laws (for these specific laws, *see* §2 of this chapter). Other examples of strict liability defined in the OZ are: (1) parents are held liable for children under 7 years of age (Article 142(1) of the OZ);[463] (2) a person that markets an object which he or she has manufactured and which entails, for reason of any type of defect, a risk of harm to people or property is liable for damage due to such defect (Article 155(1) of the OZ);[464] (3) the state or the person who should have prevented such outcome according to the regulations in force shall be liable for damage caused by death or physical injury occurring as a result of terrorist acts or during public demonstrations or manifestations (Article 156 of the OZ); (4) the organiser of a gathering of a large number of people (in an open or enclosed space) is liable for damage caused by death or personal injury from extraordinary circumstances, such as mass movement and general disorder (Article 157 of the OZ); (5) the keeper of a dangerous animal is liable for damage inflicted by the animal (Article 158(1) of the OZ); (6) the holder of the building or area from which an object fell is liable for damage inflicted by a dangerously positioned object falling or being thrown from a building (Article 159 of the OZ); (7) a person that is duty-bound to enter a contractual relationship must reimburse the damage if he or she fails to conclude the contract without delay at the request of the interested person (Article 162 of the OZ); (8) the person liable is obliged to give monetary compensation for an object which was wrongfully removed from its keeper and destroyed due to force majeure (Article 166 of the OZ).

§2. Other Provisions of Strict Liability

271. Chapter 32 of the ZKP[465] lays down the rules for strict liability of the state for damage arising from either wrongful conviction or unfounded deprivation of liberty of a person, which is already provided for by the Constitution in Article 30.

---

462. *See* ECLI:SI:VSMB:2021:I.CP.584.2021 (backhoe loader, motor vehicle), ECLI:SI:VSLJ:2021:II.CP.1991.2020 (circular saw), ECLI:SI:VSLJ:2020:II.CP.756.2020 (forklift), ECLI:SI:VSLJ:2014:II.CP.2591.2014 (pneumatic hammer), ECLI:SI:VSRS:2000:II.IPS.600.99 (detonator), ECLI:SI:VSRS:2000:II.IPS.295.99 (firearms), etc.
463. The older theory (Cigoj, *supra* n. 88, at 192) classified a number of liabilities for the acts of other as strict liability, though not all of these liabilities (employer's liability for employees, parental liability, auxiliaries' liability, etc.) can be classified as pure strict liability, as the grounds of exoneration for them are broader (for more on these types of liability *see* Part II).
464. For more on producer's liability *see* Part III, Ch. 2.
465. Official Gazette RS, No. 176/21 – UPB. *See also* ECLI:SI:VSLJ:2020:II.CP.2113.2019, ECLI:SI:VSLJ:2019:II.CP.1057.2019 and ECLI:SI:VSLJ:2018:II.CP.25.2018, where strict liability of the state was established based on the provisions from the ZKP.

272. The ZVPot-1 provides for strict liability of producers or manufacturers for the product (*see* Part III, Chapter 2).

273. The use of nuclear facilities and nuclear substances is a dangerous activity for which strict liability is imposed, just like the rules in the OZ provide for strict liability regarding the use of dangerous objects or the performance of dangerous activities. The specifics of strict liability regarding nuclear facilities and substances are regulated by the Nuclear Damage Liability Act (ZOJed-1).[466] According to the principle of exclusive or channelling liability, only the operator of a nuclear facility, that is the person who, by operating the facility, creates the possibility of an accident with serious consequences is liable for nuclear damage.[467] Any other person who might be liable under the general rules of tort law (e.g., builders of nuclear facilities or suppliers of equipment) is here excluded from direct liability.[468] Exceptionally, the state may also be liable under the conditions laid down in the ZOJed-1, which is a special feature of the regime regarding liability for nuclear damage. The liability of the state may be original (if the damage reaches a certain amount, i.e., it exceeds EUR 700 million, which is the amount up to which the operator is held liable) or subsidiary (if the damage for which the operator of the nuclear facility is liable cannot be repaid from the operator's own funds or from the funds of its insurer – Article 10 of the ZOJed-1). Article 10 of the ZOJed-1 establishes liability of the state for nuclear facilities which are directly or indirectly operated by the state and which are not obliged to insure their liability for nuclear damage under Article 11 of the ZOJed-1 (the RS and all those legal entities under public law, which were established by the RS and determined as such by the regulation of the Government of the RS). If the state grants the responsible operator an exemption from the rule of compulsory liability insurance for nuclear damage and, in the event of a nuclear accident, the operator is unable to pay for the damage up to the amount of the liability sum from its own funds, the state must provide these funds for 'its' operator. The liability of the state, which acts as a guarantor, is thus subsidiary, while the primary liability for the damage lies with the operator of the nuclear facility.

274. In railway transport, the carrier is strictly liable for death, injury to physical or mental health, or any other damage to passengers, caused by an accident or an incident during railway transport or while the passenger is on the train or ascending or descending the train (Article 19 of the Railway Transport Contracts Act).[469] Road Transport Contracts Act (ZPPCP-1)[470] provides for strict liability of the carrier for any damage occurring due to death, impaired health or injury of the passenger (Article 12 of the ZPPCP-1). The carrier can only be resolved if it is proved

466. Official Gazette RS, No. 77/10.
467. A user is a person to whom a licence for the use of a nuclear installation has been issued in accordance with the Protection against Ionising Radiation and Special Safety Measures in the Use of Nuclear Power Act (Official Gazette RS, Nos 76/17, 26/19 and 172/21), or a foreign person designated or recognised as a user by the competent national authority in accordance with its regulations.
468. Igor Sirc & Aleš Škraban, *Zakon o odgovornosti za jedrsko škodo s komentarjem* (2011), p. 8.
469. Official Gazette RS, No. 61/00.
470. Official Gazette RS, Nos 126/03, 102/07 and 49/11 – ZPCP-2C.

that the damage resulted from an act of the passenger or from an external cause that could not have been foreseen, avoided or averted (force majeure). In road transport, a carrier of cargo is liable for full or partial loss of the cargo and its damage from the moment the cargo was received to the moment it was delivered to its recipient and for any damage due to delays in delivery to the recipient. The carrier can be relieved of strict liability for reasons other than force majeure, which are defined in Article 75 of the ZPPCP-1 and include actions or omissions of the sender, the recipient, or a third person, and the properties of the cargo.

275. Strict liability is also provided in aviation, governed by Obligations and Real Rights in Aviation Act (ZOSRL),[471] which refers to the application of the provisions of the Convention for the Unification of Certain Rules for International Carriage by Air (the Montreal Convention) and the EU rules on the liability of air carriers regarding carriage by air, subject to the adjustments to the limitations of liability under the Montreal Convention (Article 20 of the ZOSRL; Article 1(2)(3) of the ZOSRL).[472]

276. The ZDLov-1 establishes strict liability of the manager of hunting grounds for game damage to agricultural and forest crops within hunting grounds or special purpose hunting grounds (Article 54(2) of the ZDLov-1). The manager of a hunting ground is also strictly liable for damage caused by deer or wild boar to agricultural and forest crops within border hunting grounds or special purpose hunting grounds (Article 54(3) of the ZDLov-1). The RS is strictly liable for damage exceeding 50% of the annual revenue from the sale of game, provided that the manager has fulfilled the annual hunting plan for the hunting ground or special purpose hunting ground. The necessary funds to reimburse such damages shall be provided by the ministry responsible for game and hunting. Furthermore, Article 53 of the ZDLov-1 imposes the so-called duty to mitigate on the injured party, meaning that the latter is obliged to act with due diligence and to take all reasonable measures to protect his or her property from damage (use appropriate safeguards, etc.).[473] The manager is also strictly liable for damage caused by hunting with firearms.[474] For other damage caused during hunting and the management of hunting grounds or special purpose hunting grounds, the injured party may also claim compensation directly from the person who caused the damage. According to Article 54 of the ZDLov-1, the RS is strictly liable also for damage caused by game in non-hunting areas.[475] However, this is a subsidiary liability if the fault for the damage does not lie with the manager of the hunting grounds.[476]

---

471. Official Gazette RS, No. 27/11 – UPB.
472. *See* ECLI:SI:VSLJ:2017:I.CP.171.2017 and ECLI:SI:VSRS:2014:II.IPS.221.2011.
473. *See* ECLI:SI:VSLJ:2014:II.CP.598.2014 in ECLI:SI:VSRS:2016:II.IPS.87.2015, where the injured parties were accused of failing to adequately protect their lambs from ravens. A possible and acceptable measure would have been for the farmer to confine the endangered individuals (pregnant ewes) in a stable for as long as necessary to ensure that the newly born lambs are no longer potential prey for ravens. Such an action does meet the standard of due care.
474. *See* ECLI:SI:VSLJ:2020:I.CP.248.2020.
475. *See* ECLI:SI:VSKP:2018:I.CP.514.2017.
476. *See* ECLI:SI:VSRS:2019:II.IPS.184.2018.

277. Under Article 22(4) of the Nature Conservation Act (ZON),[477] the owner of bred animals is strictly liable for damage caused by such animals, while the state is strictly liable for damage (material and non-material) caused by animals of protected species.

278. The Medicinal Products Act (ZZdr-2)[478] provides for strict liability for manufacturers of medicinal products and marketing authorisation holders in the RS for damage due to inadequate quality of the medicinal product (Article 27).

279. The ZNB[479] provides for strict (limited) liability of the state towards persons who suffer damage to their health as a result of compulsory vaccination leading to severe and permanent impairment of vital functions (Article 53.a(1) in conjunction with Article 53.f of the ZNB). The state is also strictly liable to the relatives of a vaccinated person (spouse, life partner, children, parents) in the event of his or her death (Article 53.a(2) in conjunction with Article 53.f of the ZNB).[480]

280. The LPC[481] provides for strict liability of the owner for any damages that result from the erection of supports and structures aimed to ensure the stability of another's immovable property during the deepening and carrying out of activities on his or her property (Article 85(3)).

281. The Environmental Protection Act (EPA-2)[482] provides in Article 161(2) strict liability for environmental damage for exhaustively defined entities causing a threat of environmental damage.[483] This is the basic principle of the polluter's responsibility.[484]

282. Strict liability is also provided for in Article 34(4) of the Copyright and Related Rights Act (ZASP),[485] referring to the responsibility of the author towards the possessor of his or her work in the event damage to the original or copy of the work is inflicted in the exercise of the author's right of access and delivery of the work.

477. Official Gazette RS, Nos 96/04 – UPB, 61/06 – ZDru-1, 8/10 – ZSKZ-B, 46/14, 21/18 – ZNOrg, 31/18 and 82/20.
478. Official Gazette RS, Nos 17/14 and 66/19.
479. Official Gazette RS, Nos 33/06 – UPB, 49/20 – ZIUZEOP, 142/20, 175/20 – ZIUOPDVE, 15/21 – ZDUOP, 82/21 and 178/21 – Constitutional Court decision.
480. *See also* ECLI:SI:VSLJ:2019:II.CP.2401.2018 and ECLI:SI:VSRS:2012:II.IPS.1253.2008.
481. Official Gazette RS, Nos 87/02, 91/13 and 23/20.
482. Official Gazette RS, Nos 44/22, 18/23 – ZDU-1O and 78/23 – ZUNPEOVE.
483. *See* ECLI:SI:VSMB:2019:I.CP.748.2018.
484. *See more* on the issue *supra* Part III, Ch. 4.
485. Official Gazette RS, Nos 16/07 – UPB, 68/08, 110/13, 56/15, 63/16 – ZKUASP and 59/19.

Part IV. Defences and Exception Clauses

Chapter 1. Limitation of Action

283. The right to demand performance of a (compensation) obligation expires with the occurrence of limitation. This is the statutory period within which a creditor may demand performance of an obligation. The statute of limitations is therefore primarily intended to protect the debtor and is based on the principle of legal certainty. This prevents the possibility of asserting claims from the distant past while forcing the creditor to actively exercise his or her rights. However, under Slovenian law, the occurrence of limitation does not extinguish the obligation, but only the civil right to demand performance (entitlement to legal protection). Thus, the obligation continues to exist and can be validly performed by the debtor, but the court cannot take the statute of limitations into consideration unless it is expressly referred to by the debtor.

284. According to Article 337 of the OZ, the limitation occurs when the last day of the statutory period of limitation has passed. The limitation period may be suspended or interrupted. Special rules on the suspension of limitation provide that the limitation period shall not run if specific circumstances arise. The OZ defines such circumstances as claims between specific persons[486] (e.g., claims between spouses or between parents and children for the duration of parental rights), claims by specific persons[487] (e.g., persons in military service), or other insurmountable obstacles because of which the creditor is unable to demand the performance of the obligation through the court.[488] Such an example is the complete lockdown due to the measures taken to contain the spread of SARS-CoV-2 (COVID-19) in March 2020.[489] If the limitation period has not yet started running because of the circumstances referred to, it shall start running when the circumstances cease. However, if the limitation period has already started running, it shall be suspended for the time

486. *See* Art. 358 of the OZ.
487. *See* Art. 359 of the OZ.
488. *See* Art. 360 of the OZ.
489. To ensure that the rules are unambiguous, the legislator of the RS prescribed the suspension of the statute of limitations in the said case in a special Act. According to Art. 3 of the Act on provisional measures for judicial, administrative, and other public matters to cope with the spread of infectious disease SARS-CoV-2 (COVID-19) the statutory deadlines for exercising the rights of parties in court proceedings did not run.

during which the circumstances exist and shall resume when such grounds cease. The time that elapsed before the suspension of limitation shall be counted towards the limitation period.[490]

285. However, the limitation period may also be interrupted. Where the circumstances for interrupting the limitation period arise, the limitation shall begin anew, with the time elapsed before the interruption not being counted as part of the limitation period. The limitation shall discontinue when the debtor acknowledges the debt or when the creditor files a suit or any other act against the debtor before the court or other competent authority for the purpose of determining, securing or collecting a claim.[491] It should be noted in particular that the acknowledgement of a debt may be explicit or indirect (e.g., payment of part of the obligation, provision of security to the creditor, etc.)[492] and that a written or oral request by the creditor demanding that the debtor fulfils the obligation is not sufficient to interrupt the limitation period.[493]

286. According to the general limitation period, claims become statute-barred five years from the moment the creditor had the right to demand performance of the obligation.[494] However, the OZ prescribes a specific time limit for non-business (tort) compensation claims. Compensation claims for damages inflicted become statute-barred three years after the injured party became aware of the damage and of the person who inflicted it (the so-called subjective limitation period), and in any event five years after the damage occurred (the so-called objective limitation period). Claims for damages for a commercial obligation become statute-barred within the limitation period prescribed for contractual obligations. Tort claims for damages from civil contracts become statute-barred after five years and claims from commercial contracts after three years.[495] The OZ prescribes two other specific limitation periods regarding claims for damages, and some more specific limitation periods are laid down in other Acts.[496]

287. When the damage was inflicted through a criminal offence and a longer limitation period is prescribed for criminal prosecution, the claim becomes statute-barred within the period prescribed for criminal prosecution.[497] In these cases, the

490. *See* Art. 361 of the OZ.
491. *See* Arts 364 and 365 of the OZ.
492. *See* Art. 364 of the OZ.
493. *See* Art. 368 of the OZ.
494. *See* Art. 346 in connection with Art. 336 of the OZ.
495. *See* Art. 352(3) of the OZ.
496. A compensation claim for damage inflicted through an act of sexual abuse of a minor shall become statute-barred fifteen years after the minor comes of age, while a compensation claim for damage inflicted through an act of corruption shall become statute-barred five years after the injured party learnt of the damage and of the person that inflicted it or at the latest fifteen years after the act was committed (Art. 352(4) of the OZ and Art. 354 of the OZ).
497. The limitation periods for criminal prosecution are prescribed in Art. 90 of the Criminal Code (KZ-1, Official Gazette RS, Nos 50/12 – official consolidated version, 6/16 – corr., 54/15, 38/16, 27/17, 23/20 and 91/20) and depend on the maximum length of the custodial sentence for a particular offence. The shortest limitation period is six years (for offences punishable by law with a penalty

limitation periods start running from the commission of the offence, while the existence of the offence must, in principle, be established by a final judgment of conviction by a criminal court.[498]

288. The limitation in case of non-commercial obligations for damages under the OZ is therefore bound by the expiry of the subjective or objective limitation period. According to Article 352(1) of the OZ, the subjective limitation period starts running when the injured party becomes aware of the damage and of the person who inflicted it. Notwithstanding the wording of the rule, the position established through case law is that the condition of familiarising oneself with damage is satisfied when, given the circumstances of the case, the injured party could have learned, with common good faith or diligence, of all the elements which enable him or her to assert a compensation claim.[499] Otherwise, it would be virtually impossible to prove that the injured party had knowledge of the damage. The injured party is presumed to be able to learn of the damage if he or she is also able to ascertain its extent. In the case of damage to property, this is possible when the extent of the damage can be expressed in monetary terms, where the injured party is not obliged to know the full extent of the damage. It is sufficient for the injured party to be familiar with the circumstances from which the amount of the damage can be determined.[500] As for non-pecuniary damage, the injured party can in principle know its extent only once his or her condition has stabilised (usually at the end of treatment).[501]

289. The objective limitation period is not dependent on the injured party's knowledge or the possibility of knowledge of the extent of the damage and the tortfeasor but only on the moment in which the damage occurred.[502] Although the moment of the damage usually coincides with the moment of the tortious event (unlawful conduct), this is not always the case, as much time may elapse between tortious conduct and the occurrence of damage. The time gap between the time of the tortious conduct and the time of the damage is particularly large in the case of diseases that take a very long time to develop (e.g., asbestosis), where symptoms might appear years or even decades after exposure to hazardous substances. This is so-called latent (hidden) damage. The European Court of Human Rights (ECHR) has also ruled on the limitation of such damage (i.e., damage that does not become

---

of up to one year in prison or a fine) and the maximum limitation period is fifty years for offences punishable by law with a penalty of thirty years in prison. According to KZ-1, the statute of limitations does not apply to specific offences (e.g., criminal offences which can be punishable by a life sentence), which is why, according to Art. 353 of the OZ, in such cases, non-applicability of the statute of limitations also regards the compensation claims.

498. ECLI:SI:VSLJ:2016:II.CP.464.2016.

499. ECLI:SI:VSRS:2014:II.IPS.357.2011.

500. ECLI:SI:VSMB:2019:I.CP.382.2019 and ECLI:SI:VSRS:2009:II.IPS.281.2007.

501. ECLI:SI:VSRS:2014:II.IPS.105.2012.

502. 'In any event the claim shall become statute-barred five years after the damage occurred', *see* Art. 352(2) of the OZ.

apparent until long after the harmful event has occurred) in *Howald Moor and others v. Switzerland*,[503] declaring that limitation periods should not be regulated in a way that impairs the effective protection of rights. This is particularly the case where, under national law, a claim for damages becomes statute-barred before the damage has even occurred (e.g., noticeable deterioration of health).

290. In Slovenian legislation, the start of the limitation period is associated with the moment in which the damage occurred rather than the moment of the tortious conduct, which is certainly more appropriate and significantly more favourable for the injured party. However, the relevance of the time when the damage occurred means that the debtor can never know with certainty that a particular (harmful) event has ceased, as damage may become evident very long after the event. For this reason, Možina believes that the term *objective limitation period* is not the most suitable for Slovenian legislation, as the moment of damage is often not externally visible and depends on numerous circumstances. In his view, from the point of view of the legal protection of the starting point of the (objective) time limit, the moment of the harmful event would therefore be more appropriate. At the same time, however, the stipulated objective limitation period should be significantly longer to ensure protection of the injured party.[504]

503. ECLI:CE:ECHR:2014:0311JUD005206710.

504. Cf. Damjan Možina, *Zastaranje nepogodbenih odškodninskih zahtevkov*, Pravni letopis (2015), p. 227.

Chapter 2. Grounds of Justification

§1. CONSENT

291. The principle of *volenti non fit injuria* which originates in Roman law states that no harm is done to one who consents to or desires specific action. Today, this principle is interpreted in the context of the institute of consent to the infringement of a right, which excludes the unlawfulness of the conduct and unlawfulness of the harm caused. According to Article 140 of the OZ, a person who has consented to an act cannot claim compensation for the damage caused by that act. The institution of consent is thus a matter of the exclusion of unlawfulness of the conduct and the damage resulting therefrom and not of a waiver of the claim for damages (since no claim for damages has arisen at all).[505]

292. However, the possibility of excluding the unlawfulness of the conduct and the harm caused thereby is not absolute, as an individual cannot (permissibly) consent to every act. A statement with which an individual consented to someone causing him or her harm by an act that is prohibited by law is null and void.[506] As a result, the rule of consent would not apply, for instance, if an individual consented to an impermissible interference with his or her body (e.g., deliberate injury).

293. Consent has the legal nature of a unilateral legal transaction, where a person's statement alone can have legal ramifications. A consent is deemed valid when all general preconditions for the validity of legal transactions are met. An individual must have legal capacity, the consent must be admissible, and there must be evidence of free, serious and unequivocal will. Consent based on insufficient knowledge of the risks, mistakes, deceit, force, or threat is invalid under the rules on defects in consent.[507] The OZ does not prescribe a specific form for proving the validity of consent, so the latter may be articulated explicitly (written or oral) or implicitly. However, particularly in the case of medical interventions, presumed consent may also be considered in cases where the patient's consent to the intervention cannot be obtained immediately and the patient is at risk of life-threatening or serious injuries to his or her health (e.g., during a surgery, it becomes evident that something other than what was agreed with the patient needs to be done).[508]

294. Consent can regard an act that will inflict damage (e.g., an individual enters into a contract with a contractor to demolish a house and agrees to the demolition) or an act that in principle does not cause damage in itself, but the damage may occur nevertheless (e.g., consent to a medical intervention on the human body, sports activities, etc.).

505. Klemen Pohar, *Pravni učinek privolitve*, Pravna praksa 1–2 (2019), pp. 33–34.
506. *See* Art. 140(2) of the OZ.
507. *See* Arts 45–49 of the OZ.
508. ECLI:SI:VSLJ:2010:I.CP.4295.2009.

295. Medical treatment or procedure involving interference with the human body is only permissible with the patient's consent, although in exceptional cases, presumed consent may be sufficient. However, the patient's consent is only valid if the patient has been provided with sufficient information on the diagnosis, possible treatment options, potential risks, the predictability of success, and possible outcomes of him or her refusing medical assistance.[509] This means that the patient can only declare his or her true will if the duty of disclosure was properly performed. The scope of the duty of disclosure depends on the circumstances of each individual case, but as a general rule, it should explain the diagnosis, the proposed treatment, and the risks.[510] The duty of disclosure is not considered to have been properly fulfilled if the patient is not warned of possible (repeated) complications during treatment.[511] However, the duty of disclosure and the validity of the consent are not assessed in the case of a medical error. Even if the doctor had informed the patient in advance, in the context of the duty of disclosure, that a medical error might occur (e.g., due to exhaustion, overwork, fatigue) and the patient consented to the procedure anyway, such consent would not be legally valid.[512]

296. In assessing the validity of consent, its scope must also be taken into consideration. Even if an individual consents to a particular act, this does not imply consent to all the possible consequences that may in fact arise in the context of that act. Thus, an individual who voluntarily participates in a sports activity only consents to the risks inherent in that sport.[513] A player in a football match as a rule consents to the possibility that certain injuries may occur as a result of the nature of the game, where his or her consent does not exclude any acts or consequences arising from a manner of playing football which is not allowed.[514] To that end, it is also necessary to establish, for each specific case of consent, what risks the individual accepted and how well he or she was informed of the extent of possible damage to which he or she consented.

§2. Necessity

297. An act committed by an individual in a state of distress or necessity is not unlawful, even if the act inflicts damage. Acting under necessity is acting with the intention of preventing harm to oneself or to another person, where the damage inflicted thereby does not outweigh the potential damage from the danger in question. There are common cases of imminent danger threatening human life, where the only way to prevent the danger is by damaging another person's property. In such cases, the protection of life is always considered to be the greater good. The risk of damage which justifies acting under necessity may be caused by a human being, an animal, or a natural event.

509. ECLI:SI:VSRS:2008:II.IPS.99.2006.
510. ECLI:SI:VSLJ:2018:II.CP.2229.2017.
511. ECLI:SI:VSLJ:2012:II.CP.3141.2011 and ECLI:SI:VSLJ:2011:II.CP.682.2011.
512. ECLI:SI:VSRS:2012:II.IPS.302.2011.
513. ECLI:SI:VSLJ:2020:II.CP.1442.2019 and ECLI:SI:VSRS:2018:II.IPS.284.2016.
514. ECLI:SI:VSCE:2012:CP.378.2012.

298. An act in a state of necessity is not considered unlawful only on condition that the risk of damage could not have been averted in a different, less harmful way.[515] Similarly, referring to necessity as justification is not admissible where an individual is fully or partly culpable for invoking the danger.[516]

299. If the specific conditions are met and the damage has been caused in a state of necessity, the injured party may only claim compensation from the person responsible for the damage risk or from the persons from whom the damage was averted, but the compensation from the latter cannot be greater than the benefit they had therefrom.[517] The person who committed the act in a state of necessity is therefore not liable for damages. Nevertheless, he or she must compensate the other persons for the damage inflicted up to the amount of the benefit received if acting under necessity was due to imminent (non-culpable) danger to himself or herself, which could not otherwise be averted.

300. Cases in which damage is inflicted on individuals who try to avert the risk of damage from another are quite common. In such cases, the individual has the right to demand compensation for the damage to which he or she was reasonably exposed from the persons from whom the risk of damage was averted. This is the so-called substituted damage. The extent of the damage that is subject to compensation depends on the facts of the case, including, in particular, an assessment of the reasonableness of the injured party's behaviour in terms of his or her own exposure to the danger, the prospects of success of the conduct, and the scale of the threatening damage.[518]

§3. Self-Help and Self-Defence

301. Self-defence and permitted self-help are both civil law institutes that exclude both the unlawfulness of the conduct and the unlawfulness of the damage. The exclusion is based on the indispensable defence of a legally protected good. The general principle of prohibition on infliction of damage is disregarded because the damage occurs as a result of defence against an attack or as a result of deterrence from an infringement. In the case of self-defence or permitted self-help, it is the unlawfulness of the conduct that is excluded, and not of the liability (fault), since the defensive act is normally committed intentionally.[519] However, the exclusion of unlawfulness does not make the individual liable for damages, irrespective of the scale of the damage caused.

302. According to Article 138 of the OZ, the person who inflicts damage on an assailant in self-defence is not obliged to reimburse the damage, except in the case

515. ECLI:SI:VSKP:2016:II.KP.49141.2014.
516. ECLI:SI:VSLJ:2011:II.CP.514.2011.
517. *See* Art. 138(2) of the OZ.
518. ECLI:SI:VSRS:2006:II.IPS.414.2005.
519. ECLI:SI:VSLJ:2019:I.CP.1125.2019.

of excessive self-defence. Self-defence is that defence which is inevitable to protect oneself or another person from an unlawful attack. The conditions that must be met for an act to be considered self-defence are as follows: unlawful attack, simultaneity of the defence and the attack, urgency of the defence, and proportionality of the conduct.

303. A precondition for a self-defence to be admissible is the existence of an unlawful attack–a conduct that is likely to cause wrongful damage to another, whether in the form of an act against a person's physical integrity or against property. According to Article 10 of the OZ, an unlawful assault is basically any conduct which causes harm to another, unless circumstances are present which exclude unlawfulness.[520] Any defence against an unlawful attack is considered a self-defence, regardless of whether the defender is protecting himself or herself, or another person.[521] It is essential that the defence is directed against the assailant. If such defence results in damage to a person other than the assailant, the rules of necessity shall apply to compensate for that damage.[522]

304. An act is considered self-defence only if the defence and the assault occur simultaneously and if the act is strictly necessary. Thus, an individual cannot claim self-defence when he or she inflicted damage after the unlawful attack had ceased.[523] As regards the issue of the necessity of the defence, what needs to be clarified specifically is whether the defender's conduct was necessary to repel the attack in the first place or could the attack have been repelled otherwise than by damaging the attacker's property.[524]

305. Even if the attacker's conduct cannot be deterred otherwise than by damaging the attacker's goods (i.e., self-defence is necessary), the defence must be proportionate to the attack. If there is no proportionality between the intensity of the attack and the defence, or between the goods attacked and the goods defended, then self-defence is deemed to be exceeded and not legally relevant.[525] In assessing proportionality, all subjective and objective circumstances of the case need to be taken into consideration, with special regard to the purpose, means and characteristics of the attack and the defence. In assessing the appropriateness of the conduct of police performing their duties, one should not consider only whether the particular method of restraint used was the most suitable (least coercive) but also whether it was used with excessive force or not.[526] Even if the attack and the defence pose a threat to

520. For example, unlawfulness is excluded in the case of permissible conduct by police, bailiffs, inspectors, and other public authorities, acting in accordance with the law or a relevant individual legal act.
521. In this specific case, an individual helped the attacked person to force the assailant to the ground and place his hands on his back (ECLI:SI:VSLJ:2016:I.CP.558.2016).
522. *See* Part IV, Ch. 2, §2.
523. ECLI:SI:VSLJ:2013:II.CP.2426.2012.
524. ECLI:SI:VSCE:2020:CP.269.2020.
525. ECLI:SI:VSCE:2016:CP.347.2016.
526. ECLI:SI:VSRS:2014:II.IPS.404.2010.

the same asset (e.g., life or physical integrity), it must be assessed for each specific case whether the threat level is the same. To be more specific, in the case of a physical attack by two stronger assailants, a defensive shot to the vital organs (following a warning shot) was not considered to be a proportionate means, since the circumstances of the specific case did not suggest that that was the only possible way of using the gun.[527]

306. The institute of permitted self-help is in its substance and its consequences very similar to the institute of self-defence, as the OZ provides for the same assumptions. Also, the individual is not liable for damages in the case of permitted self-help, as the said institute excludes both unlawfulness and damage. The main difference between self-defence and permitted self-help is that self-defence refers primarily to defence against a physical attack by an assailant, while the institute of permitted self-help has a wider application, as it establishes the right of anyone (under certain conditions) to prevent the violation of any right, thereby causing damage to the goods of the person who caused the need for self-help.

307. According to Article 139 of the OZ, a person who, during permitted self-help, inflicts damage to the person who caused the need for self-help is not obliged to reimburse the damage caused. Permitted self-help is defined as the right of any person to deter an infringement of a right if the right is in imminent danger if such protection is necessary, and if the means of deterring the infringement are appropriate for the circumstances in which the danger arises. Self-help is deemed necessary if the circumstances do not allow the right holder to seek judicial protection, that is if judicial assistance would come too late.[528] If the condition of urgency is not fulfilled, self-help is not permitted, even if a person remedies an obvious and identified unlawful situation.[529] In addition to the imminence of the danger and the urgency of the action, the action must accord with the circumstances in which the danger arises. In turn, self-help is also permissible only if the conduct (and thus the harm caused) is proportionate to the right or the legally protected good.

§4. Others

308. As a general code in the field of tort law, the OZ defines, as exceptions to the principle of *neminem laedere* (harm nobody), that conduct is not deemed impermissible or that damages are not recoverable if the damage is a result of the injured

527. ECLI:SI:VSRS:2012:II.IPS.47.2010.
528. ECLI:SI:VSLJ:2018:II.CP.613.2018.
529. In this case, an individual was held liable for damages in demolishing a small bridge that was identified as illegal construction. Although the demolition eliminated an illegal situation (unauthorised construction), the court did not rule out the unlawfulness of the conduct in question. Arbitrary conduct, even if it eliminates illegal situation, cannot enjoy legal protection if it is not strictly necessary and the individual has the appropriate (administrative) procedures at his or her disposal.

party's consent,[530] necessity[531] and self-defence or permissible self-help.[532] However, the general basis for excluding the unlawfulness of a conduct (despite the harm caused) is also set out in other legal instruments. Thus, the institute of necessity is also provided for in Article 32 of the KZ-1.

309. Also, Slovenian legislation explicitly provides for other permitted conduct that excludes unlawfulness in different legal instruments. One of the more important exceptions provided for outside the OZ is, for instance, the exclusion of the unlawfulness of expropriation, which is even laid down in the URS. Under certain conditions, the right of ownership of immovable property may be taken away or restricted for the public benefit, even against the will of the owner.[533] The specific conditions and consequences of expropriation are laid down in the Spatial Management Act (SMA).[534]

---

530. *See* Part IV, Ch. 2, §1.
531. *See* Part IV, Ch. 2, §2.
532. *See* Part IV, Ch. 2, §3.
533. *See* Art. 69 of the URS.
534. Official Gazette RS, No. 199/21.

Chapter 3. Contributory Fault

310. According to the principle of full compensation, the injured party is entitled to compensation in the amount necessary to restore the injured party's financial situation to what it would have been had the damaging act or omission not occurred.[535] However, in certain cases, the injured party may be entitled to a compensation sum lower than the amount of the damage. This is the case, for example, when the injured party contributed to the occurrence of the damage or its increase. The OZ establishes the rules on the wrongdoer's (partial) exemption from liability due to the conduct of the injured party in Article 153(3) and Article 171. According to Article 153(3) of the OZ, the keeper of a dangerous object is partly exempt from liability if the injured party contributed to the occurrence of the damage. Under Article 171 of the OZ, however, the injured party is only entitled to proportionately reduced compensation if he or she contributed to the damage or caused the damage to be greater than it would otherwise have been. The same consequence (proportionately reduced compensation) can also be reached under the rules on joint causation.[536]

311. Contributory fault of the injured party can therefore result in proportionately reduced compensation. Although objectively speaking, the injured party contributes to the occurrence of the damage in virtually any case, not every act of the injured party (e.g., crossing the road at a pedestrian crossing when the light is green) constitutes a reason to relieve the wrongdoer from liability or to proportionately reduce compensation. The reason for exemption from liability can only be conduct that is the result of negligence on the part of the injured party. The negligence of the injured party is assessed in accordance with Article 6 of the OZ based on the legal standard of care (diligence of a good manager or professional diligence) and the circumstances of the specific case. Only a person who acts in accordance with the care required and expected of him or her in given circumstances is deemed not to have contributed anything to the occurrence of the damage.[537]

312. Shared responsibility is particularly common in the case of road accidents. Traffic is organised by means of numerous rules and expected behaviours, so the level of care expected of road users is set quite high.[538] According to case law, negligent behaviour and hence contributory fault include acts, such as not wearing a safety belt,[539] crossing the road outside a crosswalk,[540] riding a motorcycle without lights despite public lighting,[541] walking on the road incorrectly (zigzagging) due to intoxication,[542] riding a bicycle on the wrong side of the road,[543] etc.

535. *See* Art. 169 of the OZ.
536. *See* Part V.
537. ECLI:SI:VSLJ:2012:II.CP.2750.2011.
538. For more *see* Part III, Ch. 1.
539. ECLI:SI:VSLJ:2009:I.CP.590.2009.
540. ECLI:SI:VSRS:2006:II.IPS.465.2004.
541. ECLI:SI:VSLJ:2015:II.CP.1148.2015.
542. ECLI:SI:VSRS:2003:II.IPS.583.2002.
543. ECLI:SI:VSLJ:2018:II.CP.168.2018.

313. However, negligent conduct does not comprise only unlawful acts (explicitly defined by peremptory rules) but also any act which, according to generally accepted norms and considering the circumstances of the case, is of such a nature that the demonstrated contributory fault is a result of a lack of care on the part of the injured party. In this specific case, the Court decided that the cyclist not wearing a helmet constituted a failure to demonstrate care (thus contributing to the damage), even though the use of a helmet was not required by law.[544] A similar ruling was reached regarding the use of reflectors. Although it is not prohibited to walk at night in dark clothes and without reflectors, this does not mean that not using a reflector does not constitute negligent conduct. It is common knowledge that a pedestrian wearing a reflector at night can be spotted sooner, so pedestrians are expected to ensure their own safety also by wearing reflectors.[545]

314. In addition to the classic contributory fault due to negligent conduct of the injured party, one should not neglect the duty of the injured party to limit the harm or the so-called duty to mitigate. According to Article 243(4) and (5) of the OZ, the injured party must take all reasonable efforts to mitigate the damage in a specific situation. If the party fails to do so, he or she may only demand proportionally reduced compensation. Although this rule primarily applies to the consequences of a breach of contract, it is also used in the cases of non-contractual obligations.

315. The duty to mitigate the damage of the injured party is based on several fundamental principles of the law of obligations, in particular the principles of good faith and fairness, due diligence, prohibition of abuse of rights, and prohibition of infliction of damage. Although the injured party did not contribute to the damage, he or she is not entitled to full compensation for the damage if reasonable conduct could have reduced the said damage (e.g., extinguishing a burning object, turning off a water valve, etc.). Reasonable efforts include any actions that do not constitute a danger or excessive risk for the injured party, and which are expected in the specific circumstances.

316. A particular example of the injured party's duty to mitigate harm is related to medical procedures such as medical treatment and rehabilitation. In certain cases, it is possible to reduce the amount of damage through (successful) medical treatment. Although the injured party's duty to mitigate damage is considered one of the underlying principles of tort law, the injured party cannot be forced, against his or her will, to undergo a medical procedure which may not result in an improvement, but which would entail considerable discomfort, pain, and risk.[546]

317. Refusing a medical procedure can have unfavourable consequences for the injured person only if there was no risk of damage associated with treatment refused. Since virtually every surgical procedure involves some level of risk or

544. ECLI:SI:VSRS:2016:II.IPS.182.2015.
545. ECLI:SI:VSLJ:2017:II.CP.744.2017.
546. ECLI:SI:VSRS:1996:II.IPS.423.94.

uncertainty as to the course and the outcome of the treatment, the refusal of a medical procedure can hardly ever be considered to the detriment of the injured party in the sense that the latter breached his or her duty to mitigate the harm.[547] Thus, the duty to mitigate harm through medical treatment would apply only to a procedure that any person would undergo under normal circumstances, using the average-patient standard as the decisive criterion rather than the criteria of medical science.[548]

318. An example of a due medical procedure is placing of a dental veneer or laminate due to a damaged tooth. This procedure can relatively easily eliminate or reduce the compensation for mental distress caused by the injury (damage to a visible tooth). Refusing such a procedure would therefore result in a proportionally reduced compensation.

547. ECLI:SI:VSLJ:2018:II.CP.2453.2017.
548. ECLI:SI:VSRS:2004:II.IPS.470.2003.

Chapter 4. Exemption Clauses

319. Liability for damages may be excluded or limited in advance by means of exemption clauses. These are particularly common in contract law, which is subject to a wide range of free dispositions. Regardless of this, the parties to a contract cannot exclude liability for intent or gross negligence in advance, as this is contrary to fundamental principles of the law of obligations, in particular the principle of good faith and fairness. However, a court may, in exceptional circumstances, rescind a contractual provision on the exclusion of liability for slight negligence if such an agreement derives from the debtor's monopoly position or from a generally unequal relationship between the contracting parties.[549]

320. There is a tendency towards excluding liability in advance also in non-contractual tort liabilities. Notifications on the exclusion of liability are particularly common with liability of the producer for the product or liability for dangerous objects and animals, etc. It should be noted that such notifications alone cannot exclude liability unless the law provides for such a possibility.[550] Nevertheless, they may have an impact on the content of the obligation, primarily as regards the duty of care exercised by the tortfeasor and the injured party. For example, a displayed 'Beware of the dog!' sign does not relieve the dog owner from liability for the damage caused by the dog's bite, but it may nevertheless influence the judgment of the care exercised by the injured party and thus the question of contributory fault of the injured party, which is reflected in a proportionately reduced compensation.[551]

321. In some cases, the law stipulates in advance that such notifications shall have no legal effect. Pursuant to Article 744 of the OZ, any declarations displayed on the premises of an eating establishment which, contrary to the provisions of the OZ, exclude, limit, or make conditional the liability of the keeper of such an establishment for any items brought by the guest, have no legal effect. The same applies to other related service providers that store items brought by guests, such as hotels, hairdressing and beauty salons, spas, health centres, hospitals, etc.

549. *See* Art. 242(2) of the OZ.
550. ECLI:SI:VSLJ:2010:II.CP.1292.2010.
551. *See* Part IV, Ch. 3.

Part V. Causation

322. Causation is one of the fundamental elements of tort law obligations, alongside unlawful conduct, damage, and liability. The term refers to the causal link between unlawful conduct and the damage inflicted. The only person who can be held liable for the damage is the wrongdoer, i.e., the person who has caused the damage by a specific active or passive act. However, as a rule, damage is a result of different causes and favourable circumstances, so the causal link must therefore be identified on a case-by-case basis. The law does not define what constitutes legally relevant causation, so it is for case law to determine, on a case-by-case basis, whether there is a legally relevant causal link in each situation or not.[552]

323. There are several theories of causation based on which a causal link between the wrongdoer's conduct and the damage in a specific case can be identified as legally relevant. According to *sine qua non* or 'but for' theory, any circumstance without which the adverse consequence would not have occurred may be considered the cause. In general, this theory cannot be legally relevant as it is too broad, treating all circumstances without which the harmful consequence would not have occurred as possible causes. This can be illustrated by the case of a car driver who collided with an oncoming vehicle because he saw a cute girl walking on the pavement. There are a few elements or circumstances that contributed to the accident (the car, other road users, the width of the road, the cute girl, etc.), which would almost certainly not have happened if the cute girl had not been walking on the pavement. The conclusion that can be drawn in this specific case is that would be illogical and inappropriate to confirm a legally relevant causal link between the girl's conduct (walking on the pavement) and the accident.

324. Among the theories of legally relevant causation, the most commonly used in judicial practice are the *ratio legis* theory and the theory of adequate causation. The latter has faced considerable criticism and is supplemented in more recent jurisprudence by the eggshell skull rule and the prospective causation analysis, which employs the criteria of threshold and sufficient probability that a particular act caused the harmful event.[553]

325. The *ratio legis* theory, which derives from legal norms, is used primarily. In the field of non-commercial liability for damages, the causes (active or passive

552. ECLI:SI:VSRS:2019:VIII.IPS.208.2018.
553. *See* Plavšak, *supra* n. 215, at 707, 729 et seq.

conduct) that are legally relevant under this theory are those that simultaneously constitute a violation of the legal norms and are considered causes by the legal norms in view of their purpose (e.g., speeding or incorrect stopping in violation of traffic regulations). The cute girl walking on the pavement did not violate any legal norm, so her conduct (even though it is highly likely that the accident would not have occurred in its absence) is not considered legally relevant under *ratio legis*, which means that causation (and thus the girl's liability for damages) is not established.

326. As regards commercial liability, however, the parties' intention to conclude a contract is taken into consideration as well as the violation of legal norms. Thus, any conduct that constitutes a breach of a contractual agreement or a violation of legal norms is regarded as a legally relevant cause giving rise to commercial liability.

327. Since in many cases not even the application of the *ratio legis* theory can provide a logical or adequate answer, this led to the development of the theory of foreseeability and the theory of adequate causation in case law. The two theories are interrelated and are founded on the fact that the possibility of damage occurring because of unlawful conduct must be objectively foreseeable. It is not necessary, however, that the person responsible should be capable of foreseeing concrete consequences. It is sufficient that he or she is (or should be) capable of foreseeing that his or her conduct may result in a wide range of harmful consequences.

328. Unlike the *sine qua non* theory and the *ratio legis* theory, the adequate causation theory does not focus on the question of the necessity or unlawfulness of the cause, but on whether a specific conduct increased the likelihood of the tortious event.[554] It is often the case that a violation of a legal norm does not increase the likelihood of a harmful consequence, either because the latter would have occurred in any event or because other causes prevail. Under the adequate causation theory, only those causes which, in the ordinary course of events, lead to a particular tortious consequence are regarded as legally relevant.[555] The key question is therefore whether a particular consequence is expected (damaging event, not the extent of damage resulting from it), normal or ordinary in relation to the cause.[556] A party is liable only for the normal consequences of his or her conduct, i.e., for the consequences which he or she should have foreseen.[557] However, a cause is not adequate if it is naturally indifferent to the occurrence of the damage and inflicts it only because of exceptional circumstances.[558] It is certainly not normal for a person to suffer cardiac arrest because a car driver honks the horn, even if this is not permissible in the specific case and constitutes a violation of a legal norm.

554. Plavšak et al., *supra* n. 95, at 511.
555. ECLI:SI:VSRS:2002:II.IPS.577.2001.
556. ECLI:SI:VSRS:1997:II.IPS.401.96.
557. ECLI:SI:VSRS:2003:II.IPS.479.2002.
558. Jadek Pensa, *supra* n. 60, at 676.

329. The theory emphasises that the adequacy of the cause should not be assessed from the point of view of the foreseeability of the extent of damage due to a violation, but rather from the point of view of the foreseeability of the occurrence of a damaging event with a certain harmful fact.[559] The extent of damage from tortious liability is – unlike contractual liability – not limited but the perpetrator owes full compensation according to Article 169 of the OZ. For example, if an official of the administrative unit issued an identity card to a wrong person due to negligence (he or she did not properly verify the applicant's identity), the state is liable for damages caused to third parties by fraud committed by the person who obtained the ID with a false identity.[560] The court considered such a damaging event to be foreseeable, and although it was 'caused' by the fraudster (and not the state), the court did not consider the fraudster's actions to be grounds for 'breaking' the causal link from the point of view of the negligent issuance of the ID card. It is also important to note that a legally relevant causal link exists and there is no shared causality if the damaging event manifests degenerative (and other) changes that were previously silent and would otherwise (probably) not have occurred in the injured party; as well as if the entire extent of damage is significantly higher due to the already poor state of health (e.g., illness) and it is necessary to attribute the (entire) cause of the problems to the damaging event (this relates to the eggshell skull theory).[561] Especially in such compensation cases, the theory of adequate causation has been used in Slovenia rather unfortunately for several years to reject larger extents of damages in the area of already ill victims who have 'suffered' more due to the injury than an 'average' individual.[562]

330. While we can find a case law example dating as far back as 1979 in which the court found a causal link between the death of an injured party that occurred

559. Plavšak, *supra* n. 215, at 709.

560. Refer to ECLI:SI:VSRS:2021:II.IPS.103.2021: The conduct of the clerk in failing to verify the identity of the applicant for an ID card by consulting other available records and posing additional questions, despite significant differences in appearance, does not meet the standard of professional care required. The damage caused to the plaintiff by the deception with a fake ID card must be attributed to the state. Even though it was caused by a 'criminal mind', it was due to the negligent behaviour of the defendant's clerk that the damage occurred. The criminal plan was always there, but it only materialised because of the actions of the defendant's clerk, who handed over a fake ID card to the holder of the criminal undertaking. This played a pivotal role in the chain of causes and effects. The damage to the plaintiff is therefore by no means atypical – it is not the result of fortuity and an objectively unforeseeable combination of circumstances.

561. *See* ECLI:SI:VSRS:2009:II.IPS.387.2007: In assessing the causal link between the injury and the specific extent of the damage suffered, the court must not delineate causes, as is typical in assessing shared responsibility (when the wrongful conduct of the tortfeasor and the contribution of the injured party concur). Instead, it must clarify whether it is probable that the plaintiff would have suffered the current issues even if the damage had not occurred. It does not matter that an average injured person (who does not suffer from rheumatism and osteoporosis) would not have experienced such an extent of damage from the same injury and that the specific extent of the plaintiff's damage is greater because of the degenerative changes that already affected her before the injury. The tortfeasor (or liable party) must accept the injured person as he or she is. ECLI:SI:VSRS:2011:II.IPS.1173.2008.

562. *See* ECLI:SI:VSRS:1998:II.IPS.217.97, ECLI:SI:VSRS:2003:II.IPS.313.2003, ECLI:SI:VSRS:2007:II.IPS.654.2005, ECLI:SI:VSLJ:2010:II.CP.1197.2010, ECLI:SI:VSRS:2003:II.IPS.552.2002, ECLI:SI:VSRS:2007:II.IPS.170.2005, etc.

during a repeat surgery of a severe leg injury six months later and a traffic accident in which the leg injury occurred,[563] there is also different case law from 2016. This newer case law considers temporally remote causes (e.g., stressful situations due to an unlawful termination of an employment contract when resuming work with the same employer after two years) as causes that do not inherently lead to damaging consequences.[564] The validity of such a legal stance is highly questionable.

331. The burden of proof is essential to establishing tort liability, as it is very difficult to prove causation in certain cases. Generally, it is the injured party who must prove the causal link between the unlawful conduct and the tortious consequence. This applies, for example, to fault-based (subjective) non-commercial tort liability and to commercial tort liability.[565] However, in certain cases, the law provides presumption of causation or other rules that lighten the injured party's position.

332. Article 149 of the OZ establishes a general presumption of causation for cases of (strict) liability for damage from a dangerous object or dangerous activity. Damage occurring in connection with a dangerous object or dangerous activity is presumed to originate from the object or activity in question unless it is proved that it was not the cause. Thus, the link between unlawful conduct and the damage inflicted is not decisive for the emergence of strict liability for damages, as causality arises from the mere possession of the object in question or from the fact that the person is involved in the dangerous activity. It is therefore a rebuttable presumption that the dangerous object or activity is the cause of the damage. The presumption is based on the abstract concept of danger.[566] Consequently, the injured party needs only to allege the existence of the presumed basis (the existence of the dangerous object or dangerous activity), while the keeper of the dangerous object or the person engaged in the dangerous activity may rebut the presumption of causation by proving that in the specific case, the object or the activity in question is not such that would give rise to increased risk.

333. The injured party's burden of proof is eased also in cases where multiple persons are liable for the same damage. For such cases, Article 186 of the OZ provides for the application of the institute of joint and several liability, which is based on the theory of concurrent, alternative, and cumulative causation. We speak of concurrent causation where there are multiple causes, each of which may lead to the same harmful consequence (e.g., two hunters shoot a runaway dog at the same time, where one shot was sufficient to kill the dog). Alternative causation is where there are multiple competing causes and we do not know which one caused the harmful consequence (e.g., two hunters fire the shot at the same time and only one shot hits

563. Jadek Pensa, *supra* n. 60, at 675. Furthermore, for more of such older case law, which recognises a causal link regardless of the time gap between the damaging event (cause) and the consequence (and does not consider the cause inadequate due to temporal distance), *see* Plavšak, *supra* n. 215, at 752.

564. *See* ECLI:SI:VSLJ:2016:I.CP.132.2016.

565. *See* Arts 131 and 239 of the OZ.

566. *See* Part II, Ch. 1, §3.

the runaway dog). Cumulative causation is when a harmful effect results from a set of individual causes but would not have arisen if each of these causes occurred individually (e.g., a runaway dog dies from two gunshot wounds, but it would not have died from a single gunshot wound).

334. As it would be extremely difficult to prove a causal link between the conduct and the damage for each individual cause in the cases in question, the law provides for the application of the institute of joint and several liability. This means that everyone involved is liable for the entire obligation to the injured party, who may demand performance thereof from any of them, in full or in arbitrary proportions.[567]

335. Hence, according to Article 186 of the OZ, the injured party does not need to substantiate a causal link between the conduct of each person involved and the damage inflicted, but must only prove that a situation exists which is grounds for the application of the rules on joint and several liability.[568] That Article provides for four general situations of joint and several liability: (1) liability for damage caused by several persons together; (2) liability of the abettor, of the aider, and of the person who participated in preventing the persons responsible from being discovered; (3) liability of persons who acted independently, where it is not possible to determine their respective shares in the damage; and (4) liability in the event of alternative causation.

336. In line with Article 186(1) of the OZ, a damage is deemed to have been inflicted jointly when several persons cause damage either by having a common intention or by acting jointly. A common intention is also present in the case of abettors, aiders, and those who help to prevent the persons responsible from being found. The determination of their liability serves the same purpose as in criminal law and is based on the preventive function of tort liability.[569] In this case, however, it is not entirely true that the injured party does not need to prove causality. In fact, the injured party must prove active conduct which had a bearing on the cause of the damage and which shows a substantively significant connection to the tortfeasor.[570] Passive conduct (e.g., omission in terms of identifying the perpetrator) is not sufficient to establish tort liability.[571] At the same time, the active conduct must be alleged in such a way that it can be established with a degree of certainty, since indicative suggestion of aiding and abetting alone is not sufficient.[572] For example, the conduct of a person who orders a physical attack on someone is also regarded as active conduct, even though that person does not take part in the beating.[573]

567. *See* rules regarding debtors' joint and several liability, specified in Arts 395–405 of the OZ.
568. ECLI:SI:VSLJ:2010:II.CP.4093.2009.
569. Plavšak, *supra* n. 215, at 1070.
570. ECLI:SI:VSLJ:2014:II.CP.387.2014.
571. ECLI:SI:VSLJ:2016:I.CP.3221.2015.
572. ECLI:SI:VSLJ:2019:I.CP.2248.2018.
573. ECLI:SI:VSLJ:2015:I.CP.1116.2015.

337. However, joint and several liability does not apply only to persons who cause the damage through joint action or common purpose, but also to persons who inflicted the damage entirely independently yet their shares in the damage cannot be determined. The use of the *a contrario* argument leads to the conclusion that where it is possible to determine the shares of those who caused the damage but acted independently, they are not jointly and severally liable. Instead. they are liable for their respective shares.[574]

338. Article 186(4) of the OZ deals with alternative causation, which is used when there is no doubt that the damage was caused by one of several possible tortfeasors, but it cannot be determined which one exactly. In this case, it is not sufficient that one of these persons claims to have caused the damage, but there must be a further condition that these persons are connected (in some way).[575] The injured party must therefore prove (with a degree of probability) that the damage was caused by one of several possible tortfeasors who are connected by a particular circumstance, conduct, or objective. For example, this would apply to the liability of four people smoking by a hayrack which was later destroyed by fire. Each of them can be blamed for failing to check whether the cigarette butts were completely extinguished or still smouldering. This omission is considered unlawful and constitutes the harmful circumstances which must be considered the legally relevant cause of the fire in this particular case.[576] The element of (substantive) connection between the people involved cannot be given, for example, in the case of a random brawl on the street.[577]

339. In addition to the general rule on the joint and several liability of several persons for the same damage, the OZ also defines joint and several liability in some specific cases, namely the liability of the representative and the represented person in the event of transgression of authorisation (Article 72 of the OZ), the liability of the parent and the child (Article 143 of the OZ), the liability of the minor and the person the minor is entrusted to (Article 144 of the OZ), the liability of the keeper of a motor vehicle for the damage suffered by others (Article 154 of the OZ), the liability of the contracting authority and the contractor (Article 187 of the OZ), the liability of the contractor and the project designer in relation to the ordering party (Article 665 of the OZ), and the liability of several carriers involved in the transport of a consignment (Article 695 of the OZ).

574. ECLI:SI:VSLJ:2010:I.CP.990.2010 and ECLI:SI:VSRS:2008:II.IPS.161.2008.
575. ECLI:SI:VSLJ:2011:I.CP.3785.2010.
576. ECLI:SI:VSRS:2013:II.IPS.316.2011.
577. ECLI:SI:VSCE:2016:CP.179.2016.

Part VI. Remedies

Chapter 1. General Principles

340. Compensation for damages is regulated in Slovenia in section 7 of the OZ (Articles 164–185). The method of compensation depends on the type of legally recognised damage. In accordance with Article 132 of the OZ, legally recognised pecuniary losses (property damage) are that which result in a diminution of the property (ordinary damage) and/or the prevention of its increase (loss of profit), as well as non-pecuniary losses (non-property damage) resulting from the infliction of physical or mental pain or fear on another, and damage to the reputation of a legal entity.[578] At this point, it should be noted that the OZ is not the only law that determines the legally recognised forms of damage.[579] Moreover, not only Slovenian law but also the law of the EU, of which Slovenia is a member, is relevant in this area. The legally recognised forms of damage in Slovenia therefore also include, for example, mental anguish caused by the loss of enjoyment during vacation.[580]

341. The fundamental task of Slovenian tort law is to remedy an unjust situation in which the injured party finds himself or herself as a result of a harmful event or to realise the injured party's interest in eliminating the negative consequences of the unlawfulness in his or her sphere.[581]

342. In the context of property damage, we speak of the compensatory or remedial function of tort law, the fundamental principle of which is to provide full compensation.[582] In addition to the compensatory function, theory and case law also emphasise

578. *See* Arts 178–185 of the OZ, which govern legally recognised forms of non-pecuniary damage in the Civil Code, where it is stipulated, among other things, that any violation of personal rights constitutes legally recognised non-pecuniary damage that can be compensated by non-monetary satisfaction (cf. Art. 178 of the OZ). Other forms of damage not provided for by law, such as mental anguish resulting from the violation of the right to vote, are not legally relevant and are not sufficient to give rise to a liability for compensation (*see* ECLI:SI:VSRS:2015:II.IPS.99.2013).

579. *See*, e.g., Art. 8 of the Employment Relationships Act (ZDR-1), which establishes the employer's liability for damages in the event of a violation of the prohibition of discrimination or harassment in the workplace (Official Gazette RS, Nos 76/17, 26/19 and 21/13, 78/13 – corr., 47/15 – ZZSDT, 33/16 – PZ-F, 52/16, 15/17 – Constitutional Court decision, 22/19 – ZPosS, 81/19, 203/20 – ZIUPOPDVE, 119/21 – ZČmIS-A, 202/21 – Constitutional Court decision, 15/22 and 54/22 – ZUPŠ-1).

580. ECLI:SI:VSRS:2022:II.IPS.69.2020. *See* more about this topic *infra* in Part VI, Ch. 2, §3.

581. *See* ECLI:SI:VSRS:2014:II.IPS.114.2012.

582. Article 169 of the OZ: 'The court, which also takes into account the circumstances that arose after the damage was caused, awards the injured party compensation in the amount necessary to make

the preventive function of compensation,[583] which is intended to provide potential wrongdoers with an appropriate incentive to act in such a way as to reduce the likelihood of harmful events occurring.[584] The OZ provides the injured party with a right of choice in the case of pecuniary damage, allowing them to decide how they wish to be compensated. They can either demand compensation in money (equivalence) or restoration to the previous state (restitution) as a means of recovering their damages.[585] However, the court has the possibility to correct the choice made by the injured party in the cases specified in Article 164 of the OZ.[586]

343. The non-pecuniary damage, where there is a violation of the immaterial or personal sphere, has no equivalent; and it is not possible to speak of compensation for the 'full' damage or its reparation, but of just compensation (Article 179(1) of the OZ). It is therefore not determined according to the same criteria as pecuniary damage. We speak of satisfaction, the aim of which is to give subjective satisfaction to the injured party. This satisfaction can be of a non-pecuniary nature (e.g., the publication of a judgment, the retraction of an insult), or it can take the form of monetary compensation if the violation of personal rights has caused certain consequential damage to a person (e.g., physical pain).[587]

344. Slovenian case law clearly emphasises that the purpose of tort law is not to punish the wrongdoer but to compensate the injured party for the damage suffered. Therefore, Slovenian case law does not recognise damages of a punitive nature as they are known in the Anglo-Saxon legal system (the so-called punitive damages).[588] Since slight negligence (*culpa levis; plain or ordinary negligence*) on the

---

his financial situation the same as it would have been if there had been no harmful act or omission.' *See* more about full compensation in Part VI, Ch. 2, §3 and §5.

583. *See* ECLI:SI:VSRS:2021:II.IPS.54.2020.
584. Plavšak et al., *supra* n. 95, at 617.
585. The restitution claim does not always have to be directed at the 'previous state.' It can also aim at the establishment of a state that did not exist before. As already argued by Cigoj, *supra* n. 88, 230, 232; cf. ECLI:SI:VSLJ:2014:II.CP.2101.2013: Compensation for it, therefore, means the establishment of a state that has not existed before, but which, if the harmful event had not occurred, would have naturally occurred.
586. *See* Part VI, Ch. 3, §1.
587. *See* Art. 179 of the OZ. In case law, two criteria have been developed for awarding monetary compensation for non-pecuniary damage, namely: the principle of objective causality and the individualisation of compensation (*see more* on compensation for non-pecuniary damage in Part VI, Ch. 2, §3, and Ch. 4, §2). For a legal entity, the mere injury to its reputation or good name, i.e., its personal rights, constitutes a legally recognised non-pecuniary damage for which the legal entity is entitled to compensation in money (*see* Art. 183 of the OZ).
588. The most notable case concerning the possibility of recognising punitive damages was the court decision in the field of medical malpractice (*see* ECLI:SI:VSRS:2012:II.IPS.130.2012). Similarly, the Slovenian Supreme Court reiterated its position on the recognition of punitive damages in cases of harassment and discrimination in the workplace (*see*, e.g., ECLI:SI:VSRS:2021:VIII.IPS.14.2021). In Slovenian law, we can also find some legal provisions in the OZ, which have a punitive character under tort law. These are referred to as 'civil fines/ penalties', as the payment of a certain amount by the responsible person is not directly related to the damage caused (*see* more on this topic in Part VI, Ch. 7, §3).

part of the tortfeasor[589] is sufficient to establish tort liability, the amount of compensation in Slovenian law only exceptionally depends on the degree of fault of the wrongdoer (*see* more on the concept of fault in Part I, Chapter 1, §2). In some cases of slight fault, the compensation can be reduced if certain other conditions are met (more on this in Part VI, Chapter 3, §4); in cases of severe fault, the court may also consider the sentimental value of the matter for the injured party when determining the amount of compensation (more on this in Part VI, Chapter 3, §1). There is also a particularity in the case of business-related liability, where in cases of slight negligence the extent of the damage is limited to the criterion of foreseeability (for more on the limitation of compensation in business-related liability, *see* Part VI, Chapter 2, §3).

589. The focus of tort law is the injured party, who is entitled to compensation in the full amount of the damage, regardless of the type of the fault inflicted by the causer (Salma, *supra* n. 125, at p. 543).

Chapter 2. Kinds of Damages

§1. Individual and Collective Damage

345. The OZ only recognises individual damages that occur to an individual and can be claimed by the individual (the injured party) under the general provisions of Slovenian civil procedure law in a so-called pecuniary (condemnatory) lawsuit. Therefore, until 21 April 2018, when the CAA[590] entered into force, it was not possible in Slovenia to collectively assert compensation claims in cases where several persons claimed to have been harmed by the same inadmissible act. The CAA defines collective damages as the sum of the individual disadvantages suffered by the members of a group from the same mass tort case.[591]

346. Prior to the adoption of the CAA, victims of mass torts had procedural mechanisms at their disposal that were governed by the ZPP,[592] such as joint litigation, joinder of claims, and causation procedures. In practice, however, it quickly became apparent that these mechanisms were only suitable if the total number of injured parties involved in the proceedings was relatively small. It also became apparent that the general provisions of civil procedure law could not effectively address the issues arising in connection with the collective enforcement of compensation claims, such as the obvious imbalance between the value of the rights violated or threatened and the potential legal costs, the lack of knowledge and passivity of the victims, the overburdening of the courts, and similar factors.[593]

347. The possibility of filing a collective lawsuit under the CAA is limited to certain predefined areas of application where individual enforcement of claims has often proven ineffective. These areas include claims related to consumer protection,[594] restrictions of competition, regulated financial markets, protection of workers' rights,[595] and environmental protection (Article 2(1) of the CAA). The CAA governs collective litigation, collective settlements, rules of collective proceedings, the content and effect of collective judgments, the procedure for disbursing aggregate compensatory damages awarded by a collective judgment, and rules regarding the costs of proceedings and the financing of collective lawsuits.[596]

---

590. Act on Collective Actions (Official Gazette of the Republic of Slovenia, No. 55/17).
591. Cf. Art. 3(5) of the CAA.
592. Civil Procedure Act (Official Gazette of the Republic of Slovenia, Nos 73/07 – official consolidated text, 45/08 – ZArbit, 45/08, 111/08 – Constitutional Court decision, 57/09 – Constitutional Court decision, 12/10 – Constitutional Court decision, 50/10 – Constitutional Court decision, 107/10 – Constitutional Court decision, 75/12 – Constitutional Court decision, 40/13 – Constitutional Court decision, 92/13 – Constitutional Court decision, 10/14 – Constitutional Court decision, 48/15 – Constitutional Court decision, 6/17 – Constitutional Court decision, 10/17, 16/19 – ZNP-1, 70/19 – Constitutional Court decision, 1/22 – Constitutional Court decision, and 3/22 – ZDeb).
593. Cf. proposal CAA, EVA 2016-2030-0007, https://e-uprava.gov.si/drzava-in-druzba/e-demokracija/predlogi-predpisov/predlog-predpisa.html?id=7418 (10 Jul. 2023), pp. 1–2.
594. *See* ECLI:SI:VSLJ:2022:I.CP.1731.2021.
595. *See* ECLI:SI:VDSS:2019:XXX.PDP.185.2019.
596. *See* Art. 1(1) of the CAA.

§2. Direct and Indirect

348. The OZ does not provide for an explicit division of damage into direct and indirect categories. However, this division is used in theory and in judicial practice.[597] One of the criteria for distinguishing between direct and indirect damage is the question of the existence of a causal link between the unlawful harmful event (the initial event) and the prohibited consequence (the harm).[598] According to the theory of Slovenian tort law, damage is considered to be direct if the harmful event or wrongful act directly causes the consequence (e.g., person A hits person B, which causes harm to person B). Damage is also considered direct if the initial event triggers a second event that is not controlled by human will, and the harm results from this intervening event. For instance, if a person throws a stone that breaks a glass, and the glass shards then fall onto the injured party and cause him or her harm, the damage is direct. However, the damage is considered to be indirect if there is an independent intermediate event between the wrongful act and the consequence (harm/damage), which is due to favourable circumstances caused by the initial event. The judicial practice has considered damages resulting from the treatment of the consequences of the harmful event as indirect damages (e.g., an injury to the right knee due to overloading during treatment of the left knee).[599]

349. The criterion for distinguishing between direct and indirect damage can also be the differentiation between direct and indirect victims, the decisive question being against whom the harmful event is directed (e.g., a person involved in a traffic accident is a direct victim). Actions directed against the direct victim may also have an impact on other persons who are consequently affected themselves – these individuals are indirect victims (e.g., the parents of the person involved in the accident).[600] Although, as a rule, the injured party within the meaning of the OZ is only the direct victim, indirect victims are explicitly defined in Article 180 of the OZ regarding non-material damage/non-pecuniary loss. In the event of death or particularly serious disability of an individual (the direct victim), the court may award fair monetary compensation to indirect victims (spouse, children, parents, and in the case of a long-term cohabitation with the direct victim, also siblings and extramarital partners) for their mental anguish. As this provision expands the legally relevant causation and the scope of the damage for which the tortfeasor is liable, the restitution of non-material damage to indirect victims is precisely delimited by an objective criterion of the catastrophic nature of the damage (only in the cases of death or particularly severe disability of a close relative – the direct victim) and a subjective

597. Cf. Cigoj, *supra* n. 88, at p. 212; *see also* ECLI:SI:VSRS:2020:II.IPS.142.2019 and ECLI:SI:VSLJ:2018:I.CPG.818.2017.

598. *See* more on causation in Part V.

599. *See* ECLI:SI:VSLJ:2016:III.CP.2648.2016.

600. Cf. ECLI:SI:VSRS:2018:II.IPS.268.2016, where it was explicitly stated that secondary damage is typically the damage of indirect victims and is recognised exceptionally.

criterion (limited circle of persons).[601] According to judicial practice, indirect damage includes both the mental anguish suffered by indirect victims due to their empathy with the direct victim, as well as the mental anguish they experience due to their own distress caused by the death or particularly severe disability of the direct victim.[602]

350. The distinction between direct and indirect damage is also important in the context of business tort liability related to seller's warranties for material or legal defects, where, in addition to warranty claims covering direct damage (i.e., damage to the thing or *damnum quoad rem*), two forms of indirect damage are recognised for the buyer (trust-based damage or *damnum circa rem* and reflexive damage or *damnum extra rem*).[603] However, these two forms are acknowledged according to different prerequisites for their assertion.[604]

§3. Pecuniary and Non-pecuniary Losses

351. Pecuniary damage in the broadest sense encompasses any interference with another's property rights (property rights, obligation rights, corporate rights, securities, and intellectual property rights) and legally protected property interests (e.g., lost profits, earnings). Under Slovenian law, not every violation of another's (the injured party's) property right is legally recognised as pecuniary damage; rather, there must be a further consequence in the form of a decrease in the injured party's assets or the prevention of their increase (lost profits).[605] A legally recognised pecuniary loss can also arise from encroachments on non-material rights and legally protected interests of another.[606]

352. According to Article 168 of the OZ, the injured party has the right to compensation for both ordinary damage and loss of profit. Ordinary damage refers to the reduction of the injured party's assets. It is the negative difference between the injured party's property before the harmful event and its value after it. Therefore, in addition to compensation for the destroyed property (*see* more in Part VI, Chapter 3, §1), the injured party is entitled, for example, to claim reimbursement of costs equal to the price paid for the repair of the damaged property.[607] In this context, the injured party may claim reimbursement of the costs of repair even if the repair of the thing has not yet taken place[608] – in such a case, the price for such repair at the

601. *See* ECLI:SI:VSRS:2015:II.IPS.252.2013.
602. Cf. ECLI:SI:VSLJ:2009:II.CP.3108.2009.
603. ECLI:SI:VSRS:2010:II.IPS.497.2009.
604. ECLI:SI:VSLJ:2015:I.CPG.934.2015.
605. Cf. ECLI:SI:VSRS:2017:II.IPS.337.2016 and ECLI:SI:VSLJ:2014:I.CPG.1460.2012.
606. The question of compensation for pecuniary loss arising from an infringement of non-pecuniary interests or personal rights of the injured party is regulated in Arts 172 to 177 of the OZ (*see* more in Part VI, Ch. 2, §4 and Part VI, Ch. 4, §1).
607. ECLI:SI:VSLJ:2019:I.CPG.703.2018.
608. ECLI:SI:VSLJ:2020:III.CP.736.2020 and ECLI:SI:VSLJ:2011:I.CP.956.2011.

time of the trial is taken into account.[609] Lost profit refers to the profit that the injured party would have made if the harmful event had not occurred. A condition for awarding compensation for lost profit is that the profit is permissible – a profit expected from an unlawful activity is not legally recognised, as it is not a profit that the injured party could reasonably expect in the normal course of events.[610] Additionally, the injured party must have an intention to make a profit.[611]

353. As previously explained (*see* Part VI, Chapter 1), the fundamental principle in determining compensation for pecuniary loss is the principle of full compensation, which follows the reparative or equalising function of tort law. Based on this principle, the court awards the injured party compensation in the amount necessary to restore his or her financial situation to what it would have been if the harmful event had not occurred, taking into account the circumstances that occurred after the damage. The principle of full compensation ensures that the injured party receives neither less nor more than the damage actually suffered (*compensatio lucri cum damno*).[612] The compensation awarded must not exceed the damage actually suffered, which is why any benefit gained by the injured party as a result of the harmful event is taken into consideration and deducted from the amount of compensation.[613]

354. The principle of full compensation, which is reflected in numerous provisions of the OZ, also knows exceptions. A reduction of compensation is possible under specific conditions in Slovenian law. This may be the case if the liable party has a weak financial situation[614] if he or she caused the damage while acting in the injured party's interest,[615] or if the injured party himself or herself contributed to the occurrence of the damage or made the damage greater than it would have been otherwise[616] (for more on these exceptions to the principle of full compensation, *see* Part VI, Chapter 3, §4).

355. In the realm of contractual tort liability,[617] the principle of full compensation is considerably limited by the principle of foreseeability. According to Article 243(1) of the OZ, the creditor (the injured party) is entitled to reimbursement for the ordinary damage and loss of profit that the debtor (the person who caused the damage) should have foreseen as a possible consequence of the breach of contract on the basis of the facts that were known to him or her at the time or that he or she

---

609. Plavšak et al., *supra* n. 95, at 621.
610. ECLI:SI:VSRS:2013:II.IPS.171.2010.
611. ECLI:SI:VSRS:2013:II.IPS.133.2010. For more information on the calculation of lost profit, please refer to Part VI, Ch. 2, §5.
612. ECLI:SI:VSRS:2002:VIII.IPS.113.2001.
613. *See* Art. 243(3) of the OZ and ECLI:SI:VSLJ:2011:I.CPG.292.2011.
614. *See* Art. 170(1) of the OZ.
615. *See* Art. 170(2) of the OZ.
616. *See* Art. 171 of the OZ.
617. *See* more on the relationship between contractual and delictual or tortious responsibility in General Introduction, §5.

should have known. The principle of foreseeability limits the scope of compensation only if the party breaching the contract acts with the mildest form of fault, namely slight negligence. In cases of fraud or intentional non-performance of the contract, as well as in cases of non-performance due to gross negligence, the creditor has the right to demand compensation from the debtor for the full extent of the damage, including damage resulting from circumstances which could not have been known to the contract breaker.[618]

356. The foreseeability of damage is assessed objectively in case law. The decisive factor is whether a reasonably diligent person (and not the specific contract breacher) would have foreseen the damage that could arise in the event of a breach of contract, based on the facts that were known to him or her at the time of the breach or that he or she should have known. The circumstances that should have been known to the contract breacher are related to the purpose of the contract or the interests of the party faithful to the contract, which is typical of the type of contract breached. These typical, most common interests are presumed to be known by the breaching party regardless of whether they were expressly pointed out by the other party. Conversely, it cannot be presumed that the contract breacher knew or should have known of specific, atypical interests or circumstances. He or she must have had actual knowledge of them. The manner in which he or she learned of them is not essential; typically, the party faithful to the contract discloses them during negotiations, at the conclusion of the contract, or prior to the contract breach. If the contract breacher was not aware of these circumstances, the damage in this respect is not foreseeable. The burden of proof that the breaching party was unaware of atypical, specific circumstances lies with the breaching party.[619]

357. Non-pecuniary damage is the kind of damage that is not financial in nature but is nevertheless legally recognised. In Slovenia, there is a subjective concept of non-pecuniary damage. The mere infringement upon the physical or mental integrity of the injured party (primary consequence) typically does not suffice to give rise to a liability for damages on the part of the responsible party. Instead, a secondary consequence must also occur in the form of physical pain, mental suffering, or fear. Compensation for non-pecuniary damage is thus awarded not for the infringement itself, but for the physical and mental anguish resulting from the infringement upon the physical and mental integrity of the injured party (e.g., not for a broken bone itself, but for the physical pain caused by the fracture; not for an insult itself, but for the mental suffering caused by it).[620] Two exceptions to this concept are non-monetary compensation (referred to as non-monetary satisfaction) for the violation of personal rights and non-pecuniary damage due to the impairment of the reputation of a legal entity.

358. Compensation for non-pecuniary damage can thus be non-monetary or monetary. Non-monetary compensation for non-pecuniary damage is regulated in

618. Cf. Art. 243(2) of the OZ.
619. Cf. ECLI:SI:VSRS:2016:II.IPS.178.2014.
620. Cf. ECLI:SI:VSRS:2016:II.IPS.251.2014 and ECLI:SI:VSRS:2014:II.IPS.63.2012.

Article 178 of the OZ. In the case of a violation of personal rights, the court may order the publication of the judgment or a rectification at the expense of the wrongdoer, or it may order the injured party to retract a statement constituting the violation or to undertake other actions that can achieve the purpose served by the compensation (e.g., an apology, a public apology, a public expression of regret). As previously explained, an objective concept of non-pecuniary damage applies to non-monetary compensation. The measures under Article 178 of the OZ are ordered by the court based on the objective fact that the personal rights of the injured party have been violated, without the need for an additional secondary consequence (such as the occurrence of physical pain, mental suffering, or fear).[621] The sanctions for violations of personal rights provided for in Article 178 of the OZ are not mutually exclusive and may be cumulated.[622] The court is limited in this respect only by the party's claim.[623]

359. Among the legally recognised forms of non-pecuniary damage in general, which already include the violation of another person's personal rights, a distinction must be made between the legally recognised forms of non-pecuniary damage for which the injured party may claim fair monetary compensation. The Slovenian legislator has introduced a 'conditionally' closed system (*numerus clausus*) of forms of non-pecuniary damage in the OZ for which monetary compensation can be claimed. For those forms of non-pecuniary damage that are not legally recognised, no compensation in money can be claimed.[624] The injured party is therefore entitled to fair monetary compensation for physical pain; for mental suffering due to restriction of life activities, disfigurement, defamation of good name and honour, infringement of freedom or personal rights, or death of a close person; for fear; and for damage to the reputation of a legal entity (Article 179(1) of the OZ and Article 183 of the OZ). However, as these legal concepts (such as mental suffering due to disfigurement;[625] and mental suffering due to infringement of personal rights)[626] are legal standards whose content is determined by the court on a case-by-case basis, their scope is open to interpretation by the court in specific instances. Monetary compensation for non-pecuniary damage is awarded to the injured party for physical or mental pain, anguish, or damage to the reputation of a legal entity only if the circumstances of the case justify such compensation.[627] In Slovenian tort law, insignificant non-pecuniary damages are not recognised and do not provide a basis for awarding fair monetary compensation.[628]

621. ECLI:SI:VSRS:2013:II.IPS.623.2009 and ECLI:SI:VSLJ:2019:II.CP.1121.2019.
622. ECLI:SI:VSLJ:2013:I.CP.2570.2012.
623. Cf. Art. 2 of the ZPP and ECLI:SI:VSLJ:2022:I.CPG.99.2022.
624. Cf. ECLI:SI:VSLJ:2018:I.CP.2623.2017, ECLI:SI:VSLJ:2009:II.CP.3323.2009, ECLI:SI:VSLJ:2011:II.CP.2597.2010, ECLI:SI:VSRS:2018:II.IPS.268.2016, ECLI:SI:VSRS:2009:II.IPS.370.2009, etc.
625. *See*, e.g., ECLI:SI:VSCE:1998:CP.83.98.
626. *See*, e.g., ECLI:SI:VSRS:2009:II.IPS.917.2008 and ECLI:SI:VSRS:2015:II.DOR.274.2014.
627. *See* Art. 179(1) and Art. 183 of the OZ.
628. *See*, e.g., ECLI:SI:VSRS:2011:II.IPS.564.2008.

360. As mentioned above, the Slovenian system of legally recognised non-pecuniary damages for which the injured party is entitled to monetary compensation is only 'conditionally' closed. This means that Slovenian tort law is not completely indifferent to changes and developments in social values, culture, and legal awareness. Its timeliness is ensured by judicial practice with a broad and open interpretation of the forms of non-pecuniary damage and sources of mental suffering defined by the legislator.[629] In this regard, the VSRS, for example, has repeatedly recognised mental suffering resulting from the violation of personal rights to a healthy living environment,[630] respect for family life,[631] freedom of choice regarding childbirth,[632] and others. Influenced by the judgment in the *Leitner* case,[633] in which the EU Court of Justice recognised compensation for loss of holiday enjoyment, Slovenian courts must also recognise non-pecuniary damages resulting from loss of holiday enjoyment or time, even if the OZ does not explicitly list this type of damage among the legally recognised forms of non-pecuniary damages. The loss of enjoyment, pleasure, or mental relaxation during a holiday constitutes a violation of the personal right to mental integrity and health. To prove this type of damage, the injured party does not need to separately assert the existence of mental suffering, as stated in Article 179 of the OZ. It is sufficient to claim that the enjoyment of the holiday was not experienced, which implies some psychological discomfort or disturbance of mental balance.[634]

361. Because non-pecuniary goods have no market value and because physical pain, mental suffering, and anguish cannot be erased as if they had never occurred, monetary compensation for non-pecuniary damage, unlike in pecuniary damage cases, is not and cannot be an equivalent for the non-pecuniary harm suffered. Instead, it has the function of satisfaction. Therefore, Article 179(1) of the OZ states that the injured party is entitled to fair monetary compensation for non-pecuniary loss and not to full compensation as specified in Article 169 of the OZ for the pecuniary loss caused. This fair monetary compensation is intended to enable the injured party to afford a level of comfort that he or she would not otherwise have been able to attain, thereby compensating for the non-pecuniary damage suffered.[635] Money is therefore not a price (equivalent) for the non-pecuniary loss suffered. Rather, it acts as an intermediary that provides the victim with a certain level of satisfaction, the purpose of which is to neutralise the pain suffered by the injured party due to the harmful event.[636]

---

629. Cf. Ana Božič Penko, *Razmislek in sodna praksa Vrhovnega sodišča o nekaterih aktualnih vprašanjih odškodninskega prava v zvezi z nepremoženjsko škodo*, Pravni letopis (2016), p. 67.
630. *See*, e.g., ECLI:SI:VSRS:2020:II.IPS.126.2019.A, ECLI:SI:VSRS:2008:II.IPS.567.2008 and ECLI:SI:VSRS:2007:II.IPS.148.2007.
631. *See*, e.g., ECLI:SI:VSRS:2008:II.IPS.53.2006 and ECLI:SI:VSRS:2014:II.IPS.195.2012.
632. ECLI:SI:VSRS:2007:II.IPS.736.2005.
633. ECLI:EU:C:2002:163.
634. *See* ECLI:SI:VSRS:2015:II.IPS.160.2013 and ECLI:SI:VSRS:2022:II.IPS.69.2020.
635. *See* ECLI:SI:VSRS:2012:II.IPS.643.2008, ECLI:SI:VSRS:2012:II.IPS.59.2011, etc.
636. Cf. Ada Polajnar-Pavčnik, *Amerikanizacija odškodninskega prava*, Podjetje in delo 7 (2004), pp. 1158–1166.

362. The amount of monetary compensation for non-pecuniary damage depends on the significance of the interest affected and the purpose of such compensation. However, it must not support tendencies that are incompatible with its nature and purpose.[637] According to established case law, the fundamental principles for determining the amount of monetary compensation for non-pecuniary damage are the principles of individualisation and objective determination of the compensation amount. The principle of individualisation stems from the recognition that each individual is a unique, unrepeatable, and indivisible entity of physical and mental being who experiences his or her physical and mental integrity and interferences with it in a specific way. The principle of individualisation of compensation requires that appropriate financial compensation be determined on the basis of the intensity and duration of the physical and mental pain and fear, taking into account also all the specific circumstances of the individual victim. In assessing these circumstances, it is necessary to consider the subjective peculiarities of the individual victim and his or her perception of physical and mental pain or fear. However, the amount of monetary compensation for non-pecuniary damage cannot solely reflect the victim's individual evaluation of specific consequences – it is important for the principle of individualisation to be balanced by the principle of objective determination. The latter requires that the harmful consequences suffered by the individual victim be assessed in comparison to the harmful consequences suffered by numerous other victims in different cases from case law, as this is a prerequisite for a uniform treatment of damages of different degrees and for determining compensation for them in appropriate proportions. The objective material possibilities of society and case law in similar cases of non-pecuniary judgments must be taken into account.[638]

§4. Pure Economic Loss

363. In the OZ, the concept of pure economic loss is not explicitly mentioned or defined. However, it is equally important to emphasise that it does not limit the forms of pecuniary damage either, so the possibility of compensation for pure economic loss is not excluded. Its recognition in Slovenian law is limited in accordance with the rules governing the compensation for pecuniary damage in the contractual and delictual spheres. Thus, in the older theory, the concept of economic loss was interpreted to include damage that may arise in both the contractual and delictual spheres, involving a situation where a party is unable to operate or produce.[639] In more recent theory, this concept refers to damage that occurs to the property of the injured party without any physical interference with his or her body or belongings.[640] Pure economic loss can thus arise either as a result of a physical interference with the body or property of another person (i.e., not the injured party)

637. *See* Art. 179(2) of the OZ.
638. Cf. ECLI:SI:VSRS:2009:II.IPS.1073.2008, ECLI:SI:VSRS:2014:II.IPS.244.2011, ECLI:SI:VSRS:2015:II.IPS.131.2013, ECLI:SI:VSRS:2019:II.IPS.356.2017, ECLI:SI:VSRS:2020:VIII.IPS.46.2020, etc.
639. *See* Cigoj, *supra* n. 88, at 214.
640. Cf. Možina, *supra* n. 98, at 10.

or without a physical interference with the body or property of another person. An example of the first type of pure economic loss is pecuniary damage suffered by one person (the indirect victim) due to death, injury, or impairment of the health of another person (the direct victim).[641]

364. The protection of pure economic interests is ensured within the framework of the principle of foreseeability in the contractual sphere. In the case of a breach of contract, the creditor is entitled to compensation for the ordinary damages and loss of profits that the debtor should have expected as a result of the breach of contract, based on facts that were known or should have been known to the debtor at the time, irrespective of whether there was interference with the creditor's person or property.[642] Pure economic loss is generally also recognised in the non-contractual (delictual) field, but usually under certain additional assumptions. For example, Slovenian case law rejects general non-contractual (delictual/tortious) liability for false information, advice, or opinions, as this would completely hinder everyday communication due to the burden of potential liability.[643] However, liability for information may be established if there is a so-called special relationship between the information provider and the information recipient (i.e., if the recipient can justifiably rely on the accuracy of the information and the information provider can foresee this) and if a violation of the duty of due care or professional standards is established.[644] Similarly, tort liability for (pure) economic loss arising from defamation or the dissemination of untrue statements is, under Article 177 of the Slovenian OZ, conditioned by an additional requirement that the person defaming the honour of another or making or disseminating untrue allegations about another's past, knowledge, abilities, or any other matter, knows or should have known that the allegations are false. However, there is no liability for pure economic loss caused by someone communicating something untrue about another without knowing it to be false, unless either the disseminator or the recipient of the false information had a genuine interest in doing so. In certain cases, recovery of pure economic loss is expressly excluded by law, such as in the case of liability of event organisers.[645]

§5. Actual and Future Damage

365. From the perspective of the moment in time at which the damage is assessed, the damage can be past (actual) damage or future (anticipated) damage.

641. *See* Arts 172 and 173 of the OZ. *See* more in Part VI, Ch. 4, §1.
642. Možina, *supra* n. 98, at 18.
643. For example, it does not constitute wrongful conduct and there is no liability for damages for advice if one person advises another to bet on a football club which then loses.
644. Cf. ECLI:SI:VSRS:2011:II.IPS.103.2009. The non-contractual liability of certain persons for information is regulated by special laws, for example, the liability of auditors under the Auditing Act (ZRev-2, Official Gazette RS, Nos 65/08, 63/13 – ZS-K, 84/18 and 115/21) and the liability related to the prospectus in a public offer of securities under the Market in Financial Instruments Act (ZTFI-1, Official Gazette RS, Nos 77/18, 17/19 – compr., 66/19 and 123/21).
645. Cf. Art. 157 of the OZ, which stipulates that the organiser of a gathering of a larger number of people indoors or outdoors is liable for 'damage caused by death or bodily injury'.

Past (actual) damage refers to the damage that has already occurred by the time the court decides on the liability for compensation. This type of damage does not need to be predicted, as it can be quantified immediately and is fully matured at the time of the trial.[646] However, the consequences of the harmful event do not necessarily end with the conclusion of the main hearing before the Court of First Instance – the damage may continue to arise or develop in the future. In accordance with the principle of full compensation, the injured party is also entitled to reimbursement for such future damage. Slovenian tort law recognises various types of future damages, both pecuniary damages, such as lost profit and earnings, loss of maintenance or support, destruction or diminution of the injured party's ability to develop and progress, and permanently increased needs of the injured party. Similarly, future non-pecuniary damages are also recognised (Article 182 of the OZ), such as mental pain due to disfigurement, loss of a loved one, and other legally recognised forms of non-pecuniary damages (for more on the latter, *see* Part VI, Chapter 2, §3).

366. The injured party's right to recover lost profit is stipulated in Article 168 of the OZ. In assessing lost profit, account is taken of the profit that could reasonably have been expected in the normal course of events or in specific circumstances, but which could not be realised due to the damaging party's act or omission thereof. From this perspective, the fact that the profit would actually occur in the future and its possible amount cannot be proven with certainty, but can only be inferred with a more or less high degree of probability.[647] According to established case law, the threshold of a sufficient probability, which exceeds 50%, is sufficient for the recognition of compensation for lost profit.[648]

367. The profit that the injured party would have made if the damaging event had not occurred is usually determined based on the normal course of events. The normal course of events refers to the conduct of business to the extent that was foreseeable from previous periods, increased or decreased by the rate of growth or decline of that business in the past.[649] To substantiate his or her claim, the injured party must specify the extent of the business prior to the damaging event, the (total) income and profit, and prove them with at least 50% probability.[650] However, the legal standard of ordinary course of events may not always be suitable for assessing lost profit. It is possible that due to certain special circumstances, such as opening of new markets or a recession, there will be a significant change (increase or decrease) in the volume of the injured party's business during the period for which the lost profit is determined. In such cases, the lost profit is assessed based on these special circumstances. The existence of special circumstances and their impact on the injured party's business must be proven with a probability of more than 50%,

646. ECLI:SI:VSLJ:2019:I.CP.646.2019 and ECLI:SI:VSLJ:2020:II.CP.1312.2020.
647. ECLI:SI:VSRS:2012:II.IPS.100.2011 and ECLI:SI:VSRS:2015:II.IPS.147.2013.
648. *See*, e.g., ECLI:SI:VSRS:2012:II.IPS.913.2008, ECLI:SI:VSRS:2015:II.IPS.147.2013, ECLI:SI:VSRS:2021:II.IPS.94.2020, etc.
649. ECLI:SI:VSRS:2013:II.IPS.107.2011.
650. ECLI:SI:VSRS:2012:II.IPS.913.2008 and ECLI:SI:VSRS:2013:II.IPS.133.2010.

with the burden of proof resting on the party invoking such circumstances.[651] Moreover, the concept of the normal or regular course of events cannot be applied if the injured party did not engage in the activity from which he or she claims the profit before the occurrence of the damaging event but only had plans to do so.[652] In such cases, the volume of business is determined by means of an appropriate market analysis, e.g., by comparing it with the profitability of the revenues of entities conducting this activity in the market.[653] If, for example, it is established that companies engaged in this activity are operating at a loss, one cannot speak of a justified expectation of profit.

368. The principles of full compensation and *compensatio lucri cum damno* must also be consistently observed in the assessment of lost profit. Namely, during the period to which the assessment pertains, the injured party would have incurred certain costs and other expenses in his or her business operations, which were not caused by the non-operation. Therefore, these expenses need to be deducted from the revenues estimated on the basis of the normal course of events or on the basis of specific circumstances.[654] However, the so-called fixed costs that arise regardless of the volume of business operations, even if the injured party is not conducting business at all (e.g., depreciation), are not deducted.[655]

369. Compensation for future damages due to loss of earnings, loss of maintenance or support, destroyed opportunities for advancement, and permanently increased needs of the injured party is regulated in Chapter III, section 7 of the OZ, which contains additional rules on the recovery of pecuniary damages in the event of death, injury, or impairment of health. The peculiarity of such compensation cases lies in the fact that the damage occurs successively over an extended period of time. Compensation for such future damages is typically awarded in the form of a cash annuity (*see* more in Part VI, Chapter 3, §5 and Chapter 4, §1).

370. Non-pecuniary damage, similar to pecuniary damage, can arise in the future, viewed from the perspective of the conclusion of the main hearing. Future non-pecuniary damage can be continuous or successive when there are recurring damages stemming from a single already concluded injurious act,[656] or independent future non-pecuniary damage if the consequences of the harmful event have not yet occurred, but

651. If the injured party claims that the volume of his or her business and the resulting business outcome would have been greater because of these circumstances, they must establish these circumstances. However, if the injuring party claims that, as a result, the volume of the injured party's business and the business outcome would have been smaller, he or she bears the burden of proof regarding this matter. *See* ECLI:SI:VSRS:2013:II.IPS.107.2011 and ECLI:SI:VSMB:2018:I.CP.591.2018.
652. Cf. ECLI:SI:VSRS:2013:II.IPS.133.2010.
653. ECLI:SI:VSRS:2021:II.IPS.94.2020 and ECLI:SI:VSLJ:2015:I.CPG.1102.2013.
654. ECLI:SI:VSRS:2003:II.IPS.17.2003, ECLI:SI:VSRS:2014:III.IPS.111.2011, ECLI:SI:VSLJ:2015:I.CPG.965.2013, etc.
655. ECLI:SI:VSRS:2021:II.IPS.66.2020.
656. The continuously recurring future non-pecuniary damage should not be equated with non-pecuniary damage that mirrors each time with its respective cause (e.g., non-pecuniary damage arising from each instance of always new emissions). The distinction is important from the perspective

it is clear from the normal course of events that they will arise later.[657] The possibility of compensation for future non-pecuniary damage is provided for in Article 182 of the OZ. Pursuant to this article, upon the injured party's request, the court awards compensation for future non-pecuniary damage as well, if it is certain, following the usual course of events, that the damage will also persist in the future. The legal standard of certainty should not be interpreted literally in this context.

371. Future non-pecuniary damage, within the meaning of Article 182 of the OZ, is that whose occurrence is foreseeable during the trial or during the negotiation of an out-of-court settlement by an average prudent injured party and liable party.[658] Established case law considers this type of damage to be encompassed within the amount of non-pecuniary damage compensation awarded by judgment or agreed upon in an out-of-court settlement.[659]

372. Future non-pecuniary damage must be distinguished from the so-called new damage. New damage is the damage, the occurrence of which during the trial or negotiation of an out-of-court settlement that could not have been foreseen following the normal course of events.[660] An issued judgment or concluded settlement does not preclude a compensation claim for these unforeseeable consequences that the injured party could not have contemplated during the trial or the conclusion of an out-of-court settlement. Therefore, the injured party can demand compensation for this new or additional damage in a new proceeding.[661]

§6. Other Costs

373. The injured party is entitled to full compensation in accordance with Article 169 of the OZ. The amount of compensation must put the injured party in the financial position he or she would have been in if the damaging event had not occurred (*see* more in Part VI, Chapter 2, §3). Under certain conditions, the injured party is also entitled to reimbursement of expenses incurred in connection with the remedy, assessment, and recovery of the damage. The expenses incurred may also constitute a financial detriment for the injured party, which the liable party must reimburse. For example, if the injured party's property is destroyed, the calculation of the amount of compensation for the property, which is typically assessed based on the

---

of the statute of limitations for compensation claims. *See* more ECLI:SI:VSRS:2011:II.IPS.68.2011 and ECLI:SI:VSRS:2011:II.IPS.223.2011. Regarding the statute of limitations of the compensation claim in general, *see* Part IV, Ch. 1.

657. ECLI:SI:VSRS:2013:II.IPS.51.2010, ECLI:SI:VSRS:2011:II.IPS.223.2011, ECLI:SI:VSLJ:2014:II.CP.954.2014.1, ECLI:SI:VSRS:2018:II.IPS.309.2016, etc.
658. ECLI:SI:VSLJ:2017:II.CP.218.2017, ECLI:SI:VSLJ:2014:II.CP.1324.2014, ECLI:SI:VSRS:2010:II.IPS.671.2007, etc.
659. ECLI:SI:VSCE:2017:CP.145.2017, ECLI:SI:VSLJ:2015:II.CP.1692.2015, ECLI:SI:VSLJ:2017:II.CP.2021.2016, ECLI:SI:VSRS:2008:II.IPS.413.2006, etc. In this regard, courts are not required to explain whether and to what extent the awarded compensation includes future non-pecuniary damage. *See* ECLI:SI:VSLJ:2017:II.CP.218.2017.
660. Cf. ECLI:SI:VSRS:2014:II.IPS.237.2012 and ECLI:SI:VSRS:2016:II.IPS.187.2014.
661. *See* ECLI:SI:VSRS:2005:VIII.IPS.270.2004 and the case law mentioned there.

fair market value at the time of the trial (*see* more in Part VI, Chapter 3, §1), should also include the costs incurred in connection with the acquisition of a new item.[662] According to Slovenian judicial practice, the legally recognised pecuniary damage also includes the costs incurred by the injured party in connection with the substitutive use of another (similar) item during the time required for the repair of the damaged item or the purchase of a new item.[663] Similarly, when recognising pecuniary damage in cases of death, injury, and health impairment, where the injured party is entitled, among other things, to compensation for the necessary expenses related to medical treatment (*see* more in Part VI, Chapter 4, §1), the costs of obtaining a medical certificate, containing at least the basic information for determining the existence and amount of the damage, may also be recognised for the injured party.[664] Furthermore, according to Article 243(4) of the OZ, the injured party who bears the duty to mitigate the damage is entitled to reimbursement of all expenses incurred in taking reasonable measures to mitigate the damage or to prevent it from increasing, even if these measures did not lead to the mitigation of the damage.[665]

374. The issue of cost allocation in court proceedings is governed by procedural law. According to Article 151 of the ZPP, litigation costs include all expenses incurred during or as a result of the proceedings, including fees for the work of attorneys and other persons entitled to a fee under the law (e.g., court experts, interpreters, detectives, notaries, etc.). The fundamental criterion for the distribution of litigation costs is the criterion of success. A party who is unsuccessful in a legal dispute must reimburse the opposing party and its intervener for all litigation costs.[666] The decisive factor for the reimbursement of costs is the final success of the party and not the success of individual procedural acts.[667] If a party is partially successful in its claim, the court may decide, based on the success achieved, that each party shall bear its own costs, or it may order one party to reimburse the other party and its intervener a reasonable part of the costs. However, if a party succeeds only with a relatively small part of its claim and no separate costs have been incurred for that part, the court may decide that the opposing party must reimburse the entire cost despite the partial defeat.[668]

375. When deciding which litigation costs are to be reimbursed to a party, the court will only take into account the costs it considers necessary for the specific litigation based on a careful assessment of all circumstances.[669] The necessity of the costs is assessed objectively; only those litigation costs are necessary without which

662. ECLI:SI:VSLJ:2021:II.CP.84.2021.
663. ECLI:SI:VSLJ:2014:I.CP.1802.2014 and ECLI:SI:VSLJ:2015:II.CP.240.2015.
664. ECLI:SI:VSLJ:2010:III.CP.2803.2010.
665. ECLI:SI:VSCE:2020:CP.69.2020.
666. Article 154(1) of the ZPP.
667. ECLI:SI:VSLJ:2018:I.CP.742.2018, ECLI:SI:VSLJ:2017:I.CP.1411.2017, ECLI:SI:VSLJ:2018:II.CP.1567.2018, ECLI:SI:VSKP:2007:I.CPG.77.2006, etc.
668. Article 154(2)(3) of the ZPP.
669. Article 155 of the ZPP.

the claim of the plaintiff or the defence of the defendant cannot be asserted.[670] In addition to the costs incurred during the litigation (expenses and fees of the legal representatives, travel expenses, costs for meals and accommodation, compensation for the wages or loss of earnings of parties, witnesses, experts and interpreters, costs for photocopies of documents, etc.), the costs incurred by the injured party prior to the litigation in connection with its preparation may also be necessary. For example, Slovenian judicial practice recognises as necessary costs incurred by the injured party prior to the litigation, such as costs incurred as a result of the injured party initially approaching the insurance company to obtain compensation for damages,[671] costs incurred as a result of hiring a private detective to obtain information on the debtor's assets for the preparation of an enforcement proposal,[672] costs incurred as a result of obtaining pre-litigation expert opinions,[673] etc. While, costs such as those incurred in drafting preparatory submissions where a party merely repeats statements,[674] costs related to responding to an appeal that does not contribute to the decision on the appeal,[675] costs for a second party representative,[676] etc. are considered unnecessary in judicial practice.

376. The correction of the principle of success in litigation is the criterion of fault as defined in Article 156 of the ZPP. Accordingly, regardless of the outcome of the litigation, a party must reimburse the opposing party for costs incurred through his or her fault or an accidental occurrence that happened to him or her (so-called separate costs). These include, for example, costs incurred as a result of the postponement of a hearing due to the failure of the parties to submit their preparatory submissions in time[677] or due to the parties' illness,[678] costs incurred as a result of the delay in withdrawing the lawsuit after the defendant has fulfilled the claim,[679] costs incurred as a result of the defendant's refusal to agree to the withdrawal of the lawsuit after fulfilling the claim,[680] etc. Despite success in the litigation, the plaintiff must bear the entire costs of the proceedings if he or she has filed the lawsuit unnecessarily.[681]

---

670. ECLI:SI:VSLJ:2016:II.CP.2532.2016, ECLI:SI:VSLJ:2018:I.CP.742.2018, ECLI:SI:VSLJ:2018:II.CP.173.2018 and ECLI:SI:VSLJ:2010:I.CP.318.2010.
671. ECLI:SI:VSLJ:2009:II.CP.2005.2009 and ECLI:SI:VSLJ:2013:II.CP.94.2013.
672. ECLI:SI:VSLJ:2000:III.CP.1732.2000.
673. Cf. ECLI:SI:VSRS:2016:II.IPS.195.2015, in which the VSRS ruled that given the severe detrimental consequences suffered by the injured party in the specific case, there was no doubt that the costs of obtaining a pre-litigation expert opinion were necessary, both for the preparation of a well-founded extrajudicial claim against the insurance company (which has its own assessors) and for the filing of a damages claim in litigation in accordance with the criteria set out in Art. 155 of the ZPP. *See also* ECLI:SI:VSLJ:2015:I.CP.1222.2015.
674. ECLI:SI:VDSS:2023:PDP.123.2023.
675. ECLI:SI:VSLJ:2022:I.CPG.212.2022, ECLI:SI:VSLJ:2019:II.CP.728.2019.1.COR, ECLI:SI:VSLJ:2020:II.CPG.375.2020, etc.
676. ECLI:SI:VSLJ:2012:I.CPG.236.2011.
677. ECLI:SI:VSLJ:2012:II.CP.1962.2011.
678. ECLI:SI:VDSS:2009:PDP.1590.2008.
679. ECLI:SI:VSLJ:2016:I.CPG.281.2016 and ECLI:SI:VSLJ:2016:I.CP.3222.2015.
680. ECLI:SI:VSLJ:2013:I.CPG.328.2013.
681. Cf. Art. 157 of the ZPP: 'If the defendant did not give cause for the lawsuit and if it acknowledged the claim made in the lawsuit in response to the lawsuit or at the main hearing, before proceeding with the main matter, the plaintiff must reimburse the defendant for litigation costs.'

377. If a lawsuit ends with a judicial settlement, each party bears its own costs, unless otherwise specified in the judicial settlement. The costs of an unsuccessful judicial settlement are considered litigation costs.[682]

378. The rules regarding the allocation of the costs of proceedings are also provided in the regulations in the area of alternative dispute resolution. In accordance with Article 39(1) of the Arbitration Act,[683] the parties are generally free to agree on the costs of proceedings. However, if the parties have not reached an agreement, the arbitral tribunal shall, at the request of a party, decide in the award or ruling concluding the arbitration proceedings which party shall be obliged and to what extent, to reimburse the opposing party for the costs of the proceedings, including representation costs and the arbitrator's fee, and to bear its own costs. The arbitral tribunal shall make this decision at its own discretion, taking into account the circumstances of each individual case and the outcome of the proceedings. The allocation of costs in mediation proceedings is similarly regulated. Unless the parties have agreed otherwise, each party bears its own costs, while the joint mediation costs are divided equally between the parties.[684]

§7. Mitigation of Damages

379. The injured party's duty to mitigate damages is stipulated in Article 243(4) of the OZ and applies to both contractual and non-contractual (tortious) liability obligations.[685] The injured party must take all reasonable measures to reduce or prevent the damage from increasing; otherwise, the responsible party may demand a reduction of the compensation (objection based on breach of the duty to mitigate damages).[686] This means that the compensation is reduced by an amount by which the damage could have been smaller if the injured party had fulfilled his or her duty to mitigate the damage (had acted proactively).

380. The injured party's duty to mitigate damages derives from fundamental principles of Slovenian law of obligations, in particular the principle of conscientiousness and honesty (*načelo vestnosti in poštenja*). It mandates that participants in obligations relationships must not solely pursue their own interests, but also consider the interests of the opposing party.[687] The duty to mitigate damages helps to establish a balance between rights and obligations in obligations relationships,

682. Article 159 of the ZPP.
683. Official Gazette RS, No. 45/08.
684. Article 18(2) of the Mediation in Civil and Commercial Matters Act (Official Gazette RS, No. 56/08).
685. Cf. Art. 243(5) of the OZ.
686. The OZ imposes an obligation on the injured party to act diligently to mitigate damages both during the occurrence of the damage and even after it has already occurred (*see* ECLI:SI:VSLJ:2015:I.CPG.1710.2014).
687. Cf. Art. 5 of the OZ.

enabling equal treatment of the parties and preventing abuse by one party to the detriment of the other. It serves to prevent unnecessary damages by promoting practical conduct and prudence on the part of the injured party, thus helping to avert unwarranted consequences and the further spread of harm. Consequently, the concept of 'duty to mitigate' also encompasses the principle of diligence as set out in Article 6 of the OZ. In this respect, the injured party is expected to be proactive rather than passive after a damaging event, actively seeking to reduce the damage by all reasonable means if feasible.[688] The fulfilment of the duty to mitigate cannot be enforced upon the injured party, as it is not a legally enforceable obligation. However, Slovenian law sanctions the passivity of the injured party by granting the responsible party the right to demand a reduction in compensation. The duty to mitigate is therefore also in the injured party's own interest.

381. Which measures of the injured party are reasonable to reduce the damage or to prevent its increase is assessed by the court, taking into account the circumstances of the specific case.[689] In Slovenian judicial practice, measures deemed reasonable may be, for example, concluding a supply contract with an alternative supplier in order to prevent disconnection from the distribution network;[690] accepting another employment contract due to removal from the position of director;[691] selling goods to a third party, even at a significant discount;[692] renting a substitute vehicle due to the inability to use one's own vehicle;[693] transporting wood across one's own property to prevent it from deteriorating,[694] etc. The injured party is never required to make disproportionate efforts or incur excessive costs. It is also significant whether the tortfeasor can rectify the cause of the damage on his or her own. Despite the injured party's duty to mitigate, the tortfeasor is not absolved of his or her own obligation to reduce or prevent further damage. If the tortfeasor can personally reduce or prevent further damage, he or she cannot demand that the injured party do so on his or her behalf. In such a case, the duty to mitigate damage does not fall upon the injured party.[695] However, this does not mean that the injured party is always unconditionally exempt from the duty to mitigate when rectifying the cause of the damage (also) falls within the sphere of the tortfeasor. This is because a situation could arise in which

688. Cf. ECLI:SI:VSLJ:2010:I.CP.4434.2009.
689. The court must appropriately assess the legal standard of 'reasonable measures' as set out in Art. 243(4) of the OZ (*see* more in ECLI:SI:VSLJ:2010:II.CP.2814.2009). Thus, in ECLI:SI:VSLJ:2010:I.CP.4434.2009, the court held that renting the apartment, in which the injured parties could not live due to mould, to a third party would not have been a reasonable measure to mitigate the damage It stated that it could not be reproached to the plaintiffs that they had not rented the apartment, concerning which they had asserted defects, to reduce the incurred damage. Due to the poor condition of the apartment (mould) as a consequence of construction defects, they had been even forced to move out themselves, and they could potentially have been held liable for damages to the tenants as well.
690. ECLI:SI:VSCE:2022:II.CPG.56.2022 and ECLI:SI:VSCE:2022:II.CPG.47.2022.
691. ECLI:SI:VDSS:2022:PDP.18.2022 and ECLI:SI:VSRS:2004:VIII.IPS.14.2004.
692. ECLI:SI:VSRS:2014:II.IPS.8.2012.
693. ECLI:SI:VSLJ:2021:I.CP.941.2021.
694. ECLI:SI:VSLJ:2022:II.CP.1363.2022.
695. ECLI:SI:VSRS:2006:III.IPS.98.2004.

such a duty is a proportionally lighter burden for the injured party than for the tortfeasor.[696] The burden of proof that the injured party did not take all reasonable measures to mitigate the damage lies with the tortfeasor.[697]

382. The injured party must not be placed in a worse position by the fulfilment of the duty to mitigate damages. Therefore, the injured party is entitled to claim reimbursement of the costs incurred as a result of taking reasonable measures to reduce or prevent the increase of the damage.[698] This applies even if the party was not able to reduce the damage despite implementing reasonable measures.[699]

696. ECLI:SI:VSRS:2017:III.IPS.86.2015.
697. ECLI:SI:VSLJ:2014:I.CP.1962.2014 and ECLI:SI:VSLJ:2013:II.CP.1768.2012.
698. ECLI:SI:VSCE:2020:CP.69.2020.
699. Damjan Možina, *Odškodninska odgovornost za kršitev pogodbe*, Podjetje in delo 2 (2016), p. 281.

Chapter 3. Assessment and Compensation of Damages

§1. Objective Versus Subjective

383. Compensation for pecuniary losses is determined in Slovenian law according to objective criteria based on prices at the time of the court decision unless the law stipulates otherwise.[700] If the victim's property was destroyed, the fair market value of the property is generally decisive for determining compensation, i.e., the value that the destroyed property would have achieved on the market in the given period.[701] The injured party, who bears the burden of proof regarding the existence and the amount of the damage, cannot succeed by claiming and proving that the destroyed property was acquired at a higher price.[702] Even if the market value cannot be determined because there is no relevant market (e.g., unique art pieces, historical clothing), the determination of compensation is not entirely arbitrary. In a specific case where there were no comparable vehicles with similar characteristics on the Slovenian market, the court applied the method of establishing the market value of equivalent vehicles (considering age, condition, and mileage) on the broader market of other EU Member States.[703] Also, in the case of damaging an object, compensation is determined according to objective criteria, specifically based on the actual cost of repairs (if the cost of repairs has already been incurred) or the prices for such repairs at the time of the trial (if the damaged object has not yet been repaired at the time of the trial). As explained in Part VI, Chapter 2, §3, the lost profit is also determined objectively, by taking into account the normal course of events or special circumstances, and not, for example, on the basis of the victim's subjective plans regarding the scope and outcome of his or her business in the future.

384. It is characteristic of all non-pecuniary damages that they cannot be valued using objective or market criteria, as non-pecuniary assets are not subject to legal transactions and therefore have no market value. Nevertheless, the method of determining monetary compensation for non-pecuniary damage is 'objectified' in terms of principles that are applied in judicial practice in the valuation (these principles include the principle of objectively conditioned amount of monetary compensation and the principle of individualisation; *see* more in Part VI, Chapter 2, §3) as well as, for example, through the publicly accessible database of non-pecuniary damages

700. Article 168(2) of the OZ. The solution where compensation is determined based on the prices at the time of the court decision (rather than, for example, based on the prices at the time of the occurrence of the damage) is of crucial importance for the consistent and full realisation of the principle of full compensation. This provision ensures that the real value of the compensation awarded is preserved. Although this provision can be found in the chapter on pecuniary damage, Slovenian judicial practice has extended its application to the assessment of non-pecuniary damage as well. Cf. ECLI:SI:VSKP:2010:CP.901.2009, ECLI:SI:VSLJ:2010:III.CP.2803.2010, etc.

701. ECLI:SI:VSLJ:2017:I.CP.267.2017, ECLI:SI:VSLJ:2021:II.CP.84.2021 and ECLI:SI:VSLJ:2019:II.CP.2232.2018.

702. ECLI:SI:VSRS:2011:III.IPS.131.2008.

703. ECLI:SI:VSLJ:2021:II.CP.84.2021.

(Non-Pecuniary Damage Database (NEGM)) maintained by the VSRS,[704] where comparisons of awarded amounts for non-pecuniary damage in similar cases are possible (*see* more in Part VI, Chapter 3, §3).

385. An exception to the objective assessment of compensation for pecuniary losses is the concept of the 'price of special affection' (*pretium affectionis*). According to Article 168(4) of the OZ, if a thing has been intentionally destroyed or damaged, the court may assess compensation based on the value that the thing had for the injured party. In this concept, elements of pecuniary and non-pecuniary damage are combined, and compensation is assessed both objectively and subjectively (or objectively-subjectively). The concept of the price of special affection is, despite its placement within the chapter of the OZ regarding the restitution of pecuniary damage, a unique manifestation of the emotional distress due to the destruction of or damage to a thing to which the injured party had a special attachment. In addition to compensation for pecuniary loss, which is objectively assessed in accordance with the principle of full compensation, the victim is entitled to compensation for the non-pecuniary damage resulting from emotional distress caused by the loss of the thing. When assessing the subjective value of the thing, the criteria developed in Slovenian judicial practice for the assessment of fair monetary compensation for non-pecuniary damages must be taken into account (*see more* in Part VI, Chapter 2, §3).[705] Since the assessment of compensation based on the price of special affection is an exception and relates to the subjective value of the destroyed or damaged thing, it must be interpreted narrowly.[706] In order to be awarded compensation based on the price of special affection, the victim must prove a genuine attachment to the destroyed or damaged thing. As per Article 131(1) of the OZ, only slight negligence is presumed as the mildest form of fault; therefore, the victim must assert and prove the tortfeasor's intention to destroy or damage his or her property.

§2. Concrete Versus Abstract

386. Based on the method of assessment, compensation can be divided into concrete and abstract categories. Concrete compensation is determined based on the specific circumstances of each case and awarded in the amount established through this process, in accordance with the fundamental principle of full compensation for pecuniary loss or fair compensation for non-pecuniary loss (*see* Part VI, Chapter 2, §3). In contrast, abstract compensation refers to situations where compensation is awarded in a predetermined amount without establishing or proving the actual extent of the damage. An example of abstract compensation is lump-sum compensation. Slovenian case law recognises the validity of agreements between contracting parties in bilateral agreements concerning the amount of possible compensation in case of breach of contract, which aims to avoid the burden of proving the extent

704. The NEGM database is accessible at https://www.sodnapraksa.si/.
705. Plavšak et al., *supra* n. 95, at 629.
706. ECLI:SI:VSRS:2001:II.IPS.17.2001.

of the damage.[707] Compensation is also abstractly determined in lump-sum amounts in cases prescribed by law, e.g., Article 180 of the ZDR-1,[708] Article 137(3) of the Public Employees Act,[709] Article 18(4) of the Compulsory Motor Vehicle Liability Insurance Act,[710] etc.

387. A type of legally prescribed abstract compensation also includes default interest on arrears as a civil sanction for delays in the fulfilment of monetary obligations. In the case of late payment, the creditor does not need to assert or prove the occurrence of specific damage due to the debtor's delay in payment; there is an indisputable presumption that the creditor has suffered damage in the amount of the default interest. However, the creditor may demand the difference up to full compensation if the actual damage incurred exceeds the amount of the default interest;[711] in this case, the compensation is determined specifically. The prescribed interest rate for default interest in Slovenia is the main rate increased by eight percentage points and applies for a six-month period starting from 1 January or 1 July.[712] Nevertheless, the prescribed interest rate for default interest does not apply if the creditor and the debtor agree otherwise.[713]

388. An example of the concrete and abstract compensation assessment can also be found in contract law within a sales contract that has been terminated. In the case of a thing with a daily or market price, Article 504 of the OZ prescribes an abstract method for assessing compensation. A party loyal to the contract may claim the difference between the price stipulated in the contract and the daily market price of the thing on the day the contract is terminated on the market where the transaction was conducted or on an alternative market (if there is no daily price on the market where the transaction took place). In this context, a loyal seller is not required to prove the cost price of the thing that would have been delivered to the buyer under the sales contract and a loyal buyer is not required to prove the selling price at which the

707. ECLI:SI:VSRS:2011:III.IPS.19.2008, ECLI:SI:VSRS:2009:II.IPS.104.2007 and ECLI:SI:VSRS:2012:III.IPS.80.2009.A.
708. 'If determining the amount of the actual damage would result in disproportionate costs, the compensation may be assessed in a lump sum determined by the collective agreement, except in the cases referred to in Article 8 of this Act.'
709. Official Gazette RS, Nos 63/07 – official consolidated text, 65/08, 69/08 – ZTFI-A, 69/08 – ZZavar-E, 40/12 – ZUJF, 158/20 – ZIntPK-C, 203/20 – ZIUPOPDVE, 202/21 – Constitutional Court decision and 3/22 – ZDeb. 'If determining the amount of damage would result in disproportionate costs, the compensation is assessed in a lump sum, if the cases of damage and the amount of the lump sum compensation are specified in the collective agreement.'
710. Official Gazette RS, Nos 93/07 – official consolidated text, 40/12 – ZUJF, 33/16 – PZ-F and 41/17 – PZ-G. 'Regardless of the provisions of the first and third paragraphs of this article, insurance companies are obliged to pay the Institute for Health Insurance of Slovenia an advance flat-rate compensation for damage caused to the institute due to the death or injuries of insured persons in traffic accidents.'
711. Cf. Art. 380 of the OZ.
712. Article 2 of the Prescribed Interest Rate For Default Interest Act (Official Gazette RS, No. 11/07 – official consolidated text).
713. Cf. Art. 379 of the OZ and Art. 1(2) of the Prescribed Interest Rate For Default Interest Act.

thing would have been resold.[714] Instead, the compensation is determined in the abstract as the difference between the agreed price and the daily market price of the thing. However, Article 505 of the OZ prescribes a concrete method for assessing the compensation. If the object of the sale is a specific quantity of substitute goods (genus) and a party loyal to the contract performs a cover sale (i.e., the seller sells the item to another buyer) or a cover purchase (i.e., the buyer buys the item from another seller), the party may claim the difference between the purchase price stipulated in the contract and the purchase price in the case of a cover sale or cover purchase. However, a party loyal to the contract who has been compensated by either an abstract or specific calculation method under Article 505 of the OZ retains the right to claim further compensation for any additional damage under Article 506 of the OZ, provided he or she proves it.

389. In Slovenian legal theory, a division of compensation into concrete and abstract is also observed in relation to the method of restoring pecuniary losses. If a situation is restored to what it would have been if the damaging event had not occurred (e.g., a damaged thing is repaired or another identical thing of the same kind is provided in place of the destroyed one), the compensation is concrete. However, if the liable party provides the injured party with compensation in money, this constitutes abstract compensation.[715] As already explained (*see* Part VI, Chapter 1, §1), the injured party has in principle the right to choose between these two methods of recovery of the pecuniary damage under Article 164(4) of the OZ.[716] There are two sets of exceptions to this rule. The injured party cannot claim restitution if the previous state (or a state that did not yet exist) is impossible to restore, or if the court believes that the liable party is not obliged to do so.[717] However, the injured party is not entitled to claim monetary compensation if the circumstances of the case justify restitution.[718] Such circumstances are rarely met according to case law, as the compensation in kind (even if feasible) often does not fully remedy the damage.[719] In the specific case, the court ruled that the injured party's object still existed, was not damaged or otherwise worn out, and the liable party was willing to return it.

714. Cf. Nina Plavšak, in: Plavšak et al., *Obligacijski zakonik (OZ) (splošni del) s komentarjem, 3. knjiga* (2004), pp. 294–295.
715. Cigoj, *supra* n. 88, at 234.
716. ECLI:SI:VSRS:2013:II.IPS.494.2009, ECLI:SI:VSCE:2020:CP.69.2020, ECLI:SI:VSLJ:2019:II.CP.333.2019, ECLI:SI:VSLJ:2017:I.CPG.1209.2016, etc.
717. Article 164(3) of the OZ. On the one hand, restoration of the previous state is not possible, for example, in the case of destruction of a specifically identified item. On the other hand, restitution in kind is not suitable, for example, in cases of so-called economic total loss, where the repair of the thing is technically feasible but would result in (significantly) higher costs than the value of the thing before the damage. Cf. ECLI:SI:VSLJ:2016:II.CPG.1244.2016 and ECLI:SI:VSLJ:2017:II.CP.1281.2017.
718. Article 164(4) of the OZ.
719. ECLI:SI:VSRS:2019:II.IPS.25.2018. If the damage is not completely eliminated by restoring the previous state, the responsible person is obliged to pay compensation in money for the remainder of the damage (Art. 164(2) of the OZ).

Since restitution is fully possible in this case, it would be unfair to impose monetary compensation on the liable party and allow him or her to keep an object that has no practical value for him or her.[720]

§3. Methods of Assessing Damages

390. The OZ does not define specific methods for assessing damages but instead provides fundamental principles that serve as a basis for determining compensation for pecuniary and non-pecuniary losses. For example, the determination of compensation based on prices at the time of the court's decision;[721] the calculation of lost profits based on the normal course of events or specific circumstances;[722] the principle of full compensation and the principle of foreseeability;[723] the rule that monetary compensation for non-pecuniary damages depends on the significance of the interest affected and the purpose of the compensation, while also ensuring that it does not endorse tendencies that are incompatible with its nature and purpose,[724] etc. The question of how to specifically calculate the amount of compensation in accordance with legal principles, given the circumstances of a particular case, is an issue addressed by both economic and legal theory as well as judicial practice. However, since courts generally lack the necessary expertise to calculate damages accurately, this task is entrusted to experts in the relevant field. The expert's method must not exclude the principles set forth by the OZ. A method that contradicts the legal principles is not considered valid.[725]

391. The baseline for the assessment of (all types of) pecuniary damage is the principle of full compensation, which in the field of contracts is limited by the principle of foreseeability (*see more* in Part VI, Chapter 2, §3). It is a matter of calculating the difference between the hypothetical financial situation of the injured party as it would have been without the damaging event and the actual financial situation of the injured party after the damaging event – this difference constitutes the compensation. However, since the injured party's financial situation might also be influenced by numerous other factors unrelated to the damaging event (e.g., changes in the capital market), the calculation must be limited to the reduction of the injured party's assets or the prevention of their growth in connection with the damaging event.[726] The determination of ordinary damages is relatively straightforward, as it pertains to past damages, which are usually determined based on expenses or costs already incurred, using documentary evidence (e.g., repair bills, bills for renting replacement items, funeral expenses, medical bills, etc.). However, when assessing ordinary damage, different methods are used in judicial practice, taking into consideration the circumstances of each specific case, such as the fair market value

720. ECLI:SI:VSLJ:2017:I.CPG.1209.2016.
721. *See* Art. 168(2) of the OZ.
722. *See* Art. 168(3) of the OZ.
723. *See* Arts 169 and 243(1) of the OZ.
724. *See* Art. 179(2) of the OZ.
725. ECLI:SI:VSRS:2010:III.IPS.122.2008.
726. Cf. Možina, *supra* n. 698, at 282.

method,[727] the cost-based method,[728] the total loss method,[729] the loss of increment due to pollution method,[730] the licensing analogy method,[731] etc.

392. A greater challenge is the calculation of lost profit. This is calculated using the equation '*revenue – variable costs = lost profit*.'[732] Similar methods are employed as in the financial forecasting of the future performance of economic entities. If the injured party was engaged in the same activity prior to the damaging event, the method of calculating lost profit based on past operations is usually applied. On the basis of past business activity, it is calculated how much revenue the injured party would have recorded if the business had proceeded normally, and how much costs such business activity would have incurred.[733]

393. If the calculation of the lost profit is not possible in this way or is inappropriate considering the circumstances of the specific case, other methods are applied (e.g., the method of a competitor's actual sales,[734] the method of comparing the profitability of the revenues of other companies engaged in the same activity on the market,[735] the method of the achieved profit of the harming party,[736] etc.).

394. A particular challenge is the calculation of future pecuniary damages in cases of death, injury, and health impairment, particularly when determining the so-called capitalised annuity (*see more* in Part VI, Chapter 3, §5).

395. Equitable monetary compensation for non-pecuniary damage, which aims to provide satisfaction to the injured party, unlike monetary compensation for pecuniary damage, cannot be quantified using mathematical formulas.[737] The basis for calculating monetary compensation for non-pecuniary loss lies in the principles of individualisation and objective conditioning (*see* more in Part VI, Chapter 2, §3). The courts establish the intensity and duration of the injured party's suffering through hearings and other evidence, usually with the help of medical experts. When assessing the consequences of damages for a particular injured party in comparison with the consequences suffered by other injured parties in similar cases, the courts use either the publicly accessible NEGM of the VSRS, which contains case law dating back to 1991 and is freely accessible to all users,[738] or collections of

727. *See* ECLI:SI:VSLJ:2011:I.CP.956.2011, ECLI:SI:VSLJ:2019:II.CP.2232.2018, etc.
728. *See* ECLI:SI:VSRS:2007:II.IPS.482.2005, ECLI:SI:VSRS:2018:III.IPS.79.2016, ECLI:SI:VSLJ:2014:III.CP.2675.2014, etc.
729. *See* ECLI:SI:VSLJ:2015:I.CPG.784.2015.
730. *See* ECLI:SI:VSLJ:2016:II.CP.511.2016.
731. *See* Art. 121.a of the Industrial Property Act (Official Gazette RS, Nos 51/06 – official consolidated text, 100/13, 23/20, 76/23) and ECLI:SI:VSRS:2018:III.IPS.102.2016.
732. The same result is achieved by a method in which fixed costs are added to income after deducting all expenses. Cf. ECLI:SI:VSLJ:2019:II.CP.772.2019.1.
733. ECLI:SI:VSLJ:2018:II.CP.2042.2017.
734. ECLI:SI:VSLJ:2016:I.CPG.1780.2015.
735. ECLI:SI:VSRS:2021:II.IPS.94.2020.
736. ECLI:SI:VSRS:2014:III.IPS.98.2013.
737. Cf. ECLI:SI:VSRS:2003:II.IPS.233.2002.
738. The NEGM database is accessible at https://www.sodnapraksa.si/.

compensation cases previously decided by the Supreme Court. As a general tool for finding and comparing similar cases, the so-called Fischer system has been adopted in Slovenian judicial practice. According to this system, injuries are classified into six basic groups based on their severity. This system facilitates a rough comparison of compensations awarded for similar injury severity across different injury groups. However, providing a definition of injury severity according to Fischer is not obligatory in a judicial decision and does not constitute a substantial violation of procedural provisions.[739]

§4. Equitable Limitation of Damages

396. In Slovenian law, as in other legal systems, it is possible to deviate from the principle of full compensation and impose the payment of reduced compensation on the liable party if equity so requires.

397. The first possibility to reduce compensation for reasons of (social) fairness is stipulated in Article 170(1) of the OZ. The court may, taking into account the financial situation of the injured party, order the liable party to pay a lesser compensation than the amount of the damage if the damage was not caused intentionally or due to gross negligence and the liable party has a weak financial situation that would lead to deprivation if he or she had to pay the full compensation. In order to apply this provision, three conditions must be cumulatively fulfilled: The financial situation of the injured party allows for a reduction of the compensation, the payment of the full compensation would lead to a deprivation of the liable party, and the damage was caused by slight negligence.[740] The reduction of compensation under this provision must be requested by the liable party; the court does not consider this on its own initiative.[741] Reduction of compensation may also occur if the wrongdoer caused the damage while acting in the interest of the injured party (e.g., a friend helps another friend move house and accidentally breaks a vase while carrying it). In this case, according to Article 170(2) of the OZ, the court may, at the request of the liable party, determine a lesser compensation, taking into account the diligence exercised by the liable party in his or her own affairs (*diligentia quam suis rebus*). The provisions concerning the reduction of compensation for pecuniary damage shall also apply mutatis mutandis to non-pecuniary damage.[742]

398. Based on equity, it is possible to reduce, exclude, or otherwise allocate compensation for damages in certain other cases as well. If a person fails to provide assistance to another whose life or health is obviously endangered without endangering himself or herself, he or she is liable for the resulting damage that should have been foreseen under the circumstances of the case. However, the court may exempt such a person from reimbursing the damage caused by the failure to render

739. ECLI:SI:VSRS:2015:II.IPS.247.2015.
740. Cf. ECLI:SI:VSRS:2014:II.IPS.34.2014.
741. Cf. ECLI:SI:VSRS:1996:II.IPS.956.94 and ECLI:SI:VSLJ:2022:II.CP.1559.2022.
742. Cf. Art. 185 of the OZ.

necessary assistance, if justice so requires.[743] In the case of a traffic accident involving motor vehicles for which no motor vehicle owner is at fault or the fault cannot be attributed to anyone, the owners shall be equally liable for the damage incurred. In this regard, the court may, if justice so requires (e.g., significant disparity in vehicle value, a substantial difference in the level of danger), allocate responsibility differently.[744] The solution, which is substantively identical, is specified in the OZ in the section on joint and several liability for damages. Jointly liable parties are obligated to cover their share of the damages in the internal (recourse) relationship. The court determines this share based on the degree of fault of each individual joint debtor and the gravity of the consequences resulting from their actions. If it is not possible to ascertain the shares, it is presumed that the shares are equal, unless justice dictates otherwise.[745]

399. In certain cases, justice requires the opposite solution, i.e., the extension of the injured party's possibilities to obtain compensation. Article 146 of the OZ addresses two instances of non-culpable liability based on fairness (responsibility in equity). The first paragraph establishes the liability of a legally incapacitated person for damages when no compensation can be obtained from the person who should have exercised control over him or her (parents, guardian, daycare, etc.). The second paragraph defines the liability of parents who are not otherwise responsible for the damage if the damage was caused by a capable minor who lacks personal assets. In both cases, an additional condition for the liability of the non-culpable party is that fairness dictates this, in particular by comparing the financial situation of the non-culpable party (the legally incapacitated wrongdoer or the parents) and the injured party. If, for example, the financial situation of the injured party allows him or her to bear the damage inflicted without major difficulties, then there may be no ground for the liability of the non-culpable party.

§5. Methods of Payment

I. Lump Sum

400. Monetary compensation is determined as a lump sum when the damage is a one-off occurrence and can be compensated with a one-off payment.[746] We refer to damage as a one-off if it results from a single event that will not happen again (e.g., if someone breaks a valuable vase, the vase cannot be broken again – it is a loss that cannot recur). Therefore, compensation is usually awarded in a single

743. Cf. Art. 161 of the OZ. Although this is not explicitly stipulated in the OZ, based on the argument *a maiori ad minus*, it is possible to infer that the court, for the sake of fairness, may also reduce compensation and not merely exempt the liable party.

744. *See* Part III, Ch. 1.

745. Cf. Art. 188 of the OZ.

746. Cigoj, *supra* n. 88, at 238.

amount for past damage that has already occurred at the time the court decides on compensation, as this damage does not need to be predicted.[747]

401. When the damage occurs periodically and gradually over an extended period of time, the monetary compensation is typically determined in the form of an annuity. An annuity comes into question especially if the pecuniary damage is due to an interference with the injured party's body or health (more on this in the next chapter). However, even in these cases, the court may award compensation in the form of a lump sum (i.e., capitalised annuity) if there is a specific vested interest on the part of the injured party.[748] Article 167(4) of the OZ explicitly provides for a scenario in which the liable party fails to provide insurance for the payment of the annuity determined by the court and the injured party may nevertheless claim compensation in the form of a lump sum for other serious reasons. Among these reasons, Slovenian judicial practice includes the (initiated or expected) procedure of termination of the liable entity,[749] the purchase of an apartment that suits the injured party's medical condition,[750] the elimination of uncertainty about future payments because the wrongdoer is a foreigner who is only temporary residing in the RS,[751] etc. The amount of the lump sum is determined based on the amount and the expected duration of the annuity, deducting appropriate interest.[752] The final decision on compensation in the form of a lump sum or an annuity rests with the court, which is not bound by the injured party's claim.[753]

II. Annuities

402. As mentioned above, compensation in the form of an annuity is determined when the damage is prospective and successive (i.e., occurs periodically and gradually over an extended period of time). This type of damage cannot be precalculated due to the uncertainty about its duration and the change in circumstances.[754] Therefore, the OZ prefers the annuity to a lump sum compensation in the discussed circumstances. The nature of an annuity better suits the gradual development of the damage, as it places the injured party in a similar position as if he or she was receiving a personal income that he or she has lost due to the damaging event.[755] An annuity compensation is also more adaptable if the circumstances on which the court based its decision change (if the damage decreases, the annuity can be reduced and

747. E.g., compensation for regular damage due to the destruction of or damage to the injured party's property, compensation for the injured party's loss of earnings during treatment, etc.
748. Cf. Art. 167(4) and 167(5) of the OZ.
749. ECLI:SI:VSLJ:2009:II.CP.2362.2009.
750. ECLI:SI:VSRS:2015:II.IPS.59.2014 and ECLI:SI:VSRS:2018:II.IPS.256.2017.
751. ECLI:SI:VSRS:2010:II.IPS.407.2009.
752. Cf. Art. 167(4) of the OZ.
753. ECLI:SI:VSRS:2010:II.IPS.407.2009, ECLI:SI:VDSS:2014:PDP.990.2013, etc.
754. ECLI:SI:VSRS:1998:II.IPS.253.96.
755. ECLI:SI:VSRS:2010:II.IPS.407.2009.

vice versa), whereas a lump sum compensation cannot be adapted to changing circumstances.[756] Lastly, an annuity is also more favourable to the liable party, who is not obligated to repay the damage all at once before it occurs.

403. The OZ does not define the term 'annuity.' Under this term, we understand a monetary compensation that is paid periodically in predetermined amounts.[757]

404. According to Article 167(1) of the OZ, compensation for death, bodily injury, or impairment of health generally takes the form of an annuity, either for life[758] or for a specified period. The latter is only exceptionally considered if it is known in advance when the right to the annuity will expire (e.g., if the deceased regularly supported a nephew in his or her studies, which the nephew will soon complete). An annuity is usually set as a monthly payment, but the court may also set an annuity for a longer period (e.g., an annual annuity) or a shorter period (e.g., a weekly annuity).[759]

405. Since death, bodily injury, and impairment of health are not in themselves pecuniary losses but may result in a financial loss recognised by the law, the following provisions of the OZ explicitly identify the types of pecuniary damage for which compensation is (usually) in the form of an annuity. These include loss of maintenance or regular support,[760] loss of earnings due to the injured party's complete or partial inability to work, damage caused by the injured party's permanently increased needs, and damage due to the destruction or reduction of the injured party's potential for further development and progress.[761]

406. Despite the many advantages of an annuity that is paid periodically over a longer period of time, it always entails a certain risk for the injured party that the liable party might later become financially incapable (insolvent). In this regard, according to Article 167(3) of the OZ, the injured party is entitled to request insurance for the payment of the annuity, unless this is not appropriate in the circumstances (e.g., if there is no risk of the debtor becoming insolvent because the debtor is an insurance company, a bank, or another stable financial organisation). If the liable party fails to provide insurance despite a court order, the injured party may demand a lump sum payment (capitalised annuity) equal to the sum of the amounts

756. Cf. ECLI:SI:VSRS:2018:II.IPS.256.2017.
757. ECLI:SI:VSRS:1998:II.IPS.253.96, ECLI:SI:VSLJ:2019:I.CP.646.2019 and ECLI:SI:VSLJ:2020:II.CP.1312.2020.
758. The term 'for life' should not be understood literally in this context, as the right to the annuity does not necessarily cease with the death of the creditor, but also for other reasons (e.g., retirement of the injured party, improvement of the injured party's health, the children whom the injured party supported acquire their own means, etc.). In this regard, a more appropriate wording is that the annuity is set for an indefinite period of time or for a specified period of time.
759. Article 167(2) of the OZ.
760. Article 173(2) of the OZ.
761. Article 174(2) of the OZ.

of the annuity payments that he or she would receive based on the projected duration of the annuity, adjusted to the current value less appropriate interest.[762] The injured party may also request payment of a lump sum instead of an annuity immediately or at a later date for other serious reasons (*see more* in the previous chapter).[763]

407. The court decides on the claim for annuity payment based on assessments of the normal course of events from the point of view of the damaging event.[764] Since certainty about future facts is conceptually excluded in such decisions, the Slovenian legislator has had to address situations where circumstances change after a judgment has been issued – circumstances that the court has taken into account when determining the annuity – or new circumstances arise that either justify a higher annuity or require its reduction or cancellation. In this regard, Article 175 of the OZ stipulates that the court may prospectively increase the annuity at the request of the injured party, or reduce or cancel it at the request of the liable party if there is a substantial change in the circumstances that were taken into account when the previous decision was issued. According to Slovenian case law, only circumstances that occurred after the conclusion of the main hearing before the Court of First Instance can serve as the basis for modifying the annuity.[765] Not every change in circumstances after the conclusion of the main hearing is sufficient, but only those that meet the legal standard for significantly changed circumstances. Reasons for increasing the annuity include, for example, a general increase in wages[766] or a substantial change in the value of money.[767] Conversely, there may be a reduction or cancellation of the annuity may occur in cases such as improvement in the injured party's health condition,[768] the injured party reaching retirement age,[769] or the exhaustion of the insurance sum.[770]

408. The right to an annuity is a personal right of the injured party, as it is granted to him or her specifically due to his or her loss. Therefore, Article 176(1) of the OZ stipulates that this right is not transferable through legal transactions between living parties (*inter vivos*). However, annuity payments already due may be transferred if the compensation amount is determined by a written agreement between the parties or by a legally binding court decision.[771]

409. Since only property rights and not personal rights are inheritable, the right to a monetary annuity is also not inheritable. However, due annuity payments are

762. Article 167(3) and 167(4) of the OZ.
763. Article 167(5) of the OZ.
764. ECLI:SI:VSRS:2016:II.IPS.3.2015, ECLI:SI:VSRS:2019:II.IPS.189.2017.
765. ECLI:SI:VSLJ:2015:II.CP.3332.2014, ECLI:SI:VSLJ:2013:II.CP.1812.2013, ECLI:SI:VSLJ:2015:II.CP.3115.2014, etc.
766. ECLI:SI:VSLJ:2009:II.CP.2147.2009.
767. ECLI:SI:VSRS:2001:II.IPS.441.2000 and ECLI:SI:VSLJ:2013:II.CP.1812.2013.
768. Cf. ECLI:SI:VSLJ:2019:I.CP.120.2019.
769. ECLI:SI:VSLJ:1999:II.CP.1376.99, ECLI:SI:VSLJ:2018:I.CP.1822.2017 and ECLI:SI:VSCE:2009:CP.425.2009.
770. ECLI:SI:VSLJ:2022:II.CP.711.2022.
771. Article 176(2) of the OZ.

inheritable, and unlike transfers between living parties, their inheritability is satisfied by the mere fact of maturity, without the need for a legally binding court decision.[772]

410. Successive damage can occur not only in the realm of property but also in the realm of non-pecuniary interests (*see* Part VI, Chapter 2, §3). Although the possibility of awarding compensation in the form of a monetary annuity is specified in the OZ only for pecuniary damage, it is an accepted position in Slovenian theory and case law that a monetary annuity may also be awarded for non-pecuniary damage if the injured party so requests and if such a form represents the most appropriate satisfaction in the specific case.[773]

III. Others

411. According to Article 164 of the OZ, damage may be compensated not only in money but also in kind (restitution or institution). A destroyed object can be replaced by another object with the same characteristics, a damaged object can be repaired, etc. As already explained (*see more* in Part VI, Chapter 1 and Part VI, Chapter 3, §2), the injured party has the right to choose between compensation in money and compensation in kind, unless the circumstances of the case dictate otherwise.

772. Cf. ECLI:SI:VSRS:2009:II.IPS.1219.2008.
773. Bilten ZS 14/81, p. 14, obr. Poročilo VSS 1/81, p. 3, Sud. praksa 10/81, p. 21, obr. PP 10/82, p. 14., Bogomir Horvat, *Denarna odškodnina za duševne bolečine zaradi zmanjšanih življenjskih aktivnosti*, Pravna praksa 31, (2002), pp. 26–30, Lidija Koman-Perenič, *Odškodninska renta*, Podjetje in delo 4 (1991), pp. 342–356.

Chapter 4. Personal Injury and Death

§1. Pecuniary Losses

412. The question of compensation for pecuniary loss caused by an infringement on the body or health of a person is specifically regulated in Chapter III, section 7 of the OZ. The reason for this is the numerous peculiarities of such tort cases: the right to compensation is granted not only to persons who have directly suffered damage (direct victims) but also to close relatives (indirect victims); the damage occurs over a future, extended period of time, periodically and successively, which is why compensation is (usually) awarded in the form of an annuity, etc.[774]

413. Articles 172 and 173 of the OZ stipulate the compensation for pecuniary loss due to the death of the (direct) victim, while Article 174 of the OZ regulates compensation for damage to property in case of bodily injury or impairment of health. Articles 175 and 176 of the OZ regulate the possibility of changing the monetary annuity and its (non-)transferability (*see* more in Part VI, Chapter 3, §5).

414. In accordance with Article 172 of the OZ, anyone who causes the death of another must pay the usual funeral expenses. According to Slovenian case law, customary funeral expenses include the cost of purchasing or leasing a burial site, funeral expenses, including the cost of purchasing flowers or wreaths according to local customs, the cost of locally customary obituary notices, the cost of customary refreshments for those attending the funeral, the cost of purchasing mourning clothes for close relatives, and the cost of arranging and maintaining the grave.[775] Legally recognised pecuniary losses, in this context, are only those funeral expenses that represent an objective necessity for the close relatives of the deceased. Expenses incurred to preserve psychological integrity as an integral part of personal mourning are not legally recognised.[776] In addition to the usual funeral expenses, the person who caused the damage must also reimburse the costs of the victim's medical treatment due to the injuries sustained and other necessary costs related to the treatment, as well as the loss of earnings due to the inability to work. These are past damages which the deceased could have claimed[777] himself or herself but was prevented from doing so by death. These claims are pecuniary rights of the deceased that arose and became due during his or her lifetime and are therefore subject to inheritance. Based on this provision, the close relatives of the deceased are also entitled to claim compensation for the costs they incurred in connection with the deceased's medical treatment.[778]

774. Jadek Pensa, *supra* n. 60, at p. 991.
775. ECLI:SI:VSRS:2008:II.IPS.146.2006, ECLI:SI:VSRS:2008:II.IPS.651.2008 and ECLI:SI:VSLJ:2015: II.CP.657.2015.
776. ECLI:SI:VSLJ:2016:II.CP.2187.2016, ECLI:SI:VSMB:2020:I.CP.612.2020 and ECLI:SI:VSRS:2011: II.IPS.588.2008.
777. *See* Art. 174(1) of the OZ.
778. Jadek Pensa, *supra* n. 60, at 992, Stojan Cigoj, *Komentar obligacijskih razmerij: veliki komentar zakona o obligacijskih razmerjih, II. knjiga* (1984), p. 746.

415. The premature death of a direct victim may also cause pecuniary loss to persons (indirect victims) whom he or she had previously supported or otherwise assisted, or whom he or she was obliged to support. In this regard, according to Article 173 of the OZ, a person who was supported or regularly assisted by the deceased, as well as a person who had the right under the law to claim maintenance from him or her, has the right to compensation for the damage suffered due to the loss of support or assistance.

416. The damage due to the loss of maintenance or regular support constitutes successively accruing damage, which is compensated by the payment of a monetary annuity.[779] The amount of damages is determined taking into account all the circumstances of the case and, in accordance with the principle of full compensation, cannot be higher than what the victim would have received from the deceased had the latter remained alive.[780] The damage for loss of actual maintenance is not determined according to the rules of family law, but by determining the specific amounts that the deceased would have spent on the victim from his or her income.[781] It is necessary to determine what income the deceased would actually have earned had he or she been alive, and how much of it he or she would realistically or factually have contributed towards the maintenance or support of the indirect victims. According to established case law, this assessment takes into account all income that the deceased could have earned under normal course of events, whether through regular or additional work.[782] For example, the earnings that the deceased received as hand money are also relevant.[783] However, if the indirect victim is also a maintenance beneficiary, he or she may claim compensation in the amount determined in accordance with the family law rules for setting alimony, if he or she can prove that the actual maintenance was lower than the alimony amount.[784]

417. In order for there to be a claim for compensation for lost maintenance, it is not necessary for the maintenance or support to have manifested itself in a monetary contribution by the deceased. Even a contribution in kind (e.g., the death of a mother who looked after the household), which must be valued in monetary terms, is sufficient.[785]

418. According to Article 174(1) of the OZ, anyone who inflicts a bodily injury on another or impairs his or her health is obligated to reimburse him or her for the costs of treatment and other necessary expenses related thereto, as well as for the

779. Exceptions to this rule are stipulated in Art. 167(4) and 167(5) of the OZ. *See* more in Part VI, Ch. 3, §5.
780. Article 173 of the OZ.
781. ECLI:SI:VSRS:2004:II.IPS.547.2003 and ECLI:SI:VSMB:2016:I.CP.1050.2015.
782. ECLI:SI:VSLJ:2010:II.CP.4485.2009.
783. ECLI:SI:VSMB:2019:I.CP.354.2019.
784. ECLI:SI:VSRS:2005:II.IPS.108.2005.
785. ECLI:SI:VSMB:2023:I.CP.798.2022.

earnings lost due to the inability to work during the treatment. This provision regulates the compensation for past damages that have already occurred due to bodily injury or impairment of health until the time of its calculation.[786]

419. Slovenian case law interprets the costs associated with medical treatment and other related necessary expenses broadly. Accordingly, the injured party is entitled to compensation for all expenses that are customary in the given circumstances, and not only for necessary expenses. The answer to the question of what constitutes necessary costs in connection with treatment should therefore be found based on the injured party's state of health and taking into account his or her circumstances.[787] Case law considers that the costs associated with treatment also include the costs of external assistance,[788] but only on condition that the assistance, in its extent, exceeds the legal obligation to provide help.[789]

420. Since the loss of earnings during the incapacity for work for the period of treatment represents past damage, its calculation does not pose any major challenges.

421. In addition to the discussed past damage, which has already occurred at the time of the decision on compensation, the injured party may also incur a pecuniary loss in the future due to a physical injury or impaired health. The question of compensation for this future pecuniary loss is regulated in Article 174(2) of the OZ. There it is stipulated that the responsible party must pay the injured party a specified annuity[790] if the injured party suffers a loss of earnings due to total or partial incapacity for work or if his or her needs are permanently increased or if the possibilities for his or her further development and advancement are destroyed or diminished. Legally recognised pecuniary loss in this context is not the injured party's mere total or partial incapacity for work, his or her increased needs, or his or her reduced or destroyed opportunities for advancement, but the resulting pecuniary loss. For example, even if the injured party has to put in more effort to perform the same job as before the damaging event, this alone does not entitle them to compensation on this basis. However, they may be entitled to fair monetary compensation for non-pecuniary losses due to psychological pain resulting from restricted life activities (*see* next chapter).[791]

---

786. ECLI:SI:VSRS:2022:II.IPS.13.2022.
787. ECLI:SI:VSRS:1994:II.IPS.562.94, ECLI:SI:VSRS:2004:II.IPS.167.2004, ECLI:SI:VSRS:2014:II.IPS.129.2012, ECLI:SI:VSRS:2015:II.IPS.2.2013, etc.
788. For example, travel expenses, parking and toll fees incurred by the injured party's relatives in connection with trips to various medical institutions (ECLI:SI:VSLJ:2012:II.CP.1139.2012), assistance with household chores such as cleaning, shopping, ironing, washing, etc. during the period when the injured party was unable to perform them due to injuries, and so on (ECLI:SI:VSRS:2018:II.IPS.160.2017).
789. ECLI:SI:VSLJ:2011:I.CP.1081.2011.
790. Exceptions to this rule are stipulated in Art. 167(4) and 167(5) of the OZ. *See* more in Part VI, Ch. 3, §5.
791. *See* ECLI:SI:VSRS:2008:II.IPS.287.2006 and ECLI:SI:VSRS:2011:II.IPS.655.2008.

422. When calculating compensation for loss of earnings due to interference with the injured party's working capacity, the principle of full compensation should be followed, and the injured party should be awarded an amount that puts him or her in the same position as if he or she were earning with the same working capacity as before the damaging event. The injured party is thus entitled to the difference between the objectively foreseeable hypothetical earnings he or she would have achieved with the working capacity before the damaging event and the actual earnings with the working capacity after the damaging event.[792] The calculation of the lost profits should be as close to reality as possible.[793] In doing so, one must consider ordinary circumstances and not possible exceptional situations, such as a temporary and exceptional increase in the injured party's income,[794] a general economic crisis,[795] an extraordinary termination of an employment contract,[796] etc. In addition to the loss of earnings, the costs that the injured party will incur in the future due to permanently increased needs are also recognised, as well as the pecuniary loss due to the injured party's reduced opportunities for advancement, provided that it can be proven that these costs or advancement would have occurred under normal circumstances.

423. Even when compensating for pecuniary losses in cases of death, bodily injury, or health impairment, one must strictly follow the principle of *compensatio lucri cum damno*. From the compensation amount, calculated based on the previously discussed criteria, all benefits received by the injured party due to the damaging event must be deducted. Given the widely established system of social security and social insurance in Slovenia, it is often necessary in practice to reconcile the compensation and the benefits that the injured party has received under this title (e.g., funeral and death benefits, family pensions, wage compensation, disability pensions, etc.).[797] In the case of pecuniary losses due to interference with the

792. ECLI:SI:VSRS:2013:VIII.IPS.182.2013.
793. For instance, what is important is the salary that the injured party was (or should have been) receiving not the average salary in the industry. In calculating the loss of earnings, it is also not necessarily the actual salary amount that the injured party received prior to the damaging event that is relevant, but rather the amount that the injured party should have been receiving according to the employment contract, the collective agreement, and other relevant regulations (ECLI:SI:VSRS:2011:II.IPS.508.2008). The concept of lost earnings may include, in addition to the regular salary, other earning which in the normal course of events, the injured party could reasonably be expected to have earned had his or her working capacity remained intact, e.g., earnings from overtime, supplementary earnings, etc. (ECLI:SI:VSRS:2021:II.IPS.103.2020, ECLI:SI:VSRS:1998:II.IPS.554.96, etc.). Loss of earnings is also recognised if the injured party did not receive a salary before the damaging event but contributed to the household with his or her work (*see* Jadek Pensa, *supra* n. 60, at p. 1002). However, the calculation of the loss of earnings does not take into account the costs of transportation and meals, which are tied to the actual presence at the workplace and do not constitute the earnings of the worker but only a reimbursement of the costs related to the work (ECLI:SI:VSLJ:2019:II.CP.1962.2018).
794. ECLI:SI:VDSS:2014:PDP.990.2013.
795. ECLI:SI:VDSS:2012:PDP.1190.2011.
796. ECLI:SI:VDSS:2021:PDP.141.2021.
797. The social insurance institutions then have a recourse claim against the responsible party. *See* Arts 190–192 of the Pension and Disability Insurance Act (Official Gazette RS, Nos 48/22 – official consolidated text, 40/23 – ZČmIS-1, 78/23 – ZORR, 84/23 – ZDOsk-1) and Arts 86–88 of the Health

injured party's body or health, the concepts of compensation reduction on grounds of fairness (*see* more in Part VI, Chapter 3, §4) or the injured party's shared liability (*see* more in Part IV, Chapter 3) also apply.

§2. Non-pecuniary Losses

424. In addition to pecuniary damage, non-pecuniary damage may also arise in the case of an infringement on the injured party's life, body, or health, in the form of physical pain (suffered and/or future), fear, or mental anguish due to a restricted life activity, disfigurement, violation of the dignity or death of a loved one.

425. Physical pain (*telesne bolečine*) may result from bodily injuries or various health impairments. According to established Slovenian judicial practice, inconveniences during treatment, such as brief unconsciousness, hospitalisation, bed confinement, infusions, transfusions, the use of a wheelchair and crutches, outpatient visits, physiotherapy, etc. are also considered physical pain.[798]

426. A reduction in life activity (*zmanjšanje življenske aktivnosti*) signifies a decline in a person's physical and mental abilities that negatively affects their involvement in various activities. When assessing the reduction in life activity, it is essential to consider the injured party's capabilities before the damaging event and the areas in which he or she was active.[799] Just compensation for reduced life activities is only awarded for the permanent limitations of the injured party's abilities that persist after medical treatment has been completed, while the temporary reduction in life activity during treatment is generally considered part of the compensation for physical pain and inconvenience during treatment.[800] The court deviated from this position in a specific case where the treatment of the injured party, who was significantly affected, was very lengthy, and awarded monetary compensation for non-pecuniary damage due to mental anguish for the temporary reduction in life activity.[801]

427. According to established judicial practice, the *disfigurement* of the injured party is assessed based on both objective and subjective criteria. Objective criteria include changes in the appearance of the injured party, their visibility or conspicuousness, the extent and the possibility of concealing them, the age of the injured party, etc. Subjective criteria refer to the influence of the objective criteria on the

Care and Health Insurance Act (Official Gazette RS, Nos 72/06 – official consolidated text, 114/06 – ZUTPG, 91/07, 76/08, 62/10 – ZUPJS, 87/11, 40/12 – ZUJF, 21/13 – ZUTD-A, 91/13, 99/13 – ZUPJS-C, 99/13 – ZSVarPre-C, 111/13 – ZMEPIZ-1, 95/14 – ZUJF-C, 47/15 – ZZSDT, 61/17 – ZUPŠ, 64/17 – ZZDej-K, 36/19, 189/20 – ZFRO, 51/21, 159/21, 196/21 – ZDOsk, 15/22, 43/22, 100/22 – ZNUZSZS, 141/22 – ZNUNBZ, 40/23 – ZČmIS-1, 78/23).

798. ECLI:SI:VSLJ:2000:II.CP.892.99, ECLI:SI:VSLJ:2020:I.CP.657.2020, etc.
799. Plavšak et al., *supra* n. 95, at 639.
800. ECLI:SI:VSLJ:2018:II.CP.607.2018.
801. ECLI:SI:VSLJ:2005:I.CP.2030.2004.

psychological balance or mental well-being of the injured party.[802] Disfigurement can develop into a reduction in life activity if it causes problems that are reflected in the area in which the injured party is active.[803]

428. Article 181 of the OZ specifically regulates the right to monetary compensation for the mental suffering of a victim, especially if he or she has been seduced into a sexual act through deceit, force, or abuse of a relationship of subordination or dependency. This also applies to victims against whom another offence against dignity, personal rights, or morals has been committed. According to theorists, the reason why the Slovenian (and previously the Yugoslav) legislator dedicated a separate article to this type of mental suffering is that the violation of a person's sexual integrity uniquely infringes upon the victim's dignity, exposing their vulnerability and weaker position in relation to the perpetrator.[804] The right to monetary compensation under this article does not exclude claims for other types of non-material damages under Article 179(1) of the OZ, provided that the conditions for them are met.[805]

429. As mentioned in the previous chapter, a unique aspect of compensation cases involving infringements on the body or health is that the right to compensation is recognised not only for direct victims but also for indirect victims. This applies to both pecuniary and non-pecuniary losses. In this regard, in the event of the death or particularly severe disability[806] of a loved one, the court may award the closest family members (spouse, children, and parents) a fair monetary compensation for their mental anguish, in accordance with Article 180 of the OZ. Siblings and the extramarital partner of the victim are also entitled to compensation under the additional condition that there was a lasting partnership between them and the direct victim. The existence of such a partnership is determined by the court, considering the specific circumstances of the case.[807] Slovenian case law has recognised the right to compensation under this provision also for certain other persons who are not explicitly mentioned in the OZ (e.g., grandchildren or grandparents), but only if

802. ECLI:SI:VSMB:2014:I.CP.1335.2014, ECLI:SI:VDSS:2013:PDP.845.2012, ECLI:SI:VSRS:2009:II.IPS.1048.2007, etc.

803. Jadek Pensa, *supra* n. 60, at 1027.

804. *Ibid.*, at 1052.

805. ECLI:SI:VSLJ:2018:I.CP.2805.2017, ECLI:SI:VSCE:2022:CP.52.2022, etc.

806. Particularly severe disability is a legal standard that requires a restrictive approach under Slovenian case law. Jurisprudence categorises only exceptional cases of disability under this standard, such as quadriplegia, removal of two limbs accompanied by severe reactive depression, dependency, inability to perform basic life activities, a completely destroyed intellectual realm of the victim's personality, etc. According to jurisprudence, a particularly severe disability can therefore also be present in the mental sphere, but it must always mean the loss of an essential life function, resulting in an inability to live independently and dependence on the care and assistance of others. *See* ECLI:SI:VSLJ:2012:I.CP.2477.2011 and the jurisprudence cited therein.

807. ECLI:SI:VSCE:2014:CP.271.2014. According to Slovenian case law, for example, permanent joint residency of siblings is not a condition for the existence of a lasting life partnership (ECLI:SI:VSRS:2009:II.IPS.406.2007). Nevertheless, the quality of relationships within the community should not deviate from those typical of closer family ties. Therefore, a sibling who creates his or her own family does not live in a lasting life partnership with other siblings, regardless of their mutual emotional and economic connection (ECLI:SI:VSRS:2008:II.IPS.620.2006).

justified by the circumstances of the case (e.g., if grandchildren live full-time with their grandparents and there is an equivalent relationship as between parents and children).[808]

430. *Fear* is a specific form of legally recognised non-pecuniary damage. In Slovenian case law, there is an established distinction of fear based on its origin or the time of its occurrence. Primary fear arises immediately before the damaging event or during its duration. It is an immediate emotional reaction to a dangerous event or situation and typically subsides when the danger ends and intellectual processing of the event begins. Secondary fear is the anxiety experienced by the injured party while dealing with the consequences of the damaging event (fear of the outcome of the treatment, fear of possible consequences, fear of surgery, etc.).[809]

431. Fair monetary compensation for the discussed forms of non-pecuniary damage is awarded to the injured party regardless of the reimbursement for pecuniary damage (even if there is no pecuniary damage at all) if the extent of the pain and fear and their duration justify it. The injured party is entitled to monetary compensation not only for physical and mental pain and fear suffered but also for future pain and anguish (*see* more in Part VI, Chapter 2, §5). The monetary compensation is determined based on the intensity, duration, and the injured party's subjective perception of the physical and mental pain and fear (principle of individualisation of compensation) and by comparing the harmful consequences of the specific injured party with the harmful consequences of numerous other injured parties in various cases from case law (principle of objective conditionality).

808. ECLI:SI:VSRS:1999:II.IPS.40.98, ECLI:SI:VSLJ:2014:II.CP.157.2014, ECLI:SI:VSLJ:2015:II.CP.2815.2014, etc.

809. ECLI:SI:VSRS:2003:II.IPS.599.2002, ECLI:SI:VSRS:2004:II.IPS.432.2003, ECLI:SI:VDSS:2008:VDS.PDP.1292.2007, ECLI:SI:VSLJ:2010:II.CP.3568.2010, etc.

Chapter 5. Various Damages

432. In the previous chapters, we introduced various types of pecuniary and non-pecuniary damages arising from the impairment of (property or personal) rights and legally protected interests of another. The injured party's right to compensation arises not only in the discussed cases of destruction of or damage to property (*see* Part VI, Chapter 2, §6 and Chapter 3, §1), breach of contract (*see* Part VI, Chapter 2, §3), interference with the injured party's life, body, or health (*see* Part VI, Chapter 4), mental or physical integrity (*see* Part VI, Chapter 2, §3 and Chapter 4), but also in all other cases of detriment recognised by law.

433. In accordance with Article 166 of the OZ, the liable party is obliged to compensate for the damage if he or she has unlawfully deprived the injured party of a thing which was then destroyed due to a so-called qualified accident (*casus mixtus*).[810] The right to compensation for pecuniary damages is also stipulated by numerous other laws, e.g., the Copyright and Related Rights Act,[811] the Industrial Property Act,[812] the ZDR-1,[813] the Act Concerning Remedying the Consequences of Work with Asbestos,[814] the Special Rights of Victims in the War for Slovenia 1991 Act,[815] the Act Regulating the Compensation for Damage Sustained as a Result of Erasure from the Register of Permanent Residents,[816] etc.

434. Special rules regarding compensation for pecuniary damage apply in cases of expropriation, nationalisation, and other acts of state and administrative bodies. In accordance with Article 69 of the URS,[817] property rights to real estate may be revoked or restricted in the public interest in return for compensation in kind or monetary compensation[818] under the conditions prescribed by law. Compensation due to expropriation as a substitute for the sacrifice of individual interests for the benefit of the common good differs significantly from compensation under civil law.

810. The OZ explicitly mentions only force majeure, but according to theorists, the provision should be interpreted broadly to also cover cases where the property of the injured party is destroyed by the act of another person who is not liable for it, or by a natural coincidence that does not meet the criteria of force majeure. Cf. Cigoj, *supra* n. 777, at 722.
811. Official Gazette RS, Nos 16/07 – official consolidated text, 68/08, 110/13, 56/15, 63/16 – ZKUASP, 59/19, 130/22. *See also* Part VI, Ch. 7, §3.
812. Official Gazette RS, Nos 51/06 – official consolidated text, 100/13, 23/20, 76/23. *See also* Part VI, Ch. 7, §3.
813. Official Gazette RS, Nos 21/13, 78/13 – App., 47/15 – ZZSDT, 33/16 – PZ-F, 52/16, 15/17 – Ord. 19 – ZPosS, 81/19, 203/20 – ZIUPOPDVE, 119/21 – ZČmIS-A, 202/21 – Constitutional Court decision, 15/22 and 54/22 – ZUPŠ-1. *See*, e.g., Art. 8 of the Employment Relationships Act (ZDR-1), which establishes the employer's liability for damages in cases of violation of the prohibition of discrimination or harassment in the workplace.
814. Official Gazette RS, Nos 15/07 – official consolidated text, 51/09.
815. Official Gazette RS, Nos 49/97, 114/06 – ZUTPG, 159/21, 43/22, 163/22.
816. Official Gazette RS, Nos 99/13, 24/18 – Constitutional Court decision, 85/18.
817. Official Gazette RS, Nos 33/91-I, 42/97 – UZS68, 66/00 – UZ80, 24/03 – UZ3a, 47, 68, 69/04 – UZ14, 69/04 – UZ43, 69/04 – UZ50, 68/06 – UZ121,140,143, 47/13 – UZ148, 47/13 – UZ90,97,99, 75/16 – UZ70a, 92/21 – UZ62a.
818. According to some theorists, the term 'compensation' is not the most appropriate because expropriation, being a coercive deprivation or limitation of ownership or other property rights for the

In fact, its function is to enable the expropriated party to acquire an item on the market that has the same value as the one taken,[819] and not to reimburse all actual and future damages suffered by the affected party that are not even related to the expropriation.[820] In this context, compensation for expropriation may be equivalent to full compensation, which is usually the rule,[821] but it may also be lower, as its determination involves a balancing of the interests of the expropriated party and the public interest. Therefore, the expropriated party sometimes has to bear certain damages himself or herself.[822] For instance, compensation for loss of profits is only recognised if the expropriated party has already carried on a business activity on the expropriated property and only for the period during which a diligent owner would have established the same use of equivalent property.[823]

435. The expropriation procedure in the RS is regulated in Articles 202 to 225 of the SMA.[824] According to Article 216 of the SMA, the owner is entitled to adequate compensation or an equivalent replacement property (compensation in kind) for the expropriated real estate. The compensation includes the value of the expropriated properties, damages, and other costs associated with the expropriation, as well as financial compensation due to restrictions on the use of the property. Compensation is determined using a methodology for valuing properties, damages to them, and other costs.[825] In certain cases, e.g., when taking ownership rights to a building or part of a building that the expropriated person uses as a residence, the beneficiary of the expropriation must provide the expropriated person with ownership rights to an equivalent building or part of a building (compensation in kind) and bear the costs associated with the expropriation.[826] However, the expropriated person may also request monetary compensation instead of compensation in kind.[827] The beneficiary of expropriation and the expropriated person may also agree on compensation or replacement by mutual consent.[828]

436. In denationalisation procedures, in which the restitution of property confiscated after the Second World War is decided on various legal bases (agrarian reform,

---

public benefit, is not unlawful conduct. Therefore, the term 'reimbursement' (which can be monetary or in kind) is more appropriate. *See* Juhart, Tratnik & Vrenčur, *Stvarno pravo* (GV Založba 2023), p. 53.

819. ECLI:SI:VSRS:2012:II.IPS.81.2012, ECLI:SI:VSRS:2013:II.IPS.262.2012, ECLI:SI:VSRS:2018:II.IPS.39.2016, etc.
820. ECLI:SI:VSRS:2018:II.IPS.276.2017.
821. *See* Virant, in: Šturm, *Komentar Ustave Republike Slovenije* (Fakulteta za podiplomske državne in evropske študije 2002), p. 682.
822. ECLI:SI:VSRS:2014:II.IPS.146.2014.
823. ECLI:SI:VSRS:2010:II.IPS.46.2010.
824. Official Gazette RS, Nos 199/21, 18/23 – ZDU-1O, 78/23 – ZUNPEOVE.
825. This regards the transitional arrangement for determining compensation in expropriation proceedings until the adoption of the methodology for assessing the value of real estate, damage to it, and other costs, *see* Art. 327 of the SMA.
826. For example, relocation costs, lost profits during the relocation, and a potential decrease in the value of the remaining property.
827. Article 218 of the SMA.
828. *See* more in Art. 217 of the SMA.

confiscation, nationalisation, etc.), compensation can also be determined if the restitution of nationalised property is not possible or not possible in full.[829] Compensation may be awarded in the form of replacement property, securities, or cash.[830]

829. Articles 2(2) and 16(2) of the Denationalisation Act (Official Gazette RS, Nos 27/91-I, 56/92 – Constitutional Court decision, 13/93 – Constitutional Court decision, 31/93, 24/95 – Constitutional Court decision, 20/97 – Constitutional Court decision, 23/97 – Constitutional Court decision, 65/98, 76/98 – Constitutional Court decision, 66/00, 66/00 – ORZDen27, 11/01 – Constitutional Court decision, 54/04 – ZDoh-1, 18/05 – Constitutional Court decision, 18/23 – ZDU-1O, 77/23 – Constitutional Court decision).
830. Article 2(2) of the Denationalisation Act.

Chapter 6. Interference with Collateral Benefits

§1. Insurance

437. One and the same damaging event may give rise to rights based on various legal grounds. The injured party's right to claim damages from the person who caused the damage is often supplemented by claims arising from premium and/or social insurance. On the one hand, the accumulation of claims improves the position of the injured party, as it increases the possibility that he or she will be compensated. On the other hand, however, the legal system must prevent the injured party from receiving more than the actual damages suffered. Similarly, it is essential to ensure that the ultimate burden of the damage lies with the one who caused it. In order to achieve these goals in the Slovenian legal system, there is a general prohibition of the accumulation of claims for damages and claims arising from (premium and/or social) insurance, as well as the regress or subrogation rights of insurance companies.

438. The two basic categories of insurances according to the OZ are property insurance and personal insurance. Property insurance provides compensation for damage that could occur to the property of the policyholder in the event of an insured incident.[831] Since the function of the insurance payment in property insurance is to compensate for damage, the injured party must not receive more from the insurance payout and compensation than he or she has suffered in damage. The injured party may choose between the claims, unless the law prescribes an order, and may also combine them.[832] However, as soon as the damage is fully compensated, the claim is extinguished.[833] Cumulation of compensation and insurance claims in such a way that the injured party would receive more than the damage incurred is not permitted. For property insurance, the right of recourse of the insurance company is also characteristic. With the payment of the insurance compensation, all rights of the policyholder against the liable party are transferred by law (*ex lege*) to the insurance company up to the amount of the payment. The liable party has all defences against the insurer that he or she would have had against the policyholder. However, there shall be no legal subrogation if the damage was caused by the policyholder's relative in the direct line or by a person for whose actions the policyholder is responsible, or by a person living in the same household as the policyholder or employed by the policyholder, unless the damage was caused intentionally or is insured against liability.[834]

831. Article 949(1) of the OZ.
832. Cf. Art. 963(3) of the OZ: 'The transfer of rights from the insured person to the insurance agency may not be to the detriment of the insured person; if the insurance payout obtained from the insurance agency is for any reason lower than the damage incurred, the insured person shall have the right to obtain a payment from the liable person's assets for the remaining compensation before the payment of the insurance agency's claim deriving from the rights transferred thereto.'
833. Ada Polajnar Pavčnik, in Plavšak et al., *Obligacijski zakonik (OZ) (posebni del) s komentarjem, 4. knjiga* (2004), p. 883.
834. Cf. Art. 963(4)(5) of the OZ.

439. A subtype of property insurance is liability insurance, which covers damage caused by the policyholder to a third party – the injured party. Particularly in the field of liability insurance, there is an increasing trend in mandatory insurance, the primary purpose of which is the socialisation of risks or ensuring a better position for the injured parties by making compensation easier and faster.[835] Mandatory insurance is widespread in various fields, and depending on its subject matter, we distinguish between mandatory traffic insurances,[836] mandatory professional liability insurances,[837] mandatory environmental insurances,[838] etc. A peculiarity of (voluntary and mandatory) liability insurance is that the insurance company usually cannot demand reimbursement of the amounts paid out from the policyholder or from the liable party who paid the premiums, except in cases specified by law or in the insurance conditions.[839]

440. The issues of claim cumulation and subrogation are regulated differently in personal (life and accident) insurances. Here the insurance payout does not constitute compensation, but with its disbursement, the insurance company fulfils its obligation under the insurance contract. Cumulation of the claim for compensation and the claim under the insurance contract is permissible in personal insurances, and the insurance company has no right of recourse against the liable party. The exception only applies to accident insurance concluded as liability insurance, as this falls under the rules of property insurance.[840]

§2. Social Security

441. Similarly to premium insurance, the social security system, which aims to ensure income security for individuals in the event of various social risks, can have a significant impact on the injured party's ability to obtain compensation. Due to the widespread mandatory pension, disability, and health insurance in the RS, an injured party receives at least partial compensation from these insurances in the event of a bodily or health impairment. The pecuniary loss of the injured party, i.e., the insured person, is covered by the social insurances with various benefits and/or services,

835. Cf. ECLI:SI:VSRS:2014:II.IPS.415.2011 and Pavliha, *Zavarovalno pravo* (GV založba 2000), p. 211.
836. *See*, e.g., Compulsory Motor Third-Party Liability Insurance Act (Official Gazette RS, Nos 93/07 – official consolidated text, 40/12 – ZUJF, 33/16 – PZ-F, 41/17 – PZ-G) and Obligations and Real Rights in Air Navigation Act (Official Gazette RS, No. 27/11 – official consolidated text).
837. *See*, e.g., Attorneys Act (Official Gazette RS, Nos 18/93, 24/96 – Constitutional Court decision, 24/01, 54/08, 35/09, 97/14, 8/16 – Constitutional Court decision, 46/16, 36/19 and 130/22) and Notariat Act (Official Gazette RS, Nos 2/07 – official consolidated text, 33/07 – ZSReg-B, 45/08, 91/13, 189/20 – ZFRO, 130/22, 49/23 – ZUS-1C).
838. *See*, e.g., Act on Liability for Nuclear Damage (Official Gazette RS, No. 77/10) and Maritime Code (Official Gazette RS, Nos 62/16 – official consolidated text, 41/17, 21/18 – ZNOrg, 31/18 – ZPVZRZECEP, 18/21, 21/21 – corr., 76/23).
839. Cigoj, 2003, p. 241. *See*, e.g., Art. 7(3) of the Compulsory Motor Third-Party Liability Insurance Act.
840. Cf. Art. 972 of the OZ.

such as wage compensation due to incapacity to work, health services, disability or family pensions, assistance and care allowances, etc.

442. Since mandatory pension, disability, and health insurance are by their nature property insurances, the injured party cannot combine a compensation claim with a claim under social insurances in such a way as to receive more than the actual damage (*compensatio lucri cum damno*). Similarly, the carriers of the pension, disability, and health insurance – the Pension and Disability Insurance Institute (ZPIZ) and the Health Insurance Institute (ZZZS) – have a subrogation claim against the party who caused the damage, another liable party (e.g., the employer in the case of damage caused by an employee during or in connection with work) or the insurance company (if the injury, health impairment, or death occurred with a vehicle).[841]

443. Contrary to the practices of institutions operating within the realm of social insurance, Slovenian judicial precedents do not grant the employer the right of a subrogation claim against the person responsible for the damage or his or her insurance provider. This is despite the provision in Article 137 of the ZDR-1,[842] which obliges employers to compensate their employees for temporary inability to work during the first twenty or thirty working days of absence.[843] This judicial approach has faced criticism in legal theory.[844]

§3. Others

444. In accordance with the general rule of *compensatio lucri cum damno*, benefits received by the injured party as a result of the damaging event are taken into account in determining the amount of compensation. However, not every benefit received by the injured party during the time for which compensation is awarded is deducted. The legal nature and purpose of the benefit received are decisive. For example, the court has ruled that a monetary allowance that is not intended to cover the injured party's financial loss resulting from the loss of working capacity, but rather to provide the beneficiary with means of subsistence, should not be offset against compensation for loss of earnings.[845] As mentioned before, the insurance benefit that an injured party receives from his or her personal insurance is also not deducted from the compensation, as it is not a replacement for the damage.

841. *See* more in Arts 190 to 193 of the Pension and Disability Insurance Act and Arts 86 to 92 of the Health Care and Health Insurance Act.
842. Official Gazette RS, Nos 21/13, 78/13 – App., 47/15 – ZZSDT, 33/16 – PZ-F, 52/16, 15/17 – Ord. 19 – ZPosS, 81/19, 203/20 – ZIUPOPDVE, 119/21 – ZČmIS-A, 202/21 – Constitutional Court decision, 15/22 and 54/22 – ZUPŠ-1.
843. *See* ECLI:SI:VSKP:2009:CPG.129.2008 and ECLI:SI:USRS:2010:U.I.116.09.
844. *See* Damjan Možina, *Delodajalci in posledice prometnih nesreč*, Podjetje in delo 8 (2014), pp. 1505–1514.
845. ECLI:SI:VSRS:2009:II.IPS.1100.2008.

Chapter 7. Other Remedies

§1. Restitution for Unjust Enrichment

445. In the Slovenian legal system, unjust enrichment is an independent basis for the occurrence of an obligation, founded on the principle of justice, which states that no one should benefit at the detriment of another. Through an unauthorised transfer of assets or rights from the legal sphere of one entity to that of another, an obligation arising by law is created, the essence of which forms the basis for the retransfer of the unjustly acquired benefits from the enriched party to the disadvantaged one.

446. Slovenian theory and judicial practice, under the influence of the Austrian ABGB/ODZ, which was in force on the territory of present-day Slovenia during the Habsburg Monarchy (*see* more in General Introduction, §2, IV), maintained a distinction between *condictiones* (*kondikcija*) or performance-based enrichments (cases in which property is transferred with the aim of fulfilling obligations) and *actio de in rem verso* (*verzija*) or non-performance-based enrichments (cases in which property is transferred in other ways). However, similar to Switzerland and Germany, Slovenia has adopted a unified concept of restitution of unjust enrichment at the statutory level, articulated through a general clause in Article 190 of the OZ. This provision stipulates that anyone who has been unjustly enriched at the expense of another without legal grounds must return what he or she has received, if possible, or otherwise compensate for the value of the benefit obtained. This includes the acquisition of benefits through services, reflecting the factual circumstances of the claim for non-performance-based enrichment (*see* Article 190(1)(2) of the OZ). Furthermore, an obligation to return a thing or compensate for its value arises when someone receives something based on a premise that did not materialise or was subsequently voided, which illustrates the factual circumstances of the claim for performance-based enrichment (*see* Article 190(3) of the OZ). For both types of claim, it is noteworthy that neither unlawfulness nor fault are prerequisites for their assertion,[846] although non-performance-based enrichment may sometimes have characteristics of unlawful conduct.[847] In the case of the latter in particular, the relationship between restitution for unjust enrichment and damage claims often comes into question, since acts leading to an unauthorised transfer of property can also meet the criteria for tort claims (e.g., the unlawful appropriation of another's property).

447. In Slovenian legal theory, the prevailing view is that tort claims and unjust enrichment claims are congruent, i.e., they are not mutually exclusive, so the creditor

846. The prerequisites for unjust enrichment claims are threefold: absence of a legal basis, a shift in property that results in the detriment of one party and enrichment of another, and there must be a causal link between the detriment and the enrichment (cf. Ada Polajnar Pavčnik, in Plavšak et al., *Obligacijski zakonik (OZ) (splošni del) s komentarjem, 2. knjiga* (2003), p. 44).

847. Karmen Lutman, *Neupravičena obogatitev* (GV Založba 2020), p. 355.

is free to choose and even combine them if necessary.[848] The limitation here is that there must be no double compensation.[849] Contrary to theorists, Slovenian case law is not consistent on this matter. Part of the jurisprudence holds the view of subsidiarity or subordination of unjust enrichment claims, i.e., an unjust enrichment claim is only possible if it does not compete with another lawsuit, especially a tort claim. According to this view, an unjust enrichment claim is only relevant if the act that led to an unjustified transfer of property is not a harmful act.[850] Other rulings suggest the opposite viewpoint, that a creditor can choose between tort claims and unjust enrichment claims.[851]

448. The OZ includes two provisions that address situations where an act, resulting in an unwarranted transfer of property, also qualifies as a tortious act. As stipulated in Article 189 of the OZ, after the expiry of the limitation period for a tort claim, the injured party may demand from the responsible person to relinquish what he or she has obtained through the tortious act, in accordance with the rules on unjust enrichment.[852] Furthermore, according to Article 198 of the OZ, the owner of a property, regardless of his or her right to damages, and even if he or she does not have this right, may claim compensation from the person who wrongfully used his or her property for the benefits derived from the use of that property. The claim for unjust enrichment based on the unauthorised use of another's property is thus, by an explicit legal provision, not subordinate to the tort claim; the creditor is free to choose between the two claims.

§2. Injunctive Relief

449. Slovenian legislation contains numerous provisions according to which an affected person may seek the prohibition of certain acts that violate or endanger his or her proprietary or non-proprietary rights or legally protected interests (injunctive relief). Pursuant to Article 134 of the OZ, any person may demand from the court or other competent authority that an act infringing upon his or her personal rights

---

848. *See* Cigoj, *supra* n. 88, at 271, Jadek Pensa, *supra* n. 60, at 1077, Polajnar Pavčnik, *supra* n. 845, at 58, Damjan Možina, *Protipravno pridobljeni dobiček kot merilo odškodninskega in obogatitvenega zahtevka*, Podjetje in delo 3–4 (2015), p. 471, Lutman, *supra* n. 846, at 340, 346, et seq.

849. Cf. Jadek Pensa, *supra* n. 60, at 1077, Lutman, *supra* n. 846, at 340, 346 and 348.

850. ECLI:SI:VSRS:2007:II.IPS.535.2005, ECLI:SI:VSRS:2013:II.IPS.145.2010 and ECLI:SI:VSRS:2015:II.IPS.147.2013.

851. ECLI:SI:VSLJ:2010:I.CPG.597.2010, ECLI:SI:VSRS:2018:II.IPS.311.2017, ECLI:SI:VSLJ:2016:II.CPG.1049.2016 and ECLI:SI:VSLJ:2018:I.CPG.688.2017.

852. A claim for damages in tort becomes statute-barred three years from the date when the injured party became aware of the damage and the person who caused it (subjective period). In any case, however, the claim expires five years from the date when the damage occurred (objective period). Tort claims for business liability expire in the timeframe specified for the expiry of contractual obligations (*see* more in Part IV, Ch. 1). Claims for unjust enrichment are subject to the general five-year limitation period under Art. 346 of the OZ, which starts to run on the first day after the day on which the creditor had the right to demand fulfilment of the obligation (cf. ECLI:SI:VSLJ:2014:II.CP.842.2014.1).

be stopped, prevented, or its consequences eliminated. The court or other competent authority may also order the infringer to cease such acts on pain of a penalty payment to the aggrieved person, imposed either as a lump sum or per unit of time. Additionally, according to Article 133 of the OZ, any person may require another to eliminate a source of danger posing a significant threat to either himself or herself or to an indeterminate number of people and to abstain from the activities from which the disturbance or risk of harm emanates. If the disturbance or harm cannot be prevented by appropriate measures, the court may, at the request of a party having a legitimate interest, mandate preventive measures against the onset of harm or disturbance or the removal of the source of danger at the expense of its possessor should the latter fail to act. If harm occurs in the course of activities which are deemed generally beneficial and for which permission has been granted by the competent authority, compensation may only be claimed for damage that exceeds the customary level. Nevertheless, adequate measures to prevent or mitigate damage can be sought even in such instances.

450. In addition to the OZ, numerous other laws contain provisions based on which the affected party may assert an injunctive relief claim, e.g., Article 167(1) of the Copyright and Related Rights Act,[853] Article 121(1) of the Industrial Property Act,[854] Article 135(2) of the Prevention of Restriction of Competition Act,[855] Article 99 of the Property Law Code,[856] etc. If damage has been caused by the act for which prohibition is sought, the injured party may also claim damages according to the rules of the law of obligations.

§3. Punitive Damages

451. As mentioned in General Introduction, §3 and Part VI, Chapter 1, the fundamental task of Slovenian tort law is to remedy the unjustified situation in which the injured party finds himself or herself, i.e., to rectify his or her detriment. In the case of pecuniary loss, compensation seeks to restore the injured party's financial position to what it would have been if the damaging event had not occurred. In the case of non-pecuniary loss, compensation aims at satisfying or subjectively appeasing the injured party, i.e., restoring his or her disrupted equilibrium. Slovenian theory and judicial practice also recognise the preventive function of tort law.[857] On the one hand, the payment of compensation should induce the perpetrator of the damage as well as other potential offenders to refrain from acts causing damage in

853. Official Gazette RS, Nos 16/07 – official consolidated text, 68/08, 110/13, 56/15, 63/16 – ZKUASP, 59/19 and 130/22.
854. Official Gazette RS, Nos 51/06 – official consolidated text, 100/13, 23/20 and 76/23.
855. Official Gazette RS, No. 130/22.
856. Official Gazette RS, Nos 87/02, 91/13 and 23/20.
857. *See* Plavšak et al., *supra* n. 95, at 651, Jadek Pensa, *supra* n. 60, at 666, Weingerl, *supra* n. 46, at 31–32, Špelca Mežnar, *Novejši trendi v odškodninskem pravu*, Podjetje in delo 6–7 (2008), pp. 1284–1293, Damjan Možina, *Naknada štete zbog diskriminacije i zlostavljanja na radnom mestu*, Harmonius: Journal of Legal and Social Studies in South East Europe 6 (2017), p. 144 et seq. For case law, *see* ECLI:SI:VSRS:2021:II.IPS.54.2020, ECLI:SI:VSLJ:2012:I.CP.2261.2011, etc.

the future (specific and general prevention). This function should not be equated with a punitive function, as compensation can have a preventive or deterrent effect even if it is (merely) proportionate to the damage suffered.[858]

452. On the other hand, Slovenian case law clearly rejects so-called punitive damages, as known in the Anglo-American legal environment, the purpose of which is to punish or take revenge on the wrongdoer. The most notable case regarding the possibility of recognising punitive damages was a court decision in the area of medical malpractice.[859] After the Court of First Instance awarded an exceptionally high monetary compensation of a punitive nature, the VSRS deliberated whether the punitive nature of the damages was compatible with the Slovenian legal system of tort law, which is based on the principle of full compensation for pecuniary damage and satisfaction or redress for non-pecuniary damage. The Supreme Court emphasised that the purpose of compensation for non-pecuniary damage was not to punish the wrongdoer. They further stated that punishment should be reserved for the state, which also had a special set of criminal law instruments for this purpose. They also noted that the latter focused on the perpetrator and also established safeguards to protect his or her fundamental rights, as he or she was a subordinate subject in relation to the state. Furthermore, they pointed out that redress belonged to the injured party due to the disruption of his or her emotional balance and not because of a desire to gain financial benefit or perhaps even to punish the alleged wrongdoer. The Supreme Court reiterated its position on not recognising punitive damages in connection with a case involving discrimination and harassment in the workplace.[860]

453. Despite the discussed aversion to punitive damages, Slovenian civil law recognises several institutions where elements of punitive damages can be identified, e.g., compensation for damage to the reputation and good name of a legal entity, civil penalty in case of violation of copyright or trade secrets, compensation based on the price of special popularity, etc.[861]

858. Cf. ECLI:SI:VSRS:2021:VIII.IPS.14.2021 and the case law cited therein, ECLI:SI:VSLJ:2012: I.CP.2261.2011, Weingerl, *supra* n. 46, at 33–34.
859. ECLI:SI:VSRS:2012:II.IPS.130.2012.
860. *See* ECLI:SI:VSRS:2021:VIII.IPS.14.2021.
861. *See* Maruša Varl, *Kaznovalna odškodnina* (GV Založba 2019), pp. 180–203, Weingerl, *supra* n. 46, at 37–46.

Selected Bibliography

§1. Tort Law in General

Stojan Cigoj. *Komentar obligacijskih razmerij: veliki komentar zakona o obligacijskih razmerjih, I. – IV. knjiga* (Uradni list SR Slovenije 1984–1986).Stojan Cigoj, *Teorija obligacij: splošni del obligacijskega prava* (Uradni list Republike Slovenije 2003).

Stojan Cigoj. *Odškodninsko pravo Jugoslavije* (Uradni list SR Slovenije 1972).

Damjan Možina. *Pogodbena in nepogodbena odškodninska odgovornost: ODZ (1811) in Obligacijski zakonik (2001)*, in: *Izročilo Občnega državljanskega zakonika* (Ada Polajnar-Pavčnik ed., Zbirka Pravna obzorja, 46, GV založba 2013), pp. 343–357.

Damjan Možina. *Obseg varstva pravnih dobrin v deliktnem pravu: kako generalna je generalna klavzula*, Pravni letopis (Inštitut za primerjalno pravo pri Pravni fakulteti v Ljubljani 2022), pp. 9–28.

Nina Plavšak et al. *Obligacijski zakonik (OZ) (splošni in posebni del) s komentarjem, 1.–4. knjiga* (Miha Juhart & Nina Plavšak ed., GV Založba 2003–2004).

Nina Plavšak, Miha Juhart & Renato Vrenčur. *Obligacijsko pravo: splošni del* (GV založba 2009).

Jožef Salma. *Obligaciono pravo* (Univerzitet u Novom Sadu, Pravni fakultet u Novom Sadu 2005).

Boris Strohsack. *Obligacijska razmerja I; Obligacijska razmerja II (odškodninsko pravo in druge neposlovne obveznosti)* (Uradni list Republike Slovenije 1998).

§2. Liability for One's Own Acts and for Acts of Others

Nataša Samec Berghaus. *Odškodninska odgovornost članov organov vodenja in nadzora gospodarskih družb in pravilo podjetniške presoje (business judgement rule)*, lecture, 24. posvetovanje Gospodarski subjekti na trgu in evropske dimenzije (2016).

Špelca Mežnar. *Odgovornost pravnih poklicev – teorija in praksa*, Pravni letopis (Inštitut za primerjalno pravo pri Pravni fakulteti v Ljubljani 2008), pp. 133–143.

Uroš Miklič. *Odškodninska odgovornost odvetnika in zavarovanje odgovornosti*, Odvetnik 96 (2020), pp. 13–16.

Damjan Možina. *Odškodninska odgovornost za nasvet in informacije ter vprašanje zahtevkov tretjih oseb*, Podjetje in delo 2 (2015), pp. 291–309.

Selected Bibliography

Damjan Možina. *Odškodninska odgovornost države*, Pravni letopis (Inštitut za primerjalno pravo pri Pravni fakulteti v Ljubljani 2013), pp. 141–165.

Bojan Podgoršek. *Odgovornost notarja*, Pravni letopis (Inštitut za primerjalno pravo pri Pravni fakulteti v Ljubljani 2008), pp. 155–166.

Vesna Bergant Rakočević. *Nepogodbeno odškodninsko pravo v Sloveniji – nekatere razvojne tendence v praksi sodišč*, in: *Razvojne tendence v obligacijskem pravu*: ob 40-letnici Zakona o obligacijskih razmerjih (Damjan Možina ed., Založba Pravne fakultete 2019), pp. 209–236.

Jan Zobec. *Odškodninska odgovornost sodnika in odgovornost države zanj*, Pravni letopis (Inštitut za primerjalno pravo pri Pravni fakulteti v Ljubljani 2013), pp. 185–321.

§3. Damages

Bogomir Horvat. *Denarna odškodnina za duševne bolečine zaradi zmanjšanih življenjskih aktivnosti*, Pravna praksa 31, (2002), pp. 26–30.

Špelca Mežnar. *Novejši trendi v odškodninskem pravu*, Podjetje in delo 6–7 (2008), pp. 1284–1293.

Damjan Možina. *Odškodninska odgovornost za kršitev pogodbe*, Podjetje in delo 2 (2016), pp. 260–289.

Damjan Možina. *Naknada štete zbog diskriminacije i zlostavljanja na radnom mestu*, Harmonius: Journal of Legal and Social Studies in South East Europe 6 (2017), pp. 127–147.

Ada Polajnar-Pavčnik. *Amerikanizacija odškodninskega prava*, Podjetje in delo 7 (2004), pp. 1158–1166.

Ana Božič Penko. *Razmislek in sodna praksa Vrhovnega sodišča o nekaterih aktualnih vprašanjih odškodninskega prava v zvezi z nepremoženjsko škodo*, Pravni letopis (Inštitut za primerjalno pravo pri Pravni fakulteti v Ljubljani 2016), pp. 67–82.

Lidija Koman-Perenič. *Odškodninska renta*, Podjetje in delo 4 (1991), pp. 342–356.

§4. Product Liability

Damjan Možina. *Odgovornost proizvajalca za proizvod z napako: evropsko obligacijsko pravo izpodriva nacionalno pravo*, Podjetje in delo 1 (2007), pp. 71–86.

Kevin Rihtar. *Odgovornost proizvajalca za proizvod: aktualna vprašanja*, Podjetje in delo 5 (2015), pp. 863–895.

Igor Strnad. *Odgovornost za izdelek*, Podjetje in delo 6–7 (1999), pp. 1280–1289.

§5. Road Traffic Act

Tomaž Pavčnik. *(Ne)dopustnost ugovora, da je za nesrečo izključno odgovoren le en voznik: (člen 154/4 OZ)*, Pravni letopis (Inštitut za primerjalno pravo pri Pravni fakulteti v Ljubljani 2014), pp. 113–126.

Igor Strnad. *Kako OZ ureja odgovornost imetnikov motornih vozil nasproti drugim?*, Pravna praksa 12 (2004), pp. 22–25.

§6. Medical Malpractice

Nataša Samec Berghaus & Rok Felicijan Pristovšek. *Nova dognanja o odškodninski odgovornosti zdravnika*, in: The patient – doctor relationship (Kraljić, Reberšek Gorišek & Rijavec ed., Pravna fakulteta: Lexonomica press 2016), pp. 109–125

Viktorija Žnidaršič Skubic. *Civilno medicinsko pravo, izbrane teme* (Uradni list RS 2018).

§7. Environmental Liability

Matija Damjan. *Množični zahtevki zaradi posegov v zdravo življenjsko okolje*, Pravni letopis (Inštitut za primerjalno pravo pri Pravni fakulteti v Ljubljani 2011), pp. 243–270.

Miha Juhart. *Okoljska odgovornost – med javnim in zasebnim pravom*, Zbornik znanstvenih razprav Pravne fakultete v Ljubljani (2008), pp. 107–127.

Miha Juhart. *Zahtevki zaradi opravljanja splošno koristne dejavnosti*, Podjetje in delo 6–7 (2009), pp. 1302–1311.

Rajko Knez. *Vpliv pravil o varovanju okolja na poslovanje podjetij*, The University of Maribor Jean Monnet Centre of Excellence, Working Paper 4 (2013) (April 1, 2023), https://jm-excellence.pf.um.si/wp-content/uploads/2013/10/WP-4-Decemebr-2013-Rajko-Knez-VPLIV-PRAVIL-O-VAROVANJU-OKOLJA-NA-POSLOVANJE-PODJETIJ.pdf.

Dušan Pichler et al. *Komentar Zakona o varstvu okolja* (Senko Pličanič ed., Inštitut za javno upravo pri Pravni fakulteti 2010).

Igor Sirc & Aleš Škraban. *Zakon o odgovornosti za jedrsko škodo s komentarjem* (RS Ministrstvo za okolje in prostor, Uprava RS za jedrsko varnost 2011).

§8. Defences and Exception Clauses

Damjan Možina. *Zastaranje nepogodbenih odškodninskih zahtevkov*, Pravni letopis (Inštitut za primerjalno pravo pri Pravni fakulteti v Ljubljani 2015), pp. 227–245.

Klemen Pohar. *Pravni učinek privolitve*, Pravna praksa 1–2 (2019), pp. 33–34.

§9. Remedies

Karmen Lutman. *Neupravičena obogatitev* (GV Založba 2020).

Damjan Možina. *Protipravno pridobljeni dobiček kot merilo odškodninskega in obogatitvenega zahtevka*, Podjetje in delo 3–4 (2015), pp. 462–478.

Damjan Možina. *Delodajalci in posledice prometnih nesreč*, Podjetje in delo 8 (2014), pp. 1505–1514.

Maruša Varl. *Kaznovalna odškodnina* (GV Založba 2019).

Petra Weingerl. *Nekompenzatorna povrnitev škode*, Pravni letopis (Inštitut za primerjalno pravo pri Pravni fakulteti v Ljubljani 2022), pp. 29–48.

Selected Bibliography

Index

The numbers here refer to paragraph numbers.

www.ingramcontent.com/pod-product-compliance
Lightning Source LLC
Chambersburg PA
CBHW070248030525
26096CB00033B/1313
9789403540382